The Light of Nakshatras

The Light of Nakshatras

A Comprehensive Work to Explain

the Functioning of 27 Mystical Energies

Author

Ajay Srivastava

Jyotirvid, Jyotirvisharad

First Edition, 2023

Published by:

Ajay Kumar Srivastava

45, Awas Vikas Colony, Betiya Hata,

Gorakhpur – 273001 (U.P.), India

Mobile No.: +91-9867837184

Disclaimer: This publication contains the opinions and ideas of its author and is designed to provide useful information in regard to the subject matter covered. The author and the publisher specifically disclaim any responsibility for liability, loss, or risk, personal or otherwise, that is incurred as a consequence, directly or indirectly, of the use and application of any of the contents of this book.

Lord Ganesha

Prayer

ॐ नमो सिद्धि विनायकाय सर्व कार्य कर्त्रे सर्व विघ्न प्रशमनाय
सर्व राज्य वश्यकरणाय सर्वजन सर्वस्त्री पुरुष आकर्षणाय
श्रीं ॐ स्वाहा ॥

(**Translation:** "O Lord of Wisdom and Happiness, only you make every endeavor and everything possible. You are the remover of all obstacles and you have enchanted every being in the Universe, you are the Lord of all women and all men, amen.")

Dedication

I dedicate this book to my father (Late) Sri R.A.L Srivastava who taught me to be an independent, courageous and determined person, and my mother Maya Srivastava whose unconditional love and support always help me to overcome all the obstacles in my life. She has a selfless spirit and served others throughout her life. Her immense patience is peerless and she always inspires me to go ahead.

Preface

Every activity on earth requires energy and without energy there is no movement. Our solar system is surrounded by 27 nakshatras and each nakshatra provides different types of energy. The energy that affects every person is a mixture of all the nine planets and nakshatras. Therefore, the placement of the same planet in different Nakshatras produces different results for each person. Hence, along with the study of planets, the study of nakshatras is also very important.

Our ancient sages developed the science of astrology and wrote many information in Vedic texts. These texts are written in codes (sutras), so they need to be decoded from time to time, new situations require new examples so that people can understand them according to the changed times. These codes provide a signal to those who take a step towards the unknown. Like, there are many types of signals present on the highway but people who drive their vehicle can see it. Similarly, when a person takes a step forward towards the unknown, that signal is visible to him. In the same way, there are innumerable signs and every sage has written what he has seen. It is a world of mystery, where something new is found every time you dig.

The knowledge of astrology reveals many secrets but it is difficult to understand. Nakshatras play an important role in knowing those secrets. The first step towards the unknown begins when a question arises in one's mind; why have I taken the birth of a human, why has another soul taken the birth of an animal, and what would I have done if I too had taken the birth of an animal. From what source did I come and by what grace did I get this human body.

When the questions of knowing the unknown start arising in the mind of a person, then his steps start moving towards the study of planets and constellations. His gaze rises up and the mysterious world of constellations starts attracting him. It is not for those who only have a certain set of mundane questions for their comfort. Astrology is to find out the most fundamental question - "Who is asking all these questions"? If it is decided that when will I get a job, when will I get married etc. then it means that someone is controlling us. So, after all who is controlling all these activities?

The study of Nakshatras is necessary to understand the nuances of astrology and whenever a person reads these ancient texts, he finds something new in his hands every time.

When I started learning astrology, I stared collecting information about nakshatras. I started observing what is the results when planets transit in these nakshatras, how this energy affects the atmosphere on the earth as well as every individual.

I have spent almost two decades of my career in corporates, visited many companies and met many people. In this book I have written all my experiences that how the energy of Nakshatras influence a person's behavior and make him to take decisions which are written in his horoscope.

This book explains the meaning of the symbol and caste related to each Nakshatra. Understanding the respective deity and planetary ruler is important and this book explains it in detail. Each Nakshatra has different characteristics and the planets placed here generate positive or negative energy, so it is important to understand both and it is written here keeping several aspects in mind. It further explains about the animal symbols and the meaning of the different padas. Some information about associated tree is also written along with its medicinal benefits, but it is only for information, not for advice, that how the energy of the nakshatra works and it affects not only humans but trees and plants also.

I give special thanks to my younger brother Abhay Srivastava for their valuable suggestions, without which such work would not have been possible. I thank God for completing this book. It is not possible for me to convert my thoughts into words without the grace of the "Almighty".

Ajay Srivastava

1st July, 2023

Navi Mumbai

Acknowledgement

The existence of this book would not have been possible without the help of my wife Seema and my daughter Saanvi. They provided me enough help to write down my thoughts which I have collected so far in my life. My wife has been instrumental as an illustrator and proof-reader and has given me enough insights to write the matter in a simple and explanatory manner.

Ajay Srivastava

Contents

Introduction

There are 27 nakshatras in Vedic astrology and each nakshatra is further divided into 4 parts known as pada. If we divide the entire 360-degree zodiac by 27 then the span of one nakshatra is 13 degrees 20 minutes. Therefore, each nakshatra is of 800 minutes, and each quarter of the nakshatra is of 200 minutes. A zodiac sign is made up of 9 pada of the nakshatra. Hence, the first sign Aries comprises four pada of Ashwini nakshatra, four pada of Bharani nakshatra, and one pada of Krittika nakshatra. The second zodiac sign Taurus contains the rest of the three pada of Krittika nakshatra, four pada of Rohini nakshatra, two pada of Mrigashira nakshatra, and so on.

The first 9 nakshatras are known as rajas nakshatra, the second 9 nakshatras are known as tamas nakshatra, and the third 9 nakshatras are known as sattva nakshatra. Again, it is divided into three categories, the first three nakshatras are rajas, the second three nakshatras are tamas and the third three nakshatras are sattva. This is divided again into three categories, the first nakshatra is rajas, the second is tamas and the third is sattva. Therefore, every nakshatra has three qualities. For example; the quality of Ashwini nakshatra is "Rajas-Rajas-Rajas" and the quality of Bharani is "Rajas-Rajas-Tamas". The 14th nakshatra Chitra is the most Tamasik nakshatra having the quality "Tamas-Tamas-Tamas" and the 27th nakshatra Revati is the most Satwik nakshatra having the quality "Sattva-Sattva-Sattva".

In the sequence of 27 nakshatras, each nakshatra is associated with an animal symbol, one is a male animal and the other is a female animal. There are 14 animals associated with all the 27 nakshatras and each animal is given its partner except "Mongoose". This animal is associated with Uttarashadha nakshatra and it has no partner and the rest 13 animals are given their partner.

The following table shows the zodiac sign, nakshatra, planetary lordship, and pada lord.

Nakshatra, Quality, Planet Lord and Pada Lord

Quality	Zodiac	Nakshatra	Planetary Lordship	Pada	Pada Lord	Degrees
Rajasic	ARIES	Ashwini	Ketu	1	Mar	0 - 3.2
				2	Ven	3.2 - 6.4
				3	Mer	6.4 - 10
				4	Moon	10 - 13.2
		Bharani	Venus	1	Sun	13.2 - 16.4
				2	Mer	16.4 - 20
				3	Ven	20 - 23.2
				4	Mar	23.2 - 26.4
Rajasic	TAURUS	Krittika	Sun	1	Jup	26.4 - 30
				2	Sat	30 - 33.2
				3	Sat	33.2 - 36.4
				4	Jup	36.4 - 40
		Rohini	Moon	1	Mar	40 - 43.2
				2	Ven	43.2 - 46.4
				3	Mer	46.4 - 50
				4	Moon	50 - 53.2
Rajasic	GEMINI	Mrigashira	Mars	1	Sun	53.2 - 56.4
				2	Mer	56.4 - 60
				3	Ven	60 - 63.2
				4	Mar	63.2 - 66.4
		Ardra	Rahu	1	Jup	66.4 - 70
				2	Sat	70 - 73.2
				3	Sat	73.2 - 76.4
				4	Jup	76.4 - 80
		Punarvasu	Jupiter	1	Mar	80 - 83.2
				2	Ven	83.2 - 86.4
				3	Mer	86.4 - 90
				4	Moon	90 - 93.2
Rajasic	CANCER	Pushya	Saturn	1	Sun	93.2 - 96.4
				2	Mer	96.4 - 100
				3	Ven	100 - 103.2
				4	Mar	103.2 - 106.4
		Aslesha	Mercury	1	Jup	106.4 - 110
				2	Sat	110 - 113.2
				3	Sat	113.2 - 116.4
				4	Jup	116.4 - 120

Quality	Zodiac	Nakshatra	Planetary Lordship	Pada	Pada Lord	Degrees
Tamasic	LEO	Magha	Ketu	1	Mar	120 - 123.2
				2	Ven	123.2 - 126.4
				3	Mer	126.4 - 130
				4	Mo	130 - 133.2
		Purva phalguni	Venus	1	Sun	133.2 - 136.4
				2	Mer	136.4 - 140
				3	Ven	140 - 143.2
				4	Mar	143.2 - 146.4
Tamasic	VIRGO	Uttara phalguni	Sun	1	Jup	146.4 - 150
				2	Sat	150 - 153.2
				3	Sat	153.2 - 156.4
				4	Jup	156.4 - 160
		Hasta	Moon	1	Mar	160 - 163.2
				2	Ven	163.2 - 166.4
				3	Mer	166.4 - 170
				4	Moon	170 - 173.2
		Chitra	Mars	1	Sun	173.2 - 176.4
				2	Mer	176.4 - 180
				3	Ven	180 - 183.2
				4	Mar	183.2 - 186.4
Tamasic	LIBRA	Swati	Rahu	1	Jup	186.4 - 190
				2	Sat	190 - 193.2
				3	Sat	193.2 - 196.4
				4	Jup	196.4 - 200
		Vishakha	Jupiter	1	Mar	200 - 203.2
				2	Ven	203.2 - 206.4
				3	Mer	206.4 - 210
				4	Mo	210 - 213.2
Tamasic	SCORPIO	Anuradha	Saturn	1	Sun	213.2 - 216.4
				2	Mer	216.4 - 220
				3	Ven	220 - 223.2
				4	Mar	223.2 - 226.4
		Jyeshtha	Mercury	1	Jup	226.4 - 230
				2	Sat	230 - 233.2
				3	Sat	233.2 - 236.4
				4	Jup	236.4 - 240

Quality	Zodiac	Nakshatra	Planetary Lordship	Pada	Pada Lord	Degrees
Sattvic	SAGITTARIUS	Mula	Ketu	1	Mar	240 - 243.2
				2	Ven	243.2 - 246.4
				3	Mer	246.4 - 250
				4	Moon	250 - 253.2
		Purva ashadha	Venus	1	Sun	253.2 - 256.4
				2	Mer	256.4 - 260
				3	Ven	260 - 263.2
				4	Mar	263.2 - 266.4
Sattvic	CAPRICORN	Uttara ashadha	Sun	1	Jup	266.4 - 270
				2	Sat	270 - 273.2
				3	Sat	273.2 - 276.4
				4	Jup	276.4 - 280
		Shravana	Moon	1	Mar	280 - 283.2
				2	Ven	283.2 - 286.4
				3	Mer	286.4 - 290
				4	Mo	290 - 293.2
		Dhanishta	Mars	1	Sun	293.2 - 296.4
				2	Mer	296.4 - 300
				3	Ven	300 - 303.2
				4	Mar	303.2 - 306.4
Sattvic	AQUARIUS	Satabhisha	Rahu	1	Jup	306.4 - 310
				2	Sat	310 - 313.2
				3	Sat	313.2 - 316.4
				4	Jup	316.4 - 320
		Purva bhadrapada	Jupiter	1	Mar	320 - 323.2
				2	Ven	323.2 - 326.4
				3	Mer	326.4 - 330
				4	Moon	330 - 333.2
Sattvic	PISCES	Uttara bhadrapada	Saturn	1	Sun	333.2 - 326.4
				2	Mer	326.4 - 340
				3	Ven	340 - 343.2
				4	Mar	343.2 - 346.4
		Revati	Mercury	1	Jup	346.4 - 350
				2	Sat	350 - 353.2
				3	Sat	353.2 - 356.4
				4	Jup	356.4 - 360

Chapter 1

Ashwini

Ashwini is the first of the 27 Nakshatras and is located at 00° 00' - 13° 20' Aries. The Sun becomes exalted here at 10 degrees. The counting of Nakshatras starts from Ashwini because the Sun is exalted here. The word Ashwini is divided into two words "Ashwa" and "Wini". Ashwa means "Horse" or "Turanga". Wini is a feminine word which means "Humble", "Winner" or "Goddess of beauty". In numerology the horse is related to "the number seven [of]".

Astronomy: In the constellation of Aries, three stars create this nakshatra and they are known as Gamma Arietis, Beta Arietis, and Alpha Arietis. The first star is visible at a magnitude of 3.87, its declination is 19° N 17' 45" and right ascension is 1h 53m 31.8s. The second star is visible at a magnitude of 2.64, its declination is 20° N 55' 1.43" and right ascension is 1h 55m 53.3s. The third star is visible at a magnitude of 2.0, its declination is 23° N 34' 3.94" and right ascension is 2h 8m 26.8s.

Deity: The deity of the nakshatra is known as Ashwini Kumaras. They are the twin brothers and gods of ayurvedic medicine. According to puranic stories, they are the son of Lord Sun and his wife Sanjana and were born when both of them took the form of horses. The twin horse deities indicate that the redness of the Sun on the horizon is approximately the same at sunrise and sunset. At the time of sunrise when the horizon is red and the Sun rises above in the sky the activities begin to intensify in the world and every person gets busy with their work. The deity of the nakshatra supports the movement and people run here and there to finish their work.

When the Sun slowly starts going down on the horizon, the activities in the world also slow down. Sunset is the time to take care of health and heal the wound. It is the time to take a cup of tea (healing through herbs). The energy of the nakshatra is deeply related to activity, intensity, medicine, care, healing activities, prevention, and knowledge. People do prayer at the time of sunrise and sunset for good fortune and good health.

The energy during this time is modest, and whose intention is always to do good. This energy does not support doing anything wrong at that time, so a person with negative intentions finds himself hapless to do anything wrong at the time of dawn. People like to be quiet.

The Twin Deity Brothers always bestow good fortune in everyone's life and this is the time to utilize this energy constructively. It is the most fortunate time; hence, every saint always says to their disciples to do morning and evening prayers. This time should never be wasted. We should always join our hands and seek the blessings of the 'Twin Brothers' for good fortune. At the time of sunrise and sunset, the redness of the sun spreads far and wide and the heat of the sun is tolerable. This is the time when a person can raise his consciousness.

Shakti (Power): The power of the constellation is known as "Shidhra Vyapani Shakti" which means "Quick access to things".

The Sight of Nakshatra: Tiryanga-mukha (Sideways)

Nature: Kshipra (Swift)

Element: Earth

Activity: Passive

TriMurti and Behaviour: Brahma and Creation

Planetary Ruler: The ruler of this nakshatra is Ketu which is related to the number seven. In Hindu mythology, the Sun god travels in a chariot driven by seven horses. Ketu is a headless and shadow planet. The head represents ego and the headless ruler indicates modesty and humbleness of the person. Ashwini people are very modest that they leave no existence of their help and generosity. They feel happy to give.

Symbol: The symbol of the nakshatra is "Twin horses" or "Horse's head". The head is the most important part of the body which indicates the beginning. Everyone is recognized by their head and an attractive face attracts the attention of people. There are five sense organs in the human body - eyes, ears, nose, tongue, and skin. Four of them are present in the head and the skin is spread all over the body. This symbol shows that they are very intelligent, beautiful and sensitive person and always alert like a horse.

Caste: The caste assigned to the nakshatra is Vaishya (Merchant). A merchant is someone who does negotiations and always comes up with a fair deal. A successful merchant is a person who always ends up the deal in a win-win situation for both parties. A merchant is always modest and understands properly the value of time. From a business perspective, a merchant is always ready because he knows that time matters. A merchant has a good network and always keeps his relationship healthy with every person.

Ashwini nakshatra people have all these qualities; they are ready to leave their comfort for work and ready to travel anytime. They want to please every person and never do any act which makes any person at workplace angry.

Characteristics: This is the first nakshatra which indicates initiation and beginning. The day begins when Sun rises in the east. Sun being the king wants a separate place for his stay because a king can't sit with the masses. The exaltation of Sun in this nakshatra indicates this energy wants a separate place for work where no one disturbs. The work of a doctor or surgeon is such an act which can't be done in front of people and at the time of operation, a surgeon needs presence of the same thought like person and the twin head indicates that these people want the company of same thought like person, they prefer to work or study with the same thought like person or prefer to do it alone.

While travelling a king needs a speedy vehicle and the twin horses of the constellation represents speed. Ashwini people are very fast and agile person. They are very energetic people and don't like to sit inactive at a place. Their body needs movement and they like to move around in different places. After a long journey, when others get tired, they look afresh, they sleep less and quickly boost their energy. They are always active at home, like to move here and there and always engage in doing some work.

The twin brothers of the Ashwini Kumaras or the sunrise and sunset on the horizon, indicate that the beginning and the end are almost identical. So, the right start is essential for a successful completion. When the beginning is wrong, people consider it inauspicious. Therefore, Morning Prayer is necessary for successful activities during the whole day. Ashwini people don't have any problem waking up early in the morning and doing Morning Prayer.

They take much interest in creative and healing activities. They look very smart, beautiful, and strong like a horse. They look younger than their actual age. They are very kind people and take an interest in religious activities. They are very sincere and caring people who like to take care of every member of the family. With the grace of twin brothers, they are fortunate and magnanimous person. They never do any harm to any other person.

At sunrise and sunset, the color of the horizon is red, so they like many shades of red. Red is the color that immediately attracts attention. Hence, they attract the attention of everyone and become the most liked person because of their humble and hardworking nature. But red also signifies isolation from others, and this Nakshatra is ruled by Ketu which signifies separation, therefore, to some extent, they are isolated from others.

Another meaning of Ashwa is Turanga which means fast going. A horse is a very loyal animal, obeying the orders of its master and sometimes even sacrifices its life. Ashwini people are agile, trustworthy, and reliable people and they are always ready to help others. To complete their work they sacrifice their food, sleep, etc. but completing the work is very important for them. They are good at time management and always complete their work on time. They are very straightforward people, never dodge anyone, and always want every matter to be clear. They are very agile and finish their work quickly. They like to be independent and do not like to be dominated by anyone.

The deity of the Nakshatra is always shown as a twin, so it is difficult for them to be alone and they always want someone or the other's company. They love their friends and family, are quick to organize group gatherings, and love light jokes. They are adventurous and eager to discover new things. They want to explore something new and are always ready to travel somewhere. Traveling gives them excitement and they don't want anything motionless in their life. They find it very uncomfortable to sit idle in one place and in such a situation they want to break all bonds.

Running requires space and oxygen, the closed doors and windows restrict fresh air and oxygen. So, the first thing they do immediately after entering a room is to open all the doors and windows and let fresh air enter the room. This nakshatra is closely related to the breath and long breath is required for healing and singing.

The first sound of the universe is "Om" and being the first Nakshatra, this is associated with everything that starts from the beginning. The people of Ashwini Nakshatra are very sensitive to sound and speech. Their voice is very sweet and they are fond of music and singing. Hence, they are good singers and have a deep understanding of phonetics. They can pronounce even difficult words easily, and their pronunciation is very clear.

According to mythology, the twin deities – Ashwini Kumars are the physicians of the gods and they cured the blindness of the yogi Chyavana.That's why the people of Ashwini Nakshatra feel great sympathy with the blind person or the one-eyed person and they work as ophthalmologists and provide all their support to such people.

They feel compassion for the injured person. They have strong knowledge of medical science and work as doctors, surgeons, nurses, or any other profession related to this field. Being the first Nakshatra, they are involved in every work of child development. They are very kind people and work as kinder garden teachers, child care centers etc., where children's needs and activities are taken care of for their development.

They work as a teacher or a professor in the education department. They work in colleges, universities, and other places where students come and learn skills and face the challenges of the world. They act as a coach and never get angry on repeated questioning and like a mother their punishment is never harsh and wants all round development of their students. This energy is related to the beginning, so these people do any work related to the beginning. It is highly altruistic energy and it can never do anything wrong to any person. If anything goes wrong, they immediately say "sorry", a word that is always on their tongue.

The planetary ruler of the nakshatra is Ketu, which is a mysterious planet and a significator of Moksha (salvation). Ketu's behaviour is sudden and unpredictable and its energy is separative. Ashwini

Nakshatra people's behaviour is mysterious and unpredictable and many unexpected events happen in their life. They are secretive and it is very difficult for others to know what is in their mind. They never reveal their feelings, ideas and thoughts. Sometimes, they find it difficult to express their thoughts in words, so, they speak very slowly, say only a few words, and expect that the other person will understand the rest, especially Ashwini females.

Their intuition is very strong and their understanding is very deep. They are the person who takes decisions from their heart. So, they are very liberal and unable to take tough decisions. People take undue advantage of their benevolent behavior but this humble energy cannot do anything drastic. Sometimes they make the situation bad due to their extremely liberal behavior but they think that what they have done is right. They take wrong decisions because of their liberal behavior but they do not like anything harsh and stiff in their life, neither the behaviour of a person nor the food. That's why such people like to watch comedy serials and funny movies and enjoy delicious food.

People born in Ketu Nakshatra have many unfulfilled desires from their past lives. Therefore, they crave speed in life, don't like anything static, and get bored easily. Running around all day never frustrates them, but in a few minutes of traffic jams, they soon become frustrated and tired.

The first nakshatra indicates the beginning of something new in life. They can produce new and innovative ideas, they research new thoughts and anything fresh and new always excites them. They often use these terms in their discussions; fresh, new, advanced, modern, latest, original, unique, recent, brand-new, up-to-date, etc.

Ashwini Nakshatra is the first Gandanta Nakshatra where the water energy of Pisces ends and the fiery energy of Aries begins. Water and fire have no relation and are opposed to each other. The divisive energy of Ketu indicates that they have no attachment with the past and always believe in new beginnings. Therefore, they have strong abilities to produce new things and can make some great discoveries in life.

On the higher aspects, this energy signifies the return of the soul to the kingdom of God. According to Hindu scriptures, each soul is separated from God, and in millions of births, the Jiva (soul) wanders in the mundane world in various yonis and goes through many experiences.

One day the soul wakes up and starts stopping its futile activities. The Sun begins to set on the horizon and then the beauty of the sunset cannot be compared. Such a person's hands are automatically joined and his head is bowed down, now he has no ego, he has completed his journey.

Negative Traits: They go into a headless state of mind, do not listen to anyone's advice, and become very rigid due to rulership of Ketu and Mars indicates anger, a person with full anger and a headless state of mind creates a big problem, such a person doesn't know what they are doing, they are impatient and take irrational decisions. Although, they calm down soon but such behaviour is non-acceptable in society.

They are very stubborn, get frustrated easily, and get nervous very soon. They believe in running from the situation, they are not visionary people and often take wrong decisions. They run around aimlessly but cannot stay at one place. Their liberal decision creates a big problem for others but they are never ready to accept their mistake. They complete their work or project soon but want to see the result quickly due to their impatient behavior.

Anything new ignites their mind; therefore, they start a lot of things, make messes and waste resources. They work in an unorganized manner and are unable to handle large-scale projects. They lack direction and are poor at navigation. Due to their impatient behaviour, they never learn from their mistakes and keep repeating the same mistake again and again.

Gender: Its gender is Male. It indicates high activity.

Animal Symbol: Its animal symbol is a 'Male Horse', and its counterpart is Satabhisha nakshatra whose animal symbol is female horse. It is inimical to Swati and Hasta nakshatra whose animal symbol is buffalo.

Horses are social animals, and they need the company of other horses in order to be happy. They are very active animals, have a keen sense of smell and hearing, and can see forward with one eye and backward with the other. This is one of the reasons why sometimes they are a blindfold. Horses are assertive, can be easily dominated but not aggressive. They are also known to have excellent memory, have high retention and never forget anything.

Sun's Ingress: The Sun enters Ashwini nakshatra from 14th April – 28th April every year. During this time the temperature starts rising in India. Various new initiatives start taking place, students start taking new admission in various schools and colleges. Nature itself supports the new beginning.

Profession: This constellation has a strong relation with travel, so, they do transport-related business. They do medicines and drug-related jobs and work as doctors, pediatricians, physiotherapists, and psychologists. They work in anything related to the beginning, as toy makers or sellers, children's books writers, kindergarten teachers, and tutors. They work as singers or any work related to voice and sound. They do work related to nurturing, counselors, social workers, and education-related work. They run fast, work as sports person and take participation in fun and adventurous sports.

Favourable Activities: The energy of the nakshatra supports starting anything new in life. It is good for starting a new journey or a new project or travelling to a new place etc. It is good for medical activities, it is good for learning something new in life, and taking initiative, it is good for yoga and breathing practices.

Unfavorable Activities: Not auspicious for marriage and closing of anything.

Gana (Type): Its Gana is Dev. They are not demanding and calm down easily.

Guna (Quality): The quality of the constellation is "Rajasic-Rajasic-Rajasic". They prefer to do work when some motivation is there.

Body Parts: Upper part of foot is related to this nakshatra.

Tree: The tree associated with the nakshatra is Ashwagandha. The scientific name of the tree is '*Withania somnifera*' which is also known as Winter Cherry. Ashwagandha in Sanskrit means "smell of the horse," indicating that the herb has the ability to provide the strength and power of a horse. Ashwagandha is one of the most important herbs in Ayurveda and is used for various kinds of disease processes and especially as a nervine tonic. It is useful to treat insomnia and ease pain and inflammation.

Padas: The first pada of this nakshatra is 0°0' - 3° 20' in Aries and ruled by Mars (Aries Navamsha). The energy of this pada indicates the most dauntless and courageous nature of the person. They are very quick; possess strong commanding power, and ability to move forward against all odds. They are impulsive people, they are initiative takers and do not hesitate to take risks. They like to win at any cost, no matter what. They prefer to go alone and do not wait for others to join them.

The second pada of this nakshatra is 3° 20' - 6° 40' in Aries and ruled by Venus (Taurus Navamsha). The energy in this pada indicates they are very reliable, loyal, and creative person. They have a strong sense of humor and are fond of pleasure. They are dress-conscious people; take an interest in gatherings, and like music and arts. They avoid taking risks of any kind.

The third pada of this nakshatra is 6° 40' - 10° 00' in Aries and ruled by Mercury (Gemini Navamsha). These natives are good at communication and logic. They are witty and like gossip. They are very cooperative, good at teamwork, and strong in negotiations. They generate strong ideas and are good at writing, editing and publishing. They are very talkative people and have many friends. They are always updated with every latest news and information. They are curious, but restless individuals.

The fourth pada of this nakshatra is 10° 0' - 13° 20' in Aries and ruled by Moon (Cancer Navamsha). They are very emotional and moody people. They prefer a safe environment and are always ready to help others. They are keen observers and have strong intuition. They are very productive persons and give good results. They take interest in taking care of others; these people have a lot of sensitivity and imagination.

Chapter 2

Bharani

Bharani is the 2nd of 27 nakshatras and is situated at 13° 20' - 26° 40' Aries. Bharani comes from the Sanskrit word Bharana, which means "Nurture", "Filling up" or "Compensation to be made when something gets damaged". Hence, Bharani means "The Bearer" or "One who maintains". In this nakshatra Saturn gets debilitated at 20°.

Astronomy: In the constellation of Aries and a visual magnitude of 3.63, the main star of this nakshatra is known as "41 Arietis". The star can be seen at the declination 27° N 21' 6.77" and right ascension 2h 51m 18.9s in the clear sky.

Deity: The deities of the nakshatra are known as Yami and Yama. They are twins and the gods of life and death. Yama is the god of death and Yami (Yamuna) is his twin sister. Yama – the God of Death has the greatest power to give life back to a person and

Goddess Yami represents the connection of this Nakshatra with water.

The deity indicates that one can see a death-like experience and then he gets his life back. When a sperm enters the egg, the sperm's identity is lost and a baby begins to take shape and it gets a new life when comes out from the mother's womb. When a person dies and the soul leaves the body, it does not enter the same body again. The association of lord of death indicates this nakshatra has strong relation with death; therefore, Bharani natives take interest in life after death and read literature related to this topic.

Kali is another deity associated with the nakshatra. Mythology says, when Kali entered the battle, she started fiercely killing all the demons and they started running here and there to save their lives. This Nakshatra has a strong power to dispel the infinite darkness quickly and impart knowledge. This calm energy can suddenly become terrifying and swiftly dispel all the devils of darkness.

Shakti (Power): The power of the Nakshatra is known as "Apabharani Shakti". Ap is the Sanskrit term for "Water", which means "The power to take things away from water" or "The power to remove or cleanse impurities".

The Sight of Nakshatra: It is Adhomukhi Nakshatra – Facing Downward.

Nature: Ugra (Dreadful)

Element: The element of the nakshatra is "Earth". Bharani people are very firm in their commitment.

Activity: The activity of the nakshatra is "Balanced". Bharani people bring balance among critical circumstances, do justice, and prefer to balance in every sphere of life.

TriMurti and Behaviour: Vishnu and Maintenance

Planetary Ruler: The planetary lord of the Nakshatra is Venus which is related to the reproductive part of the body. Venus is the lord of sexual energy which has the power to transform and give new birth.

Symbol: The symbol of the nakshatra is Vagina (Yoni). It is a female sexual organ and it is the source of existence. It is a way of birth where a sperm enters and takes a shape of a baby. It is very mysterious, a sperm is not visible from the naked eye, but when it enters the vagina, its transformation begins and starts to cross the various stages one after the other. Nature (Prakriti) works silently in the mother's womb and everything is in deep darkness (Tamas). After some time, everyone jumps with joy when the child comes out of the mother's womb.

Boat is another symbol of the nakshatra. A boat always floats on top of the water and saves one's life. No matter how deep the water, but a narrow and small boat is enough to save from drowning and give new life. This energy saves the person from drowning in the deep sea of this material world and helps the person to reach safely on the river bank (Ultimate wisdom).

The third symbol is a shape of an "Inverted Triangle". It indicates the shape of the uterus. The uterus is the place where the fertilized egg begins to take shape. The uterus carries this fertilized egg for the next nine months; therefore, this nakshatra has strong relation with bearing and carrying.

Caste: The caste assigned to the asterism by our ancient sages is Mleccha (Outcaste). Mleccha are those who are unable to live in the society. Bharani Nakshatra people do such things which people do not do in front of others and which are not accepted by a group or society. They prefer to live in a secluded place or a place where other outcasts are living.

Characteristics: Existence manifests itself in various forms; among them humans are the best. For birth every soul requires a womb and the vagina is the source which provides entry of a sperm to takes shape of a baby. This is the way nature's greatest creation come into existence. The power of this nakshatra is to take away things from water or to clean impurities and water is the essential element for cleaning.

A baby in the womb of mother float in the water and when the time comes it starts pushing down to come out. The energy works is downward direction and help the baby to come out from the womb. This process requires patience, deep understanding and much caring of the child. Hence, midwives and doctors are called during this time and Bharani people work related to these professions.

The personality of these people has imbibed all these qualities and they are very mature and mysterious people. They keep patience, their understanding is very deep and they always keep everything secret. They are very hard-working person and like a mother they are very caring in nature and take care of every person in the family. A pregnant woman never takes any wrong step and takes utmost care of the fetus. In the same way, Bharani people take extreme level of caution in their work and never do any mistake. They keep every file well organized and remember everything even after many years.

Ashwini is the energy that starts the work and Bharani is the one that completes the work. They never leave anything in between and anyone in lurch. Once they offer their hand, they drag the person (task) on the bank of the river (final completion). Ashwini represents the male who initiates and Bharani represents the female who holds and sustains.

Ashwini represents the man who throws the sperm into the womb of a female, but it is the job of the woman to protect the sperm, and provide due care until it transforms into a baby. It takes months to complete but Bharani have such strength and patience, that's why Bharani people are never in a hurry and hate any kind of haste.

They are adept at keeping things safe and providing proper security. They keep valuables in a safe place and protect them like a pregnant woman protects her fetus. They work to prepare strong boxes, and keep everything safe in the warehouse. Planets in Bharani indicate a person who is always ready to defend his things and becomes extremely fierce if someone attacks to snatch his things from his hands. Hence, they act as a guard who is always ready to protect the valuables.

However, they do not initiate. When there is any sign of danger, they immediately create a circle to safe their belongings and do not allow anyone to enter in that circle. They are the best protectors. They always take step carefully and move ahead only when everything is safe and secure. Their first priority is always to protect the valuables.

They are very honest, loyal and faithful person and never cheat anyone, they patiently do their work and wait for the outcome. They never demand the fruits of their loyalty and hard work. They are silent person but nothing can be missed from their sharp eye. They have compassion and provide necessary guidance to others.

The energy of this nakshatra works as to take things from water. A human body contains 70% water and after death our soul leaves this watery body. The association of the lord of life and death shows that they recognize any dead thing immediately and as

Yama comes to take the soul and the body is left behind, they save life by removing the dead. They immediately recognize the signs of life and do everything possible to save it. They are the best physicians who save a person's life by removing any dead matter from the body. They have a strong desire to save the dying person and get the person out of danger.

They are too perfectionistic to take anything out very slowly, as by gently pushing the baby comes out of the womb. Yama pulls the soul silently from the body. Bharani people do their work silently and show only the result, till they keep patience and involve in the process with full concentration and sacrifice everything to complete the work.

They are much disciplined and live a moral life. They are good to fill the gap and bring order and justice. They have strong patience to bear immense pain without making any complaint.

The energy of the nakshatra is dreadful due to association with Yama. Yama keeps no mercy and pull the soul from the body. Similarly, the people of Bharani do not show mercy to anyone during their work. A midwife may scold the child's father at the time of childbirth. There is no matter of any delay, the situation can become critical, the baby has to come out and no one dares to interrupt the process. Hence, Bharani nakshatra people anger is very fierce. They want to destroy everything like Yama. On hearing the name of death, people get scared and the relation of the lord of death with this nakshatra makes them outcaste (Mleccha) from the society.

They do things that other people hesitate to do. They are very calm and believe in silently doing their work. They provide out of the box ideas because their mind doesn't like to think in a traditional manner. They prefer to live at isolated place or spend time alone in their room. They are taboo-breakers.

The process of birth requires sexual energy. Bharani - The star of transformation, signifies that a person's transformation begins when his or her sexual energy begins to transform.

Sex is closely related to food, and food is closely related to blood. Blood is needed to save someone's life and it slowly enters the sick body and gives new life to the person. Hence, Bharani people work in the blood bank; they patiently collect the blood and work hard to save the life of the wounded and sick persons. They take interest in cooking and they cook good food. They take keen interest in every activity of creation and it manifest in various aspect of life.

Life and death both are connected with this asterism. For a new life sexual energy is required and where there is life, there is death. Hence, they take interest in sex, occult and tantric activities. Life and death mean beginning and end. They work in most of the jobs where something is related to beginning or something is going to end.

On the higher aspect, Vagina indicates 'Cosmic Yoni' where billions of stars take birth. The whole existence is coming out from that 'Cosmic Yoni'. When a person sees above into the sky everything looks very mysterious. Different stages of transformation indicate that this energy transforms a person from lower conscious level to superconscious level.

Negative Traits: This nakshatra is deeply related with the female sexual organs. If the energy has gone into wrong direction, then they become sexually perverted and deeply indulge in notorious activities. This fierce energy is not ready to listen anyone's advice, they have strong desire for pleasure and can indulge too much on the matter related with sex. They become extremely possessive and furious when someone comes to take something from their possession. They are not ready to share anything and keep everything secret.

They always feel afraid of unknown danger. They always take utmost care on every step and become very fearful. They lose their confidence, always feel gloomy and lose the trust of every person.

Gender: The gender of the nakshatra is "Female". This energy brings feminine traits to the planets placed in this nakshatra.

Animal Symbol: Its animal symbol is 'Male Elephant', and it is compatible with Revati nakshatra whose animal symbol is a female elephant. It is inimical to Purva Bhadrapada and Dhanishta nakshatra whose animal symbol is lion.

Elephants are the largest living land mammals and male elephants are bigger than females. They leave the family unit between 12 and 15 years of age and are solitary. They are mainly active in the morning and evening (twilight) when the atmosphere is cooler and tend to roam on their own or in a small group. The association with the male elephant shows how powerful this energy is when calm and uncontrollable when agitated.

Sun's Ingress: Sun enters Bharani nakshatra from 28th April to 12th May every year. This is the time when the temperature is at its peak in the country.

Profession: Doctors, Surgeons, Gynecologists, Midwives, IVF experts, and Pediatricians. They work for the entertainment & film industry, amusements, theme parks, play rounds, hospitality sectors like hotels and caterers, meat production, leather industry, construction, farming, and cosmetics. All activities connected with funerals and morgues, birth & death record-keeping officer, coffin makers, and obituary writer. They work for the tea, coffee, and tobacco industry. They work as geologists, and volcanic & earthquake experts. They are excellent at protecting someone, hence, they work as bodyguards.

Favorable Activities: Tantric activities, research, drilling, digging, fencing, trenching, nurturing and caring activities, sex and childbirth-related activities, and life-saving activities.

Unfavorable Activities: It is not auspicious for marriage and travel-related activities. It is not auspicious for ceremonial and destructive activities. It is not good to take initiative in any matter. It is not good for the declaration of war and any offensive activity.

Gana (Type): The Gana assigned to the nakshatra is "Manushya" (Humans). Humans are the middle between gods and devils. The people of Bharani has many humanitarian qualities, they are very compassionate person and bring balance to life.

Guna (Quality): Under the category of three Guna the quality of Bharani is "Rajasic-Rajasic-Tamasic". They are not initiators and like some motivation to perform the tasks and money is the greatest motivator. If motivation is high, they act quickly; otherwise they remain in their deep darkness.

Body Parts: The bottom of the feet is related to this nakshatra.

Tree: It is related to the Amla tree, also known as Indian Gooseberry. Its scientific name is "*Phyllanthus emblica*". It is a medium-sized tree up to 8 meters in height. It has various medicinal benefits; it strengthens the body's defense mechanism and flushes out toxins. It improves eyesight and controls blood sugar. It is considered a sacred tree and is worshiped in the country.

Padas: The first pada of this asterism is 13° 20' - 16° 40' in Aries and ruled by Sun (Leo Navamsha). Such a person is very energetic with high creative abilities. They are bold and courageous and can command people. They are good at administration and are big-hearted.

The second pada of this asterism is 16° 40' - 20° 00' in Aries and ruled by Mercury (Virgo Navamsha). They are intelligent and good at cooperation. They like to win debates and are strong in negotiations. They are curious, explorers and take quick action.

The third pada of this asterism is 20° 00' - 23° 20' in Aries and ruled by Venus (Libra Navamsha). They are diplomatic and have a strong business quality. They are very active in their social life but do not like any controversial matter. They are very popular and adept at maintaining relationships.

The fourth pada of this asterism is 23° 20' - 26° 40' in Aries and ruled by Mars (Scorpio Navamsha). The fierce form of Bharani is visible in this pada. The position of the Moon is very important; a weak Moon makes a person extremist, cruel, stubborn, egoistic, and obsessive. Here, the negative qualities of sex are visible and the person can become a sexually perverted person. On the higher aspect, such a person uses this energy to uncover the mystery of the universe and penetrate deep into Tantra and Occult.

Chapter 3

Krittika

Krittika is the 3rd of 27 nakshatras and situated at 26° 40' Aries – 10° Taurus. It is a cluster of six stars depicted as nymphs acting as nurses of "Lord Kartikeya - The god of war". The word Krittika is divided into "Kriti" and "Ka". Kriti means "Creation", "Work done", "Action" or "Creative work has done by someone" and "Ka" is a preposition of relation. Therefore, the word Krittika means relation among the cluster of six stars and that relation is only for creation and for a specific aim or object. When the six stars focus on only one goal, their energy is very sharp and penetrating. Hence, another meaning of Krittika is "The Cutter".

Astronomy: In the constellation of Taurus, and at a visual magnitude of 2.87, the main star of this nakshatra is known as "Alcyone (Eta Taurus)". It is the third brightest star in this constellation after Aldebaran and Elnath. This star can be easily seen at the declination 24° N 10' 22.69" and right ascension 3h 48m 49.6s in the sky with the naked eye.

Deity: Lord Karttikeya who is also known as Skanda is the primary deity of this constellation. He is also called Shanmuka (six-faced Lord) and is considered commander-in-chief of the army of demigods.

According to mythology, a demon named Tarakasura was invincible and could not be killed by anyone. Only the son of Lord Shiva can kill him. Tarakasura knew that Lord Shiva had no son yet, so he could not be killed. Later the story goes ahead and the son of Lord Shiva is born, who was nurtured by the six wives of Saptirishis. When the boy becomes six years old, the battle begins between demigods and demons and Karttikeya killed the demon Tarakasura.

This story indicates that the energy of the constellation works for protection against evil. Krittika nakshatra people never misuse their weapons and when any difficult situation comes in someone's life, they are always ready to protect them. Lord Karttikeya is worshipped in South India as the protector of dharma and is known as Lord Murugan.

'Agni – The God of Fire', is the secondary deity of the constellation which indicates that this nakshatra has a strong connection with heat. Sun is the source of energy and when it conjoins with Mars, it produces excessive heat and becomes extremely powerful. Agni (fire) is the source of power and energy, and the symbol of fire of this nakshatra represents the same.

Fire is necessary for transformation; it is necessary for purification. Fire provides us light, heat, and brightness. Fire removes darkness and burns every sinful and inauspicious thing. The process of creation continues when the fire burns and the celestial creation continues going on with the heat of the Sun. The symbol of fire indicates that this nakshatra has a strong connection with creation.

Shakti (Power): The Shakti (power) of the star is known as "Dahana Shakti". Dahana means; the act of burning or producing heat and flame or burning of a substance or combustion. It means the power to destroy something by flames.

The Sight of Nakshatra: It is Adhomukhi Nakshatra – Facing Downward.

Nature: The nature of this energy is "Sharp and Soft". It shows the quality of fire, sometimes it is sharp if not utilized with proper caution and sometimes it is soft and produces favorable results and is helpful to us when we use it with proper caution.

Element: Earth

Activity: Active

TriMurti and Behaviour: Shiva and Dissolution

Planetary Ruler: The Sun is the ruler of this nakshatra. The nature of the Sun is sharp and soft, and both are necessary to maintain the environment on Earth. The Sun in the summer season is sharp but the same Sun during the winter season is soft. A king cannot remain heated all the time, for a declaration of war heat is necessary but for signing a peaceful agreement soft nature is required.

Symbol: The symbol of the constellation is a sharp object as a kind of razor or knife or axe or anything which has a sharp edge. The tip of the flame is sharp since hot air rises. The symbol represents the intense nature of the Nakshatra; its energy is very sharp and has strong ability to penetrate deeply.

The symbol indicates that Krittika people never hesitate to cut anything but being protective in nature they never take the initiative to harm others. When they find something wrong or there is no point in keeping it, they are ready to cut it without any hesitation. Just as a sharp arrow can pierce the target, they always do only purposeful and meaningful things. If the arrow has no target, they never shoot it from their bow i.e., they do not indulge in doing anything worthlessly. They don't like to wander here and there and always do something which has a purpose in life. They don't like gossip and say only a few words, they believe in saying short sentences and don't like lengthy discussions and meetings. The aim of their discussion is to get straight to the point, and they don't like to circumrotate.

Caste: The caste assigned to the constellation is 'Brahmin'. A Brahmin is a person who works on his mind and can think deeply. They are knowledgeable and visionary person, and have a strong ability to guide others. The caste indicates an inclination towards purification. Although it is a very aggressive nakshatra, they never fight for anything wrong and believe that what they are doing is always right.

Characteristics: Krittika's energy is a very high fiery energy. When the energy is high it can't sit idle. These people never hesitate to take initiative; they are adventurous and never afraid to take step towards the unknown path. Due to their penetrating insight and ability to play with sharp objects, they properly assess the depth of the risk and prepare their planning accordingly.

As the symbol indicates, their logics are very sharp and with their penetrating eyes they can see the hidden truth or hidden motive of a person. Their focus is always on a direction and immediately cut all those things which have lost its direction. In a meeting they cut the worthless discussions, they cut the relations; they leave their work and place without hesitation. They are the first who speak in a meeting and when no one dare to ask, they ask questions and as the fire is visible from a long distance, they get attracted immediately. This energy is a unique mix of sharpness and softness, they are very aggressive people but their personality also has softness and they never use their aggression for wrong deeds. The fiery energy of Krittika never does any harm to anyone unless it is teased. This energy always works for protection.

They can catch a flying knife by their hands but they keep its sharp edge always down and raise only when danger arises. They are very sharp but on face always appear to be a soft and polite person. They like calm and peace in their surroundings.

Krittika's natives are not afraid of trials; being courageous they always take their step forward and want to see the outcome from their eyes. They lack consistency and want to enrich their experience, so, they leave their job, they leave their city and country too. Years of relations they cut within seconds, they are not social person, they are not diplomats.

They see various ups and downs in their life and till the middle age their life is full with trials and experiences. They are very rich in many experiences but lag behind socially. They never look back; they are very optimistic and go ahead soon. The second half of their life is completely a changed life. They have knowledge of various arts and subjects; they learn from their trials, their experience is vast, which many people do not have.

The energy of the nakshatra favors cutting and burning for creation. Cooking is one such activity where both are required. Hence, they take great interest in cooking activities. This nakshatra has strong connection with source of energy and power, and it deals with fire and metabolism in our body. So, many Krittika people work with fire related jobs. The nature of the nakhashatra is sharp and soft. The process of cooking requires softness with the heat of fire otherwise food will burn. They are soft in nature but often burn their outcome or food, because they lack patience.

The food looks delicious when it is hot but we have to eat it with caution. Hence, Krittika natives look very smart and charming but inside a razor-sharp person is sitting and this heat is not an ordinary heat, but it is excessive and fierce. Krittika people always like to eat hot food and they can drink a hot cup of tea very fast.

When they find anything wrong or untruthful or someone take undue advantage of their soft behaviour, then immediately a sharp knife comes out. They are ready to cut immediately everything and burn it forever. Their move is totally unexpected and surprises others but they are not negotiators. When they leave anything, they leave it forever. There are no negotiations with fire only it has to calm down by removing fuels.

Fire is sharp and also provides comfort; it is both friend and enemy. An uncontrolled fire is dangerous, but when it is controlled, it works as a friend; it cooks our food, and makes us warm. A small quantity of fire we require in everyday of our life, without which everything would become freeze.

Fire is necessary to create something, and the Sun is the creator of everything that exists on the universe. So, this nakshatra has strong connection with creation. Krittika nakshatra people are very creative and always produce innovative ideas. As strong fire is required to create something big, they have capacity to create something big and often use the term; big, large, great, broad, tremendous in their discussions.

They are very liberal and broad-minded person. They are very good advisors. They always think about an aim or a purpose or how to penetrate a difficult task. They do deep enquiry and easily identify the cause of imperfection. Their eyes are like scanners, who can easily detect anything wrong in the piles of luggage. Hence, they always look for perfection and are not ready to accept anything below the quality. Their vision is very deep and they have a strong mind which does not satisfy by only superficial observations. They are deep thinkers and have ability to see the root cause of the problem.

According to science, when the oxygen in the air combines with the carbon and hydrogen in the fuel, a chemical reaction occurs. In this process energy is released in the form of heat and light, which is called fire. Fire burns everything and never shows any mercy. To play with fire is very dangerous as it can create serious harm on a slight mistake. Hence, it is not good to play with Krittika people, their hidden fire can burn anytime when necessary chemical reaction takes place.

A very soft person can convert into a very fiery person, a big danger exists on the next level, and the chain reaction begins with no time. Following are some points that describe the quality of fire and the characteristics of Krittika people;

1. Fire sparks suddenly, so they are blunt.

2. Fire provides protection, so they are protective.

3. Fire provides strength and support; they are ready to provide strength and support.

4. Fire provides light and the way out from darkness, they always provide proper and valuable guidance to others.

5. Fire provides warmth and care, so other people feel comfortable in their vicinity.

6. Fire is sharp, so, their logics and reasoning are very sharp and penetrating.

7. Fire creates a distance; therefore, they always maintain a distance and are unable to come too close to anyone.

8. Fire creates isolation, so they are lonely people and keep friendship with very few people.

When the process of burning starts it is difficult to control till the fuel exist, in the same way, Krittika people do not listen to anyone. Fire has the property of burning everything around it, similarly if they are doing one thing and they find something similar nearby, they want to finish (burn) it too. They finish it half, leave in between and want to complete another task (another burn). As fuel (motivation) is high, their process (involvement) is also high; when fuel runs out (no motivation) they drop it immediately and never regret doing so. Fire never repents, fire has no tears, it is the quality of fire to burn.

Fire indicates purity and thirst for knowledge. They are very honest person and always thirsty for knowledge. For knowledge they can travel anywhere and they keep on learning always something new in life. Having wide knowledge on multiple subjects they become good trainer, master and spiritual person.

They are very hard working and focused person. Being aggressive and adventurous in nature, they like to travel farther places and like to travel alone. They do not hesitate to accept any job which is far away from their native place. They are always ready to help others but never accept any help from others, if taken then they try to return it soon.

The puranic story of Karttikeya says that the six wives of saptirishis brought up the little boy and taught him various subjects. Hence, Krittika people are very close to their mother or any other woman like mother. They are multi-talented person but never show their ego. In many cases, those born in Krittika Nakshatra are brought up by their mother with another woman.

The puranic story states that the six-year-old Karttikeya killed the invincible demon Tarakasura, which tells us that the Krittika people have the ability to accomplish a difficult task with minimal resources. They do heroic deeds and never give up in any difficult situation.

On higher aspects, the constant burning fire indicates they are the seekers of the truth. This energy has strong power to penetrate the hidden chakras in the human body. They can become great mystics, philosophers and have ability to provide guidance to the masses. Their blunt behaviour can transform into a wise person who has ability to speak on various topics and instantly provide answer on various complex questions.

Negative Traits: The fire element produces a short-tempered person who can be provoked easily and take any sharp object in his hand. Although they calm down quickly such behavior in front of others makes them unpopular. They are very straightforward and a non-diplomatic person. Their blunt behavior makes them unacceptable people. They never listen to the advice of others and often burn their fingers. They prefer to go alone and lack the spirit of teamwork which makes them misfits in the social circle.

They like to enjoy their penetrating power and to say stinging words to others. Instead of protecting others, they misuse the power of fire and prefer to burn others. These are criminals who like to insert sharp objects into the body of others. They are unfit to live in society and live near a cremation ground or any other place where the fire burns continuously. When a person is unable to control such fiery energy, he indulges in illicit relations and finds it an easy way to calm down his energy.

Gender: The female gender of the nakshatra indicates feminine quality of this energy.

Animal Symbol: The animal symbol assigned to this constellation is Female Goat or Sheep. It is compatible with Pushya nakshatra whose symbol is a Male goat and inimical with Purva Ashadha and Shravana nakshatra whose animal symbol is monkey.

Goats are very resilient and can climb up hills with their small legs. Goats are gentle and ready to sacrifice their life. Goats avoid danger at first and become defensive. Goats are very reliable and sensitive.

These people consider all aspects deeply before taking any action. Their aim is always far and high and like a goat can climb on the mountain to eat green grass they can cross any terrain to achieve their objective. They are courageous people and do very adventurous deeds.

Goats are adept at mountain climbs by balancing their bodies and feet. Similarly, Krittika native makes the best plan to complete any difficult task. They do heroic deeds and are able to reach the top of the mountain like a goat.

Sun's Ingress: Sun enters Krittika nakshatra from 12th May to 25th May every year. During this period the temperature is at its peak in India. People try to avoid going out during the day time and use umbrellas or head caps to protect themselves from the heat. The Sun is sultry and burns the skin if precaution has not been taken.

Profession: They work as heads of state or organizations, advisors, or administrative officers. They work for those jobs where cutting is involved, through a knife, blade, or some other sharp object. They work as surgeons, carpenters, butchers, barbers, tailors, blacksmiths, and chefs. They work for the power department, arms industry, military and police department. They work as a trainer, professor, spiritual teacher, discoverers, inventors, metaphysicians, and astronomers. They work for any work-related to fire, gold, furnace, and cooking. They do best for all those works where individual performance is considered and work as an entrepreneur.

Favorable Activities: Pooja and performing yajna, fire purify everything, so it is good to do activities related to purification, cooking, cutting, and shaving. Such energy is useful to do penetrating activities like sewing, embroidery, etc.

Unfavorable Activities: This nakshatra is not auspicious for marriage and any activity related to water, social activities, and diplomacy.

Gana (Type): The gana of the nakshatra is Rakshasa (Monster). Rakshasa is unable to live in society and is too prone to anger and violence. Krittika people don't like to mingle with people and prefer to live in isolation.

Guna (Quality): The Guna of the constellation is 'Rajasic-Rajasic-Satwic'. Under the category of three gunas, the first two are rajasic indicating they are a very active person and constantly work on doing something, but their action is high when the rational motivation exists. Satwic quality indicates the final creation is always for the benefit of others.

Body Parts: The head is related to this nakshatra.

Tree: The tree associated with the constellation is Cluster fig, which is also known as the Gular or Umber tree, the scientific name of the plant is '*Ficus racemosa*'. The fruits of the tree always grow in clusters and are edible. The tree is a symbol of good luck and its plant is used for an ornamental purpose. The fruits of the plant have antibacterial, antifungal, and antimicrobial properties and have many other beneficial aspects.

Padas: The first pada of this nakshatra is 26° 40' - 30° 00' in Aries and ruled by Jupiter (Sagittarius Navamsha). Due to Sun-Mars-Jupiter energy, the level of heat is highest in this pada. They are very aggressive and dare to challenge anyone and are never afraid of the circumstances and its outcome. They are very energetic and passionate and able to perform those daring tasks which others never think to do so. They are arrogant and bossy and don't like to accept orders from others. They never accept the help of anyone and never show their back, they prefer to die than surrender. They are mystical people, possess strong knowledge of the occult, and are proficient in mantras. They have penetrating eyes, think very deeply, and are born detectives. They prefer to live alone.

The second pada of this nakshatra is 00° 00' - 3° 20' in Taurus and ruled by Saturn (Capricorn Navamsha). The aggression of Krittika turns into benevolence and compassion. The focus of energy is more on the material aspect. They like to nurture others and provide proper help and guidance. Moon is exalted here at 3° which indicates fertility and pada lord Saturn means ethics and morality are high.

The third pada of this nakshatra is 03° 20' - 06° 40 in Taurus and ruled by Saturn (Aquarius Navamsha). The creation of the Sun and the benevolence of the Moon turn into a humanitarian aspect. They believe to preserve things, focusing on collecting knowledge, and utilizing their energy in a constructive manner which will be beneficial for the public at large. They never manipulate or support anything harmful to others.

The fourth pada of this nakshatra is 06° 40' - 10° 00' in Taurus and ruled by Jupiter (Pisces Navamsha). They are a very sensitive and emotional person. They are very religious, perform spiritual practices, and have an inclination toward occultism. They are imaginative, intuitive, and selfless people. They are peaceful people, love cultural activities, and like to experience more through travelling.

Chapter 4

Rohini

Rohini is the 4th of 27 Nakshatras and is located at 10° 00' - 23° 20' Taurus. Rohini comes from the Sanskrit word Rohana which means to ascend, thrive, and prosper. The word Rohini means fertility and growth, it is also known as the mother of all cows. Rohini is known as "The red one", because of the bright color of this star. Red is the colour of excitement, enthusiasm, and passion. It is the colour of energy and action. Red attracts attention, so it is the color of success and it is also the color of danger. The association of Rohini with the color red signifies all the above-mentioned qualities in a person.

Astronomy: In the constellation of Taurus and a visual magnitude of 0.85, the star of Rohini is known as Alpha Tauri (Aldebaran). Its declination is 16° N 33' 9.68" and right ascension is 4h 37m 12.9s. It is the brightest star in Taurus and one of the easiest to find in the night sky.

Deity: The deity of the constellation is "Prajapati Brahma". He is the creator of the universe. Rohini is a perpetual fertile energy that supports the creation of existence in every matter and this mundane world runs from the seed of fertility. Mythology states that Brahma created the world with the help of Rohini, as this is the only star with the ability to create such a vast creation. Since Brahma is the creator of the constellations, Rohini becomes his daughter.

Shakti (Power): The Shakti of the nakshatra is known as 'Rohana Shakti', it is the power of growth, and growth is not possible without nurture, and nurture requires care, protection, and feeding. Without fertility, there is no feeding, so the power of this nakshatra works for fertilization and nourishment which supports growth, and every life seeks its growth. That's why every mother feeds cow's milk to her children because it is for their development. This energy only supports for growth and development.

The Sight of Nakshatra: It is an Urdhvamukhi Nakshatra i.e., Facing Upward.

Nature: The nature of the Nakshatra is Dhruva (fixed).

Element: Earth

Activity: Balanced

TriMurti and Behaviour: Brahma and Creation

Planetary Ruler: The lord of this Nakshatra is Moon. Rohini is a very soft energy and cannot become harsh at any point in time. When the moon rises above the horizon, all soft activities begin to take shape and people take interest in pleasurable activities. Dancing, music, and singing begin and aggression disappears. The energy of love starts spreading all around and creativity starts happening and the great creativity of the world continues with the energy of the Sun and Moon. So, Rohini comes after Krittika, the energy of the Moon comes after the Sun.

Every great creation begins in deep silence and the moon is our mind. When a person's mind is completely calm, he is capable of doing creative work. Only a calm person can do creation because a restless mind cannot catch subtle nuances and when the mind is unable to catch the finer details it is unable to understand the art. When the light of the moon is high, the power of creation is high, so great things are done on the full moon day. Lord Buddha was born on the full moon day and he attained enlightenment also on the full moon day.

Symbol: The main symbol of Rohini is an oxcart pulled by two bulls. People use bullock carts for travel and supply of goods, a bullock cart provides support to the legs and people feel comfortable and secure during the journey. Before the advent of machines, bullock carts pulled by two bulls were used to transport agricultural products from one place to another. Two bulls indicate strength, fertility and upward movement. A bullock cart indicates *safety and comfort* and these two are the first priority of Rohini people.

Prosperity enters when supplies reach the door. People in the market eagerly wait for the supply and this energy feeds them. The wheels of the bullock cart support the motion without which there is no prosperity and development. In the present day the oxcart has been replaced by cars and trucks, but the function remains the same.

Rohini natives want speed in their life, they move faster than others. They are very active people and deep down they know that prosperity will come only when supplies reaches, if they rest then prosperity will be delayed. So, they work hard to complete the task and immediately accept another work after the first because prosperity is wanted. They are very honest, hardworking and self-respecting people, they work hard to get money but never cheat anyone. They always take interest in feeding and share their food with others. They like to travel with full of music, song and dance and make the environment pleasant.

Another symbol of this nakshatra is a 'Chariot', pulled by horses is a sign of luxurious travel. This symbol strengthens the desire for comfort, momentum and luxury to Rohini natives.

Caste: The caste of the nakshatra is 'Shudra'. A shudra is a very hardworking person who earns his bread with whole day of hard work. They run hither and thither to supply all the necessary things and do not sit down for rest. They make an infertile land into a fertile land with their hard work and feed the people. They are the pillars of the society.

The shudra caste of this nakshatra indicates they are very hardworking person. They take care of every person in the family, and supply all the required things. To fulfill their obligation, they never take rest and work for long hours. They are individuals who are determined to help, overcome every obstacle and emerge victorious with their hard work.

Characteristics: Rohini people are good looking, well-mannered and stable mind person. They are truthful and loyal person. They are soft and benign having tender qualities and hate any kind of tricks, malpractice and conspiracy. They like comfort of every kind and a pleasant environment around their surroundings. They are very emotional person, possess feminine qualities and their power exists in their eyes. Rohini people are very intuitive and their eyes are very attractive and mystical.

Agriculture and fertility lead to civilization. So, this energy indicates every kind of development which is necessary for humanity, it is good for sowing the seeds whose fruits are eaten for generations. Rohini people take active participation to increase production and are always conscious about nature and environment.

The lord of Rohini is Moon, it comes under the sign of Venus, and both are female planets. So, the highest feminine qualities come under this nakshatra because the combination of Moon and Venus nowhere exists. So, Rohini people are very sensual and it is not in a negative way. It means the senses of their body are strong enough to catch any slight variation and only such a person can excel in arts and literature whose senses are very strong. So, they take an interest in dance, song, music, and all those activities which provide soft and soothing pleasure to the mind. People eagerly wait for the dance of the Rohini people, they are great dancers.

Moon rules our mind and mind control all the senses. Venus represents sexual energy that take part in fertility. Due to the combination of both, the senses are attracted towards sexuality, and it compels them to indulge in the desire of the senses through sexuality. As per Hindu mythology, Moon is also known for making relation with the wife of Jupiter.

But there is a difference between sexual energy and sexuality, fertility does not mean sexuality but high sexual energy. When sexual energy is high, the power of creation is high and creativity manifests in various forms. When a person controls his senses, this energy is manifested for many creative works. Then such a person's creativity starts emerging in various forms, dance, music, songs, arts are the way to manifest such energy. Venus represents attraction, and it draws it to itself. Venus is represented by diamond, and diamond always attracts attention wherever it resides.

No one can ignore the brilliance and attraction of Rohini; it brings abundance of physical pleasures to the native. Such a person draws attention with their voice and work. They are very productive and always engage in the creative work, they are very active person and they never get tired while doing creative activities.

In present corporate world, Rohini people demand productive report from their employees and prefer to take a meeting on, 'how to improve productivity'. They don't like anything unproductive and nurture to improve it. Being of the Shudra caste, their feet are always energetic, ready to run and work to increase productivity.

Taurus is a highly fertile place of the zodiac and Moon and Venus both represents water. To understand it better, we can imagine a beautiful place where river is flowing, showers are running, fresh breeze is blowing, people are dancing and singing songs. Lord Krishna's 'Rasleela' continues and whoever hears it gets instantly attracted.

Such an attraction Rohini has, so mythological story says that the Moon does not want to leave such a place and starts ignoring about other nakshatra. In Hindu mythology, these 27 constellations are the 27 wives of the Moon, but Moon likes Rohini more than other wives and gets a curse from Prajapati of waxing and waning.

Negative Traits: Rohini people use their charm for distraction and manipulation. To fulfill their desire, they can go up to any extreme and make multiple relations. They want the finest and costliest things in life that can provide some pleasure to their senses. They always like to eat rich food and indulge more in food and drink. If the Moon is weak, they are a very moody and unstable person and change their words immediately.

They are possessive, feel jealous, stubborn, and don't like to change their opinion under any circumstances. They want full comfort in their life, don't like to do any kind of work, and are ready to sacrifice other things for their comfort. If Moon is not strongly placed or affected by malefics, such a person is weak and submissive. They are timid, lack courage and immediately run away from adverse circumstances.

Gender: The gender of the nakshatra is 'Female'. It indicates all tender qualities of the person; Soft voice, attractive appearance, beauty, well-mannered and caring abilities.

Animal Symbol: The animal symbol associated with the nakshatra is the 'Male Serpent'. Its counterpart is Mrigashira, whose animal symbol is the female serpent. It is inimical to Uttara Ashadha, whose animal symbol is Mongoose.

Rohini people always take caution of their skin and clothes, like a snake shed its skin a few times a year, they change their clothes fast, and whatever is left never looks it again. Snakes are limbless and use their muscles to bend and unbend their bodies. In the same way, Rohini Nakshatra natives have a very flexible body and this skill is essential for dancing. Snakes can make soundless movements, that quality is also possessed by these people. Snakes are very intuitive and sensitive animals with charming eyes.

Among many qualities a lethal danger also exists with Rohini. Snake is a symbol of such danger, whose mouth poisons and kills the offender instantly. Its attack is sudden, fast and fatal.

But why is there such a threat in this nakshatra, which only provides support for growth and development?

Snakes eat rats and other species that damage the produce. This indicates that this energy cannot accept anything that hinders growth and annihilate that obstacle forever like a snake. Just like a mother can go to any extent to save her child, Rohini can go to any extent to save their creation. Rohini always bestows fertility and growth, and when someone tries to destroy it, then she turns fatal.

Therefore, according to the author's opinion, Lord Krishna chose to take birth in Rohini Nakshatra. When many demons started creating problems for humanity, He annihilated them forever one by one and said in Geeta, *"Whenever virtue diminishes and immorality prevails, then I come again and again to help the world"*. This "red star" always takes care of its fertility, and whoever harms it, it destroys him forever.

Sun's Ingress: Sun enters this Nakshatra every year on 25th May and stays there till 8th June. During this time marriages and ceremonies starts in India.

Profession: Banker, Accountant, Financial Advisor, Treasurer, Dancer, Musician, Singer, Fashion designer, Car designer, Model, Artist, Actor, Farmer, Cosmetics, Textiles, Environmentalist, and any work-related to agriculture, feeding, and creation.

Favorable Activities: It is auspicious for marriage, and buying clothes, jewellery. It is good for farming, gardening, and plantation.

Unfavorable Activities: It is not suitable for any harsh activity.

Gana (Type): The gana of the nakshatra is Manushya (Human). It indicates a level of consciousness that has the power to choose. Human nakshatras have enough potential to move in either direction (ups and downs) and such choices always exist in their hands.

Guna (Quality): The quality of the nakshatra is "Rajasic-Tamasic-Rajasic". It is a very active Nakshatra that inspires to fulfill the desire which otherwise remains in a passive state. This indicates that after sufficient rajasic activities, they prefer to go on a long vacation where they are unaware of the activities of the outside world and then they are as active as before.

Body Parts: The body part related to this nakshatra is the 'forehead'. In Hindu culture, ladies wear 'bindi' at this place, a mark known as 'tilak' made on the forehead. On the higher aspect, the center of the forehead is the place of the third eye.

Tree: The tree associated with Rohini is "Jamun", also known as *'Syzygium cumini'*. It is an evergreen tree, that grows very tall and bears fruits in May and June. Its fruits are very soft and perishable, so it is picked and sold fresh daily. It cures diabetes, diarrhea, and ringworm and has many other medicinal properties.

Padas: The first pada of this asterism is 10° 00' - 13° 20' in Taurus and ruled by Mars (Aries Navamsha). They are a passionate, impulsive, and action-oriented person. They are a confident person and take on new challenges. Mars is a forceful planet, any relation with Rahu will increase the force, and such a person will indulge in deep materialism and take any initiative to fulfill his desire.

The second pada of this asterism is 13° 20' - 16° 40' in Taurus and ruled by Venus (Taurus Navamsha). The highest quality of Venus is present in this pada. They are a creative and well-mannered person. They take an interest only in the finest things and are not ready to compromise with others. They always look for luxury, comfort, and pleasure. They are truthful, loyal, and hardworking people. They take interest in arts, social activities and are always ready to help others.

The third pada of this asterism is 13° 20' - 16° 40' in Taurus and ruled by Mercury (Gemini Navamsha). They are cooperative people, express their ideas in strong words, and do arguments with logic. They are inquisitive people, good in negotiations, and have strong business acumen. They always prefer light discussion and hate any kind of rough word. They are good at writing.

The fourth pada of this asterism is 16° 40' - 20° 00' in Taurus and ruled by the Moon (Cancer Navamsha). This pada indicates a very moody person, who changes his word immediately after saying them. Such a person is a fickle-minded person and unable to take any decision. They will take a step when everything is in their favor and secured. They are a highly possessive, extremally materialistic person and don't have any capacity to think beyond the box. Such a person always thinks about themselves, the demerit of flattery and sycophancy is also visible in this pada.

Chapter 5

Mrigashira

Mrigashira is the 5th of 27 Nakshatras and is located at 23° 20' Taurus – 06° 40' Gemini. The word Mrigashira comes from the two Sanskrit words, 'Mriga' means deer and 'Shira' means head, so it means 'Deer's head'.

It is the star of search, and the greatest search is the search for God. Where is 'He' hiding, the scriptures say that 'He' is there and if 'He' is, then we have to find 'Him', but where to find, this Nakshatra provides energy to search for the unknown.

Astronomy: In the constellation of Orion, Rigel (Beta Orion) and Bellatrix (Gamma Orion) are the two brightest stars visible in the night sky at the magnitude of 0.12 and 1.64 respectively. Its declination; 8° S 10' 38.19" and 6° N 22' 5.6", and right ascensions; 5h 15m 37.2s and 5h 26m 20.3s, respectively.

Deity: The presiding deity of the nakshatra is Soma, who is known as the god of immortality. Soma is known as the moon and is also the name of an elixir of the gods, by drinking that they always look young and attractive. Every quest begins with a thirst, and when there is a thirst then the person is ready to travel and recognizes every sign along the way. The God of immortality indicates that the search for the unknown ultimately leads the seeker to the path of immortality.

There are many mythological stories that tell about the effort of a person to achieve immortality. It means that which is not easily available, one has to make tireless efforts to achieve it, one has to search through countless paths and the energy of this Nakshatra gives the power to do so.

Shakti (Power): The Shakti of the nakshatra is "Prinana shakti", i.e., the power of fulfillment.

The Sight of Nakshatra: Tiryanga-mukha (Sideways)

Nature: Mridu (Soft)

Element: Earth

Activity: Passive

Planetary Ruler: Mars is the ruler of this nakshatra. It is the seeking energy, and such a person seeks every hidden thing, and the most hidden one is the Supreme Soul. The soul searches for it everywhere, and it does not find it, yet this Nakshatra keeps on giving energy and does not sit idle. Because such a discovery requires incessant energy, that's why Mars is the lord of this Nakshatra.

Symbol: The associated symbol is "Deer or Deer's head". According to Hindu mythology, there is a story of the birth of this nakshatra. Lord Brahma falls in love with her daughter Rohini, is obsessed with her charm, and starts chasing to make a sexual relationship with her. Then Lord Shiva was very upset, he knew that the creator's head was causing problems, in the form of a hunter he immediately shoots an arrow and cut the head. Where the head falls leads to the birth of this constellation.

This story has great significance, on the lower aspect it indicates incest but it has a very deep meaning that people do not understand. Every person falls in love with one's creation and it becomes very difficult for him to leave it.

For instance;

1) A worker's month-end salary is the creation of his hard work and imagine the reaction of that worker when someone says to leave that forever.

2) A person reached a top position in his life after years of hard work, and how he will react to listen to the words that leave it immediately.

3) After many battles a king has built an empire, can he give it up to get some other superior things, which is unknown?

It is totally impossible for a person to leave his creation, so how a seeker of the truth can leave his hard-earned penance? Daughter is the best example taken by our ancient sages to describe such a situation. Every daughter is the most beautiful creation of her father, and Brahma falling in lust with his daughter Rohini indicates that the last obstacle on the path of ultimate truth is to love one's creation (penance). After much wanderings, now the journey of the seeker is about to end, but he must get rid of all his penance, he has to leave all the attachments that he has created till now and this becomes impossible for a seeker.

The story says that Brahma chases Rohini for lust indicates that the seeker is ready to fall from the top but he is not ready to leave the charm of his penance and without leaving that charm this journey will never reach its destination. The biggest obstacle in the search for excellence is the seeker's beautiful creation, and without cutting that attraction, his search for truth will never be complete. Hunter indicates the help of the guru, and with that help, the seeker understands his fault, he immediately wakes up and bows down in front of the Lord, his search has been completed.

The stories written in our Vedic texts should not be taken literally; each story reflects some great meaning and provides necessary guidance. It is the compassion of our ancient sages that they have written it in the form of stories.

Caste: The caste of the nakshatra is Framer or Servant. Farmer's mind is sharp in understanding the signs of the sky. In ancient times, when satellite data was not available, farmers used to estimate rain by looking at the position of the stars. Even today, many farmers in India understand the mood of the weather by looking at the sky and decide the sowing of their crops accordingly.

A servant runs to fulfill the task after hearing the signal of the master and waits until the signal is received. Mrigashira people are smart enough to understand the signals and they prefer to wait till the signal is received.

Characteristics: Mrigashira natives are deeply influenced by the qualities of a deer. Deer are calm and gentle animal; they are very sensitive, innocent, and gracious animal. They are social but shy animal; they live and travel in groups. They are generally timid and can be tamed if trusted. The hearing and smelling power of deer is very high. They quickly smell impending danger, give a silent signal of warning to others through their tail, and flee the area.

Mrigashira is a seeker. Such a person enjoys searching, he sets out to find from a very small clue. Their brains are quick to pick up signals, like a hunter looking for his prey, they keep on searching for their target. They work for research and investigation where such skills are required. They love to explore new things and like to travel new places. They have a penchant for finding the unusual and they immediately catch it, even they can catch the change in millimeters through their naked eyes. They are very intuitive people and can sense danger quickly.

The ruling deity indicates these native looks very charming, take interest in those activities which help them to look young and are very cautious about their diets. Their focus is always to take those drinks and foods that make them always younger. They are always in search of those medicines which help them to live longer. Medicines save our lives and help us live longer. Hence, these people have strong knowledge of medicines and can identify the trees for medical benefits.

Because of their vast experiences of different places, they are good advisors and prevent others from going in the wrong direction. They do the work of a map worker, navigator and their mind are sharp to catch the signals available along the way, like a farmer catches signals from the sky, they recognize distant signals.

These natives always take interest to find out hidden things, search is the purpose of their life and planets in Mrigashira indicates that such a person is ready to burn his fingers but the desire to know the unknown always pulls him. They chase for an object or a dream for their whole life. They keep rare collection of things, it also means rare books and rare knowledge, with that they always look confident and put a step forward without getting afraid. Search on the unknown path requires courage and they are very courageous person.

According to the legend of the Ramayana, the deer also symbolizes false attraction, and Lord Rama lost his wife because of going after the golden deer. It indicates trouble in married life where there is a possibility of losing the partner due to following after the mirage.

Its first two pada come in Taurus where the energy of Venus is there and the remaining two pada come in Gemini where the energy of Mercury influences. In the pada of Venus, the focus is on productivity and they always work very hard to improve it. Their focus is on the materialistic things, they like to enjoy all the pleasures of life and they keep a collection of rare luxuries in their house. They perform better in their job and gets praise, because their work immediately attracts the attention of others. Hence, they are inclined towards works like corporate presentation, speaking, music, dance etc.

They take great interest in searching by applying their mind. They like to play with their mind and deep intelligence is visible in their work. They are not interested in showing before their search is over. They love to do in-depth research and write up their findings. In fact, they find great pleasure in searching them, not in showing them.

Negative Traits: Moon indicates our mind but it is also known for its fickle mindedness and lust. The searching energy can shift in wrong direction and they take interest in finding wrong things in life. They become passionate, and to fulfill their desire they use the path of immorality. They are unable to make a difference between good and bad and get easily influenced by the attractions. They never hesitate to take any wrong step in life because steps are important for them not the direction.

Their enthusiasm can go in wrong direction and they blindly trust upon others. They are always suspicious on every information and don't believe on anyone. They are extreme desirous person and have too much attachment to their things, they become highly possessive and doesn't allow anyone to touch their things.

Gender: The gender of the nakshatra is neutral. They are not interested in making any connection with other Nakshatras and prefer only the association of other neutral gender Nakshatras.

Animal Symbol: Its animal symbol is a 'Female Serpent'. They make good relation with their counterpart animal male serpent, that is Rohini nakshatra, and inimical to Uttara Ashadha whose animal symbol is Mongoose.

The symbol of snake is used for protection. Serpents are considered as protectors of wealth. So, every asset Mrigashira person create they are very firm for its protection and they will not let their creation get destroyed at any cost and if anyone tampers even a little, they will become as dangerous as a snake. Just like snakes prevent crops from being destroyed by eating rats and attack without warning, they will not spare anyone. The attachment of a female with her produce is more than a male, that's why Mrigashira people get more attached with their creation, than Rohini people.

Sun's Ingress: Sun enters this Nakshatra every year on 8th June and stays there till 22nd June. June is the best month to visit because of the high temperature. To get relief from the heat, tourists prefer to go to the mountains. This is the month of competitive exams in India.

Profession: Mrigashira people prefer to work where movement is part of a profession. They don't like full day table jobs. They work as; Navigators, Explorers, Hunters, Writers, Salesman, Fashion designers, Farmers, Gardeners, Travel agents. They work for manufacturing and construction sector. Their eyes are always searching for some signal or their aim; hence, they work for defense sector. The ultimate search is for God, so they are Mystics.

Favorable Activities: Travel, itinerary, education, shifting, socializing with people, healing, communication and doing spiritual practices are good.

Unfavorable Activities: Unnecessary suspension and misunderstanding is not right. It is not favorable for marriage ceremonies.

Gana (Type): Its gana is Deva, indicates such a person take interest in higher aspects of life.

Guna (Quality): The quality of the nakshatra is "Rajasic-Tamasic-Tamasic". Such a person is highly active person but deep down they are very secretive and never reveal their activities to others. They keep on searching their dream without intimating to their nearest one.

Body Parts: The associated body parts are "Eyes & eyebrows".

Tree: The associated tree is known as Khadira, also known as Kattha and its scientific name is '*Acacia catechu*'. Its tree is up to the height of 10-15 meters and flowers are white and yellow. Kattha it is an important ingredient in beetle that gives red colour while chewing and mixed with lime. It is an effective herb that controls bleeding disorders, it is a great blood purifier and used for skin problems. Its decoction is used on wounds to stop bleeding and speed up the healing process.

Padas: The first pada of this asterism is 23° 20' - 26° 40' in Taurus and ruled by Sun (Leo Navamsha). They are very courageous person, take initiative and bold decisions. They are a warm, passionate and self-centered person. They are independent person, and attract attention.

The second pada of this asterism is 26° 40' - 30° 00' in Taurus and ruled by Mercury (Virgo Navamsha). They are very energetic people, concentrate on their work and do things smartly. They are intelligent and sensible person, like to cooperate with others, strong in negotiations and good in criticism.

The third pada of this asterism is 00° 00' - 03° 20' in Gemini and ruled by Venus (Libra Navamsha). The focus is more on analytics and they are quick to decipher the meaning of signals. They know that the result is an output of the process, so they do everything in an organized manner and the focus is on the right use of mind more than the end result.

The fourth pada of this asterism is 03° 20' - 06° 40' in Gemini and ruled by Mars (Scorpio Navamsha). This pada indicates a very high level of research and investigative capability. They quickly understand the hidden meaning of words, symbols, gestures, motives. They take interest in writing and pen down their experiences. They take interest in occultism and mysticism and love to travel in search of knowledge. However, if Moon is weak, negative qualities of Mrigashira can't be ruled out.

Chapter 6

Ardra

Ardra is the 6th of 27 Nakshatras and is located at 06° 40' - 20° 00' Gemini. The Sanskrit word Ardra is coming from the word "Aadra" which means "wet" or "moist". Hence, Ardra is related to water which means "fresh" or "green". These words indicate its relation with cleaning, herbs, cure, compassion, etc.

Astronomy: At sidereal longitude 04° 53' 44" Gemini and a visual magnitude of 0.4 to 1.3, the second brightest star in the Orion constellation is known as "Betelgeuse (Alpha Orion)". Its declination is 7° N 24' 33.85" and its right ascension is 5h 56m 23.4s. The second star is Alhena (Gamma Geminorum), longitude 15° 14' 44" Gemini, magnitude 1.93, declination 16° N 22' 41.36" and right ascension is 6h 39m 0.7s.

Deity: The deity of the nakshatra is known as "Rudra", the fierce form of Lord Shiva. The birth of Rudra is related to the wet and angry eyes of Shiva. Mythology says that upon hearing the news of the death of his wife Sati, Lord Shiva became furious, his eyes became moist and tears started flowing.

Who can believe that Lord Shiva is crying, but circumstances forced the Lord to cry too, when His beloved wife immolated herself in the sacrificial fire of her father Daksha. Lord Shiva could not bear this news and his eyes filled with tears and he became extremely angry.

Till then, the universe was unaware of the fierce form of Lord Shiva. But this sudden incident has changed Him completely, His tears soon turn into a storm and Rudra was born. He is a very fierce and destructive form of Shiva, full of tears and anger and ready to destroy anything that comes in front. The destruction of Daksha yagna begins and everyone starts running here and there to save their lives.

He beheaded Daksha and destroyed everything, yet his anger was out of control and invincible. The story further states that Rudra's tears become the sacred Rudraksha and where the body parts of Sati fell became a place of worship. Rudra is also called the god of storms.

Shakti (Power): The Shakti of this nakshatra is known as "Yatna Shakti". Yatna means anguish and pain; it indicates that the energy of the nakshatra works for taking efforts and endeavors. This energy gives pain to clean.

The Sight of Nakshatra: It is an Urdhvamukhi Nakshatra i.e., Facing Upward.

Nature: The nature of the Nakshatra is Tikshna (Sharp).

Element: Water

Activity: The activity of the nakshatra is "Balanced."

TriMurti and Behaviour: Shiva and Dissolution

Planetary Ruler: The planet of disorder and chaos "Rahu" is the ruler of this nakshatra. The presence of Rahu indicates inconsistency i.e., the functioning of this energy is not smooth. Rahu doesn't like to follow the rules, having the ability to break any barrier, the lordship of this nakshatra is provided to Rahu.

The water related to this Nakshatra is not ordinary silent water, it is extremely powerful like the flood that does not follow any rules and breaks all barriers. The flood water washes away all the old structures and makes significant changes to the soil, nothing happens in nature without a reason.

Symbol: The first symbol of the nakshatra is the "Teardrop". Tear starts coming from our eyes when our mind is unable to control the load of emotions, then our eyes release tears in both phases; sorrow and delight. It is a process to release the emotions and the person feels relaxed.

The second symbol is "Diamond", it is a very valuable gem and is not easily available. Due to extreme pressure and temperature over millions of years the carbon atoms are slowly converted into diamonds. Hence, every pressure that comes into the life of Ardra natives is slowly turning them into precious human beings.

The third symbol of the nakshatra is the "Human Head." The head is related to our brain and tears are related to our eyes. Hence, Ardra has a deep connection with our minds and eyes.

Caste: The caste assigned to the nakshatra is "Butcher." Its counterpart nakshatra Mula also has the same caste. The butcher cuts the flesh mercilessly. Their eyes are penetrating and their hands are powerful. Therefore, the behavior of Ardra people is sharp, they immediately cut off those things which have become unwanted or give pain.

Characteristics: Ardra is a very powerful transformational energy but these people appear to be very stable minded and calm. They are very intelligent person and possess quality of quick-thinking; they are very hard-working but stubborn. They wear simple clothes and prefers to lead an isolated life. They prefer to wear their tattered clothes and worn-out slippers, even if their wardrobe is full of clothes. They do not give any importance to the wealth, looks and clothes of others and they laugh heartily when people consider them poor. They have a very few friends and do not take any interest in maintaining relationships. They do not have any arrogance of their position and power and are always ready to help others. It is difficult for them to fit in with a group of people due to their unusual behaviour.

As they grow up, they become very mature and wise person. They always take interest in development and give up all their negative habits. They are very responsible person and attract the attention in a meeting due to their humor. They are very intuitive person and good to understand psychology as well. Due to their compassion, they always listen to the voices of others. They are very daring and courageous person and always ready to accept challenges. Due to their audacious nature, they learn from their own experiences.

Their behaviour is never constant and even they don't know what next they are going to do. They never do the same type of work in their whole life and prefer to do different types of work which have no relation with each other. They do not believe the stagnant pattern and prefer to change it. Their such behaviour create chaos among those who don't want to change their orthodoxical beliefs.

But Ardra is a very forceful and dreadful energy. Hence, they do not care about opinion of others and they think that it is a process of cleaning. They are merciless person like flood, who brings change by force and throws down all obstacles.

Water has the quality of purification and it takes away all the dirt. Showers of rain clean the dust accumulated in the atmosphere and make it pleasant. Things start changing with the first drop of rain and after the sultry weather of summer, people eagerly wait for the rains and enjoy listening to the sound of thunder in the sky. Rain brings life and people start dancing when they see the first shower of rain. It brings growth and sowing begins. So, Ardra people take interest in agricultural activities and have deep understanding of herbs and medicines. But these rains also create floods, destroy many villages and wash away everything that comes in between. In the same way, when they are angry they become very fierce and ready to destroy everything.

They look very tough from outside, but inside they have soft feminine qualities and always think about nurturing. They are very sensitive people and can understand the difference of emotions. They have knowledge of various subjects and are always in search of enhancing it. They are rebels and do not hesitate to destroy old beliefs, ideas and structures. This energy brings subtle changes and paves the path for a new life.

They have a quick mind to check things and can find fault within seconds. They quickly understand the complexity of the matter and are able to find out the solution. They observe every development and are oriented towards knowing the hidden truth, so they are never satisfied with what others say. They are deep thinkers and write about innovative ideas and revolutionary thoughts. They take a keen interest in activities related to the removal of old things and the creation of new.

Their life is full with twist and turns, but they never frustrate to walk on the difficult path of life. The energy of this nakshatra works for cleanliness, hence they are perfectionists and can find mistakes too on those files which are fully corrected and checked by others, nothing can miss from the eyes of Ardra people. They are very sensitive about failures so they prefer to check again before sending. They are very dominant person and show their superiority. They have strong ability to do in-depth research and surprise others with their findings.

Ardra person cannot work for others throughout his life, controlling an Ardra person is like controlling storm. New challenges and new projects always excite them, this energy works for creating freshness, hence, their personality shines when challenges exist, then quality of sharpness and innovation excels in their mind. Hence, they are best for an independent profile and entrepreneurship. They do best in marketing when there is no pressure upon them, if you put pressure on an Ardra person, he will take no time to leave that place.

Rahu has the quality to distract and attract attention; hence, they have strong ability to control a chaotic situation. Their life is not a stable life and Rahu indicates abnormality. Their professional life is also unstable, but they are never afraid of any unexpected event and witness sudden changes. The planets in this Nakshatra indicate that the person will have to learn various hard lessons in life, so the disorder created by Rahu is a process of clearance.

Success in the life of Ardra people is not easy. Planets placed in this nakshatra indicate that many efforts are required for achievement. It is like cleaning clothes, where soaking and beating is necessary and this rubbing and beating is not in an order (Rahu indicates disorder), temperature is also needed to clean stains and strong dirt. When the cleaning process starts, with each beating the dirt starts to get removed and gradually the clothes start to shine. When the process is over only dazzling shine remains and people cannot believe it that this is the same old clothe. Hence, their involvement in all these tough circumstances is in fact a process of cleaning. Gradually, the qualities inherent in them start coming out and one day they start shining like a diamond.

Ardra is a very powerful cleaning energy. In the same way a washer uses temperature and chemicals to remove stains and strong dirt from clothes, this energy indicates the use of temperatures and different chemicals to achieve the end result. Ardra people are excellent in finding those chemicals that can clean tough dirt. It is related with pharmaceuticals industry which uses various chemicals to clean the diseases (dirt) from the body. Beating is an important part of Ardra by the wet cleaning process, so they work for arms and ammunition industry where temperature, water and chemicals are required.

They are the washermen of the society and do not hesitate to use any means to clean up the system. They are excellent physicians and possess strong knowledge of medicines. The medicines are nothing but to flush out the dirt from the body and generally they recommend using warm water while taking the medicine.

This is the life of Ardra natives, initial success in their life are difficult. It takes a lot of effort to move even an inch. Although they are very hardworking person but success is far away from them. Due to their attire and behaviour many people think that they are a worthless person and can't do anything in life. Their life is full of chaos and they have experiences in many directions. This energy gives extreme pain but no matter how much it hurts, they believe in making one more effort.

The story of Daksha beheading indicates that this energy will cut the ego of those who abuse their power and position and underestimate the power of God. Hence, Ardra natives do not associate with arrogant persons, they immediately recognize the hidden ego and when the person's ego starts crossing its limits, they become fierce like Rudra. History is full of such incidents where a very arrogant person was beheaded by a very ordinary looking person.

Negative Traits: They are highly self-centered person and always hide their activities from others. They show lack of gratitude and abruptly cut the discussion and phone calls. They have malice nature and never show their true intention. They are greedy for materialistic things and do not hesitate in doing mean activities. They have a habit of lying and cheating people and their entire intelligence is involved in fraudulent activities.

They are lawless and cruel person; they enjoy in disobeying the orders and create difficulties for others. Rather than finding solutions they make the situation complex and create a mess. They indulge in unsocial activities; make relationship with notorious people and like worthless gossips. They are highly reckless and dogmatic person and suddenly raise their voice and shout. They are sadist person, rather than looking the bright aspect they always look the negative side and feel jealous on success of others.

The disorder in their mind, behavior and personality is manifested by their actions. They like to live in dirty places and never change their clothes for years. They enjoy torturing others, are cold-blooded killers, and willingly do things that harm others. They live only to do destruction.

Gender: The gender of the nakshatra is "Female". Its association with moisture indicates that it is not a dry (male) energy. The moist and feminine nakshatra indicates intense emotion, sacrifice and transformation.

Animal Symbol: The animal symbol associated is "Female Dog", its counterpart is Mula nakshatra whose symbol is a male dog and it is inimical to Jyestha and Anuradha nakshatra whose animal symbol is deer.

Female dogs are able to focus for longer periods of time and learn tasks more easily than male counterparts. The dog has a strong power to smell everything. In the same manner Ardra people have ability to focus more and can smell if there is something wrong. They are very moody and their aggression takes time to heat up.

Sun's Ingress: Sun enters this Nakshatra every year on 22nd June and stays there till 6th July. This is the time of onset of rainy season in India.

Profession: They work for investigation, analysis and jobs that require a high level of research work. They do better in psychology, pharmaceuticals, homeopathy, chemistry, biochemistry. They take a keen interest in storms and study weather and meteorology. They work for innovation and technology, computer science, electricity, photography, electronic music and weapon industry. They patiently wait for their time and work as a sniper.

Favourable Activities: It is good for discarding old things; Favourable for that destruction which creates barrier for arrival of new; Killing insects; Leaving unwanted jobs and relations; Good for investigation and research.

Unfavorable Activities: It is not auspicious for marriage and ceremony, it is not good for beginning, it is not good to receive anything auspicious like, awards, etc.

Gana (Type): The type of Nakshatra is Manushya (Human). This energy works to find the middle way. When one misses the true journey of life, Ardra (Rudra) comes to teach a lesson.

Guna (Quality): They are highly action-oriented individuals but remain passive until things start crossing their limits.

Body Parts: The body parts related to this nakshatra is; Hair, Scalp and Eyes.

Tree: The tree of the nakshatra is known as "Krushna Agaru" or "Agar Wood". It is known as "*Aquilaria Agallocha*". The Agaru tree has a special unique fragrance. Its herbs are useful to clean wounds and skin diseases and provide relief from cold, asthma, bronchitis. It is used in the treatment of ear, nose and throat infections etc.

Padas: The first pada of this asterism is 06° 40' - 10° 00' in Gemini and ruled by Jupiter (Sagittarius Navamsha). It represents a kind-hearted person who is thirsty for knowledge. They have strong intellect, good in communication and able to attract others by their voice and wisdom.

The second pada of this asterism is 10° 00' - 13° 20' in Gemini and ruled by Saturn (Capricorn Navamsha). This pada reflects the ability to control the tough situation, they never frustrate to see the mess, and their mind works very quickly to put things in an organized manner. They are very dogmatic, give very firm orders, desire to control everyone and never forgive anyone who disobeys their rules.

The third pada of this asterism is 13° 20' - 16° 40' in Gemini and ruled by Saturn (Aquarius Navamsha). They have deep desire to accumulate information from multiple sources and keep a network of people. They involve in reforms and innovations and are very helpful person.

The fourth pada of this asterism is 16° 40' - 20° 00' in Gemini and ruled by Jupiter (Pisces Navamsha). They are very intelligent and religious people. They are very kind, loyal but moody person. They try to avoid any kind of conflict and act as a mediator. They are very receptive, sensitive person and good in advisory. The storm which starts from the first pada and gets intense in the second and third pada, starts to subside here. They are deep observer and work to pacify the situation

Chapter 7

Punarvasu

Punarvasu is the 7th nakshatra and is situated at 20° 00' Gemini - 3° 20' Cancer. The word Punarvasu comes from the two words 'Punar' and 'Vasu'. Punar means 'Again', 'Afresh', 'Another', or 'Anew' and Vasu means 'Bright', 'Excellent', 'A ray of light', 'Beneficial', or 'Wealth'. Hence, Punarvasu means 'Bright again', 'Wealthy again', 'Another ray of light', 'Afresh again' or 'Excellent again'.

Astronomy: The two bright stars in constellation of Gemini are known as Castor (Alpha Geminorum) and Pollux (Beta Geminorum). The first star is visible at a visual magnitude of 1.95, its declination is 31° N 50' 14.13" and right ascension is 7h 36m 2s. The second star is visible at a visual magnitude of 1.14, its declination is 27° N 58' 12.03" and right ascension is 7h 46m 41.4s.

Deity: The deity of the nakshatra is "Aditi - The universal mother". The Sanskrit word Aditi means boundless or limitless. Aditi is known as the Goddess of the sky and the mother of the 12 Adityas (celestial deities). The nature of motherhood is visible among these persons and they take care of people and surroundings. They are soft-spoken and take care of everyone.

Shakti (Power): The power of the nakshatra known as "Vasutva Prapana Shakti". The power to regain wealth and objectives.

The Sight of Nakshatra: Tiryanga-mukha (Sideways)

Nature: Its nature is Chara (Movable). People of this nakshatra like to travel and being soft they feel satisfied with what they have.

Element: The element is watery and the dominion of the watery planet Jupiter shows the nourishing and nurturing quality of this nakshatra.

Activity: Its activity is Passive.

TriMurti and Behaviour: Brahma and creation.

Planetary Ruler: Only the planet that provides endless hope can become the lord of this nakshatra. Hence, Jupiter is the lord of this nakshatra.

Symbol: The symbol of Punarvasu is "Quiver of arrows" which indicates that if one arrow misses the target then another will hit and the process will go on until the target has been achieved.

Caste: The caste of Nakshatra is Vaishya (merchant). Merchants are the provider of necessary means to society but in exchange for that, they want something in their pocket. A merchant is that person;

1. Who is not aggressive and uses gentle words.

2. One who is proficient in dealings.

3. One who knows better the time value of money.

4. One who can recognize the hidden value of a thing and has patience for its fruits

5. One who knows about the surroundings, environment, and place of the goods produced.

6. One who is willing to cooperate with others.

7. One who is willing to go anywhere for a good deal.

8. One who can adapt quickly to changing times and is ready to let go of the past without attachment.

9. One who does not have the arrogance to meet anyone from business perspective.

10. One who is not easily discouraged by unsuccessful attempts.

11. One who respects talent and is willing to pay for it.

Balance is the most important thing in business and those who can bring balance and avoid conflict are the ones who are successful in business.This Nakshatra has all these qualities. That's why ancient sages have given it the Vaishya caste.

Characteristics: Punarvasu people are generous and magnanimous people and are always ready to help others. They are soft-spoken, social, friendly, and humorous people. They provide support to everyone whom they see in difficulty. They readily give their goods to others who need them. They know the right use of available resources and can create something new with limited resources and never complain about the lack of resources. They are protectors and do their duties very well.

They are benign and like to do charity. If someone demands something from the Punarvasu people then he never returns empty-handed. They are simple, benevolent, and maintain good relations with everyone. They are Intelligent and never harm others.

Punarvasu people are kind and humble, their life makes them humble. The ego is like a rock, where everything is fixed, but rocks become sand through weathering and erosion over the years. Success is difficult for Punarvasu people in the first attempt and this gives birth to a very determined and humble person who learns from the roller-coaster ride of life.

Since this energy supports many attempts, therefore, one thing is certain and that is success in the first attempt is doubtful. But Punarvasu is not for taking only one attempt. They do not take interest in those works in which only one attempt or limited attempt is available. Because their talent does not come out properly, they show no interest or give up very soon on tasks, where efforts are limited.

They don't like any monotonous work that doesn't offer any challenge to their mind. They say, "Try this and try that...", they like to sit late at night on the table to solve the problem. Till the problem exists their mind can't take peace and they continuously think about various possibilities to resolve it. The symbol of the nakshatra signifies that the "Quiver is full of arrows"; So, they don't want any kind of restrictions. It is better to give them a free hand and such people will give their best results, if you try to limit them then they will leave it.

They prefer to go for jobs like computer programming, scientific research, music, sports, etc., where many attempts are required before the final result. This type of work allows them to make proper use of their talent. They love to hone their skills; 'Practice makes a man perfect' is his motto. More effort means a skilled mind and a shining personality, then they show their success with gusto.

They believe that failure means coming close to success. Like a mother encouraging her child to get up when he falls, they always inspire others to keep trying.

After multiple failures, frustration is obvious to anyone but not to Punarvasu people. They never get discouraged and come back again with full energy. They will keep doing it until they get success. They become passionate to get the desired thing and forget day and night, forget food and clothes, forget friends and relations. They constantly throw their arrows to hit the target.

It may be possible that such a person may lose everything in that process but they never lose their hope and they can get it back. By the grace of Jupiter, a new ray of light comes into their life and they are re-established with renewed vigour.

Punarvasu persons are those who always motivate their team members to make another attempt. They often say, "I know that you can do it, try one more time and do your best". They respect talents and provide proper support. They never shout about failures and when they find that people are disheartened then they make the situation pleasant by using their jovial behaviour.

The ancient sages have given the Vaishya (Merchant) caste to this nakshatra. A merchant should be firm on his decisions and ready to explore unknown territory. When nothing is visible to others, he can see what is hidden and what is coming, and once he decided to go ahead, he should not deviate his mind from external forces. Because every decision cost money and for a merchant every rupee is important. One who does not know the value of money can't become a good merchant. Punarvasu people have all these qualities.

Punarvasu native always looks fresh and their mind is always ready for the next attempt. Their subconscious mind is always traveling to explore; Hence, they are always ready for a trip and surprise others by making untimely visits.

It is very difficult for Punarvasu people to sit idle in one place. They like to roam here and there, discuss with everyone and make the environment pleasant with their humorous behaviour. They are very social, have many friends, and mingle easily with others. Such a person likes to wander around and prefers a job where short travelling is involved. In their discussions, they often use the term; trip, tour, transit, ride, run, and go. They have a lot of energy to travel and if Mars is situated in this Nakshatra, then such a person can walk miles on his feet.

They are very good at time management and after completing one task, they immediately move to another task and have the ability to complete the third one in between. They reach just before the commencement of the process or journey and never miss the bus.

This Nakshatra has the potential to make one an expert as it is not only making many attempts but also knowing the various causes of failures. By the time the person reaches the result, he has experienced many things in life. Such a person can become a great master in his life.

On the higher aspect, searching into the territory of the unknown is not easy. When no one knows the way, direction and required resources, a person decides to find solutions that seem ridiculous to others. But the thought of seeking is so intense for a Punarvasu person that if he does not work in that direction, he cannot sleep peacefully and then the search for the unknown begins.

This energy signifies that after so many lives wandering in this material world, one starts searching for the 'unknown' who is present everywhere but not visible to the eyes. The person starts searching around and asks everyone who has seen "Him". When the thirst for the "unknown" begins, this energy compels the individual to seek and cannot stop until he finds the "Ultimate Truth".

Lord Ram was born in this nakshatra. His life shows how strong this energy is in doing 'good again' in the life of the person.

Negative Traits: Punarvasu people have the power to solve complexities and this brings happiness to their mind. Therefore, they often like to invite complexity and feel happy to be involved in that matter. Sometimes they make a simple matter very complicated and run around to solve it.

Because deep down in their subconscious mind they want to run. Wandering unnecessarily is not good, so they deliberately create confusion and like to run away. In that process, they involve others and love to show off their problem-solving skills. They assign some tasks to everyone to reduce the problem and when everyone is busy, they feel satisfied.

They are always ready to go somewhere, whether their health or other situation allows it or not, they are not ready to listen to anyone. They blame others who do not support their plan. They are fickle-minded people and do not like anything stable in life, not even relationships. They do not like to stay at one place for a long time and like to change the place or city or country.

Gender: Its gender is male.

Animal Symbol: Its animal symbol is a 'Female Cat'. It is highly compatible with Ashlesha nakshatra whose symbol is a male cat and inimical to Magha and Purva Phalguni whose animal symbol is rat.

All three Jupiterian nakshatra animals belong to Cat or Felidae family. Vishakha nakshatra animal symbol is a 'Male Tiger' and Purva Bhadrapada animal symbol is a 'Male Lion'. The quality of these animals indicates that they cannot remain silent and are ready to raise their voice without hesitation. Their throat is strong and they can speak well for hours. They can make a strong presentation and can become a good singer and orator. A few more characteristics of cats influence them:

1. Cats are moody and like cleanliness. These people like to live in a clean environment and are very moody people.

2. Cats do not make any noise. When other family members are sleeping these people quietly go to the kitchen and eat delicious food without making any noise.

3. Cats are very clever: These people are very smart and intelligent and no one can fool them.

4. Cats can be funny too. These people love watching funny movies and can make funny expressions to make others laugh.

5. Female cats are very loyal. They are sober and steadfast, but if someone scolds them loudly, they remain silent for a long time.

Sun's Ingress: Sun enters Punarvasu nakshatra from 6th - 20th July every year. It indicates a period when people are working for recreation. In India, Kharif crops are usually sown with the beginning of the first rains in July, during the southwest monsoon season.

Profession: Such a person works for those jobs where success comes after multiple attempts, such as a job of computer programmer, sports, aerospace industry, medical research and development, and other testing jobs where multiple attempts are required to hit the target. They work as musicians where a person is able to play an instrument after several attempts.

They work with recycling industry and antique products. They work for construction industry, dam, bridges, roads, travel & tourism industry, transport industry, Postal services, Communication, Newspaper and Media, Hotels, Delivery services, Travelers, etc. They are great masters and hermits.

Favourable Activities: It is highly favourable where multiple attempts and caring requires to finish something. It is favourable for travelling, exploration, scientific discoveries, medical treatment, agriculture related activities, construction, pursuing something, studies, taking admission in a new course, purchase a car, renovation of home, starting a new project, etc.

Unfavorable Activities: It is not good to do any act where aggression is required.

Gana (Type): It is considered a Dev nakshatra. It reflects satwic qualities of the person.

Guna (Quality): The behaviour of the person does not remain the same at all the time and the associated action could be positive, negative or neutral. When we divide the 27 nakshatras into 3 groups and in to 3 times then each nakshatra quality is divided three times. A nakshatra contains not only one quality but it is a mix of all the three qualities as a person is a mix of three qualities Satwic, Rajasic and Tamasic. Hence, the quality of this nakshatra is 'Rajasic-Satwic-Rajasic'. Therefore, such a person has not only Satwic qualities but also rajasic qualities and when the situation demands, he comes to the fore.

Body Parts: Nose and Fingers

Tree: The tree associated with the nakshatra is bamboo. Bamboo is hallowed and moves back and forth as per the wind fluctuation. Bamboo is used for creating musical instruments. Passing wind among bamboo trees create music, indicates close association of music with this nakshatra.

Punarvasu people are humble, benevolent, simple and easily accessible to anyone as bamboo is easily accessible. People used to keep bamboo plant at home to bring good luck, wealth and fortune. Bamboo has various medicinal properties and their leaves are used as a food wrapping material to prevent food deterioration. They are resilient in nature as bamboo has strong bending properties.

Padas: The first three pada comes under Gemini and fourth pada comes under Cancer. The lord of Gemini is Mercury indicates strong intellect and business acumen of the person. Cancer lord Moon indicates generosity of the person.

The first pada falls in 20°-23.2° Gemini and lord is Mars (Aries Navamsha). It indicates energy of Jupiter-Mercury-Mars. Hence, they are benevolent, intelligent and active person.

The second pada falls in 23.2°-26.4° Gemini and lord is Venus (Taurus Navamsha). It indicates energy of Jupiter-Mercury-Venus. In this case, in place of Martian qualities, Venusian qualities play role and manners and etiquettes reflect in their personality.

The third pada falls in 26.4°-30° Gemini and lord is Mercury (Gemini Navamsha). It indicates energy of Jupiter-Mercury-Mercury. Hence, along with generosity, intelligence and business comes.

The fourth pada falls in 0°-3° 20' Cancer and lord is Moon (Cancer Navamsha). It indicates energy of Jupiter-Moon-Moon. Many positive feminine qualities come under this pada. The person is charitable and has a natural tendency to nurture others. Fickle mind can also be seen in this pada.

Chapter 8

Pushya

Pushya is the 8th of 27 nakshatras and situated at 03° 20' - 16° 40' Cancer. Pushya means the one who nourishes, the one who gives energy and strength. Another meaning of the word is blossom, flower, the best, the uppermost, or the topmost of anything. A flower is a final outcome of a tree and it blossoms with full grace when the vital energy of the tree moves in an upward direction.

"Tishya" and "Sidhya" are the two other names of this nakshatra. The meaning of Tishya is 'auspicious' or 'lucky' and the meaning of Sidhya is 'one who is accomplished' or 'one who has attained a siddhi'. The name itself signifies its association with luck, prosperity, accomplishment, and the best in every aspect of life.

Astronomy: At sidereal longitude 01° 55' 21" Cancer and a visual magnitude of 0.38, the main star in this constellation is known as "Alpha Cancri". Its declination is 5° N 9' 56.68" and its right ascension is 7h 40m 28.7s. The other two stars are known as Theta Cancri and Delta Cancri (Asellus Australis).

Deity: Lord Brihaspati – the god of benevolence and wisdom is the deity of this nakshatra. This Nakshatra has an inherent instinct of nurturing and no intention of causing any harm to others.

Shakti (Power): The energy of the nakshatra is known as "Brahmavarchava Shakti". It means "To create spiritual energy". Sexual energy is transformed into spiritual energy when one follows the path of Brahmacharya (Celibacy).

The Sight of Nakshatra: It is an Urdhvamukhi Nakshatra i.e., Facing Upward. When sexual energy moves in an upward direction, it blossoms.

Nature: Kshipra (Swift)

Element: Water

Activity: Passive

TriMurti and Behaviour: Vishnu and Maintenance

Planetary Ruler: The activities of caring, nurturing and teaching require maturity. Therefore, the lordship of this Nakshatra is given to Saturn.

Symbol: The first symbol of the nakshatra is the 'Teat of cow'. The stars in this constellation make the shape of a "Cow's udder" and the cow provides us with milk. Cow's milk has innumerable health benefits and has some unique nutrients that cannot be compared to any other milk. Similarly, in this Nakshatra, the quality of nurturing prevails, which cannot be compared with any other power.

Another symbol of the nakshatra is the 'Lotus Flower'. A lotus flower only grows in the mud, but when it blossoms it becomes the most beautiful flower. It is a symbol of growth and enlightenment. The symbol indicates the transformation of sexual energy into spiritual energy and when it reaches the crown chakra it blossoms.

Another symbol of the nakshatra is "an arrow", which indicates that this energy has a strong ability to concentrate. An arrow always goes in one direction and never deviates from the chosen target. When it is released from the bow it has to hit the target, that is the task and it has to be done, there is no going back. Similarly, sexual energy has a task to reach the crown chakra. The energy of this Nakshatra provides support for the upward movement and follows the path of celibacy.

Caste: The caste assigned to this nakshatra is Kshatriya or Warrior, which means a person who is always ready to defend and does not give up the battle until victorious. Kshatriyas are not interested in dealings and negotiations. If there is a battle and it has to be a win at any cost then no negotiations and no surrender.

Such a person has to do everything to win the battle. In the same way, there are no negotiations when a person decides to move his sexual energy in an upward direction. It has to go up and every effort has to be made to take it in an upward direction. But winning such a battle is not easy and requires determination. The warrior has to fulfill his duty at all costs and there is no way back.

If the lotus flower has to blossom, then this inner war has to be won and only one with the qualities of a warrior can do that. That's why our sages have assigned the Kshatriya caste to this nakshatra.

Characteristics: This is the most positive asterism; this energy works only for the upliftment of the native. Such a person has wealth, prosperity, opulence, growth in many aspects of life and luck always favors him. They are very gentle, selfless and altruistic. Like a cow gives us milk from its teat, they always take interest in nurturing the mental, emotional, physical and spiritual aspects of life. Such persons always do everything for the betterment of others and they gain fame and popularity by their gentle behavior and knowledge.

The entire 13° 20' span of the nakshatra falls into the watery sign of Cancer. The water of Cancer is a fresh water and for nourishment fresh water is required. In natural zodiac fourth house represents mother. This is the place where the planet of benevolence and abundance Jupiter feels comfortable and gets exalted at 5°. Jupiter represents wisdom and highly beneficial energy supports knowledge when one follows the path of celibacy. A flower blooms but it needs proper care, hence, the quality of nurturing and caring is inherent in these natives.

Calmness, moral, ethics, selfless nature, patience, giving due respect to others and many other positive human characters automatically come into their personality. They are full of generosity and it is impossible for them to harm others and always have a sense of kindness and goodness towards others. Being full of compassion, these people always want to help others but at the same time they also take care of the circumstances, so that, while helping the ego of the person is not affected. So, they give their help in deep silence that the recipient never knows who was that person who came silently like a thief and went away after showing his generosity.

It is written in Hora Sara that, "The person of Pushya Nakshatra will be very short-tempered, intelligent, fearless, talkative, expert in many branches, helping his relatives, a thief, wealthy and independent."

Amidst all the positive qualities, why has Hora Sara given these people the quality of a thief?

A thief has the quality of working without the knowledge of others. Being full of compassion, such people always want to help others but at the same time they also take care of the circumstances, so that while helping, the person's self-esteem does not get hurt.

They are very hard-working person always try to give their best and never take anything lightly. They always take interest in progressive activities, they always encourage others and provide their necessary support, they support everything for the upward momentum in life.

They silently engage in fulfilling their obligations and patiently wait for the final result (flower). If a Pushya person is entrusted with a task, be sure that something great will result, although it may take some time, as they seek perfection. They don't accept anything below quality, so they always choose the best things in life.

They like to wear branded clothes and buy expensive things which are better in quality. Their eyesight is so sharp that they can catch even the tiniest of mistakes, but instead of scolding, they prefer to teach in the right way.They never take any harsh decision for someone's poor performance and listen patiently to their problem and provide proper guidance.

One should understand all the possible advantages and disadvantages with a sense of empathy, then only one can fulfill the responsibilities of a mother. Pushya people are great teacher who nurtures their students like a mother. They never abuse anyone nor do they like to quarrel with anyone. As a mother, they have a sense of protection of their surroundings. They raise their hands, but always for protection, not to beat someone.

They are very honest and anything in the hands of these people is always safe. Neither they do any wrong nor do they accept any wrong and are ready to fight for truth. When they feel that people are not giving them proper respect and their knowledge and wisdom have no value, they prefer to leave such a place. They are not greedy and the temptation of money cannot allure them. The arrow symbol shows that once they have decided, they never turn back.

The people born in Pushya Nakshatra always desire for their spiritual development. Deep in their hearts, they have a desire to follow the path of celibacy; they practice yoga and meditation to transform sexual energy into spiritual energy. Hence, they take less interest in sexual activities and more in religious activities. They read religious texts and often perform puja and yagna at their home.

When a person knows the secret of sexual energy, he works hard to change its momentum. Then begins a battle between material desire and spirituality and only a person with the quality of a Kshatriya (warrior) can win this battle. Similarly, when the individuals of this Nakshatra are involved in solving a problem, they sit for hours with full concentration to solve it. They don't even bother to eat and drink in between, because the 'arrow' symbol represents a single-minded person.

This energy has a deep connection with rhythm and music. When the fresh air passes through the trees on the banks of the river, when the freshwater of the flowing stream produces sweet and soft sound, wonderful music is produced. Rhythmicity is inherent in the people of Pushya Nakshatra which is reflected in their speech and general body language.

They are very talented in multiple aspects and possess knowledge of various things. They are very kind in nature but if someone scolds them, they get hurt easily. Their speech is very sweet and they always expect others to speak in a soft tone.

They are foody and like to travel long distances for delicious food. They know every good restaurant around them and know where the best food is available. They prefer to eat dairy products like paneer, cheese, ghee, cream, milk, curd etc. They like to have some extra cheese, ghee, cream in their food. Their focus is always is on nutritional products and before picking any packet they like to read its nutritional content.

They love to cook at home to prepare delicious food. They have a keen sense of mixing things and do not mix anything unnecessary. In the same way, they have a strong power to handle large-scale projects and never get disheartened with a bundle of files. They keep the important matter under confidence and wherever necessary they have a habit of preserving all important items. They keep everything in a proper sequence and remember everything easily even after years.

They are very intelligent person and scholars of many subjects. They are soft-spoken people and have a dignity in their personality. They take care of every person but do not take care of themselves. Like a mother first feeds her children and then eats herself, they like to ask others before eating anything.

On the higher aspect, this energy indicates the upward momentum of sexual energy from Muladhara chakra to Sahasrara Chakra (Crown chakra). It is possible only when the person follows the path of celibacy and the symbol of arrow indicates no deviation from the chosen path. Once an arrow left the bow it forcefully moves only towards one direction to hit the target and the new dimension of the unknown world starts opening in front of the native. With the blessing of Lord Jupiter, the person is successfully able to accomplish it and the Lotus Flower blossoms.

Negative Traits: Such a benevolent energy can covert only to show off their wealth and charity. They become haughty, arrogant, and loose temper quickly. They ignore their responsibilities in pursuit of materialism and lose some important thing in life as Brihaspati keeps busy in the court of Indra, and his wife Tara elopes with Moon.

An arrow likely to take the spiritual path may wander in the lower aspects of life and such a person may be busy only in collecting costly objects and feel satisfaction. Instead of knowledge and wisdom, the focus can be only on branded items and money related discussions. The altruistic attitude may turn into a low level of popularity and the person may only be interested in gossips.

Water has the quality of cleaning everything and also has the power to dissolve. The quality of cleanliness can be negative and a person can waste his energy only in this work. They become obsessed and suffer from depression, mood swings and fear of the unknown.

Gender: Male

Animal Symbol: The animal symbol of the nakshatra is a "Male Goat" or a "Male Sheep". Its counterpart is Krittika nakshatra whose symbol is a female goat and it is inimical to Purva Ashadha and Shravana nakshatra whose animal symbol is monkey.

Like a goat they are sociable people and feel uncomforted if they are separated or isolated from their companions. They are very intelligent and curious person and always wear neat and clean clothes. They are selective in communication and don't like worthless communication. They are ready to sacrifice their lives and their own interest for a great cause. Male goats usually have a beard. Hence, many Pushya nakshatra people like to grow their beard.

Sun's Ingress: Sun enters Pushya nakshatra from 20th July – 03 August every year. When Sun comes darkness is removed and the energy of this nakshatra support spiritual growth. Hence, many positive activities take pace and progress starts.

Profession: Teaching, advisory and counselling services, investment planners, charity and non-profit organization workers, profession related with child care and nurturing, restaurant and hotels, dairy industry, music and art, personal secretary and hosts, priests and gurus, politicians and ministers, education department, volunteers and self-service persons, construction and water related work.

Favourable Activities: It is supportive for laying foundation or beginning of a new thing. It is supportive to go anything in upward direction. It is supportive for investments, planning, gathering and organizing. Activities related with music, dance, travel, cooking, nurturing, and gardening are good. Work related with fresh water, food and dairy industry. This energy supports for healing, charity, teaching, advisory and counselling activities. Mentors, Masters, Spiritual persons are associated with this nakshatra.

Unfavorable Activities: This energy supports the path of celibacy; hence, it is not good for marriage. Any act which requires aggression, demolition, destruction is not good.

Gana (Type): The gana of the nakshatra is "Dev". They are very compassionate people and like a Dev, they always think about giving and doing something good for others.

Guna (Quality): The category of three Guna of this nakshatra are "Rajasic-Satwic-Tamasic". They are very active, passionate and generous persons but when the required enthusiasm is lacking, they show no interest and prefer to remain in a passive state.

Body Parts: Face

Tree: The tree associated with the constellation is the Ashwattha (Peepal) tree. Hindus consider it a sacred tree. Gautama Buddha is believed to have attained enlightenment under a Peepal tree, also known as the Bodhi tree. The tree has many medicinal aspects and is used for many chronic diseases. Studies show that the Peepal tree plays an important role in the protection of the ozone layer.

Padas: The first pada of this nakshatra is 03° 20' - 06° 40' in Cancer and ruled by Sun (Leo Navamsha). The heat of the Sun in this watery sign is not scorching. It makes magnanimous and humble. They are frank, outspoken and broad-minded person. They are responsible person but it gives aloofness through some extent and they like to live a reserved life.

The second pada of this nakshatra is 06° 40' - 10° 00' in Cancer and ruled by Mercury (Virgo Navamsha). A very benign personality with a high level of intelligence comes here. They are scholars and very hardworking people. They are experts and have in-depth knowledge of many subjects.

The third pada of this nakshatra is 10° 00' - 13° 20' in Cancer and ruled by Venus (Libra Navamsha). They are humble, polite and soft-spoken person. Being a highly social person, they have many friends. They are always ready to help others and don't like to beat the drum. The level of politeness, etiquettes and manners are highest in this pada. They like to wear fancy items and are always busy attending seminars, wedding ceremonies, parties, celebrations. They are very busy people but never disappoint anyone.

The fourth pada of this nakshatra is 13° 20' - 16° 40' in Cancer and ruled by Mars (Scorpio Navamsha). This position gives birth to a person who has energy with compassion. Such a person has a strong ability to find the root cause. When the question of going to a distant place in search of cause or truth (meetings at various places, going to distant places), or solving a problem required several journeys, they never hesitate to go there. They are determined and work oriented people. Vengeance, deviousness and obsession is also visible on the negative side. If both Jupiter and Moon are afflicted then the native may take his life journey on the wrong path.

Chapter 9

Ashlesha

Ashlesha is the 9th of 27 Nakshatras and is located at 16° 40' – 30° Cancer. The word Ashlesha means to embrace, entwine, adhere, and have a close connection. It is a tenacious energy with focus on persistancy, grasping firmly, intuition and transformation. It is known as 'The Clinging Star'.

Astronomy: This constellation falls in the Hydra constellation; it is one of the largest constellations and is represented in the form of a water serpent. One of the brightest stars in this constellation is known as Alphard (Alpha Hydra) which appears at magnitude 1.98, declination 8° S 45' 25.93", right ascension 9h 28m 41.6s. The other stars that make up this constellation are known as Beta, Gamma, Epsilon, Delta, Sigma, and Zeta Hydra. The shape of the hydra constellation resembles that of a twisted snake.

Deity: The deity of the nakshatra is "Nagas - the divine serpents". It is represented as a serpent with many heads. According to

Hindu mythology, Lord Vishnu is resting in the cosmic ocean on the coiled body of Sheshnag, a multi-headed serpent. Another story states that on the request of Lord Brahma, Sheshnag went to Pataal lok (netherworld) and raised his hood to balance the earth; he became the bearer of the earth and came to be known as Anant Shesha.

The story indicates that serpents are the protectors. Whenever the imbalance is witnessed on the earth they will come to provide protection. In Ramayana, Lakshman and in Mahabharat Balram is said to be the incarnation of Sheshnag.

Ashlesha supports the person they believe in, it also indicates a blind faith where they simply follow orders without questioning.

Shakti (power): The Shakti of the nakshatra is "Vish Ashleshana Shakti", i.e. the power to embrace or adhere to the poison.

The Sight of Nakshatra: It is Adhomukhi Nakshatra – Facing Downward.

Activity: Active

Nature: Its nature is Tikshna (sharp), which indicates sudden attack or action.

Element: Its element is "Water", which can dissolve many other substances. Water is life, and where water exists, life exists. Water brings life back, so these natives take an interest in all those activities that bring life back. They can convert even poison into medicine. Such a person can prepare those medicines that bring life to many people.

Planetary Ruler: The ruler of the planet is Mercury. It is known as a prince among all the nine planets. Mercury represents the child and adolescent stage where the muscles of the body can bend easily. If something is in a rigid state or an excessive liquid state, it cannot bend, and to coil means to bend. A child's muscles can flex more easily than an adult. Ashlesha has the quality of bending, so the lord of this constellation is given to Mercury.

Bending signifies diplomacy and Mercury is known for this. It represents our intelligence, awareness, curiosity, and search for mysteries. It indicates news and information, correspondence, connections, ideas, and thoughts. So, Ashlesha people are always aware of the latest information, they have many connections and respect innovative ideas.

Mercury has impatience, as children are immature and want quick results. That's why Ashlesha people make decisions based on external circumstances only.

Symbol: The symbol of the nakshatra is a 'Coiled snake'. Ashlesha comes under Cancer which is a watery sign. Among nine rajasic nakshatras, it is the last, and thereafter, a new series of the next nine tamasic nakshatras begins. The water of Cancer ends here and fire starts from the 10th nakshatra. It signifies that a new journey begins from where Ashlesha ends, but there is no synergy between the two, as the first journey is ending in a water sign and the new journey is starting in a fire sign, and water and fire do not support each other, they are opposite to each other. It means that such a person has to give up his previous path; whatever he did till now is over forever.

It is like crossing the border where there is no bridge and it requires a lot of courage to cross such a bridge. It is only possible when the person is not ready to live on this side at any cost and now the soul is extremely thirsty to cross such border, but it requires a big push. So, such a person starts accumulating the energy to take that jump and the formation of a coil begins. Therefore, the symbol of the nakshatra is a 'Coiled snake'.

It indicates the accumulation of energy in a circular formation at one place and when a thing accumulates in a circular pattern gradually it becomes very powerful to provide a big push. For instance, a spring becomes powerful and able to provide a big push which is not possible with a straight wire. When such energy is ready then the journey of the person starts in a new direction.

Ashlesha people do those works where there is no bridge or connection, if the bridge is available then people can easily cross it, but when there is no connection then work becomes difficult. Hence, these people do those difficult tasks that others cannot even think of daring. They are quick to make connections, they are courageous people and handle even the toughest situations easily. They recognize danger quickly and duck easily which is an essential skill for their survival.

Caste: The caste of the nakshatra is Mleccha (outcaste). Outcastes are those who are not accepted by society. This indicates that this energy works for those tasks that are generally not performed by a group of people. Because of his work, such a person has no place in the society. A hermit and a bandit both are unable to live in the society and Ashlesha has power to produce both.

They work an isolated place at night when others are sleeping. They work in a secluded place where no one can come. They prefer odd time for work, when most of the people return from their work then it is their time to go. They support those ideas which are not accepted by others, they are revolutionists and taboo breakers.

They fight for a noble cause, create revolution and bring drastic changes in the system. They write many articles and struggle to change the old beliefs and system but when the goal is achieved their own people sideline them. People respect them but are not ready to accept them, now they become an outcaste for the new system. It is a bitter irony for these people.

Characteristics: Ashlesha people are wise, philosophical, and intuitive. They are receptive and sensitive but lazy and self-indulgent people. They have charismatic personalities, with charming and penetrating eyes, and they are known to be experts in the art of seduction. They always have a tight approach towards money and are reluctant to help when it comes to money; their help is more verbal than actual.

Ashlesha is associated with poison and poison produces heat. This star falls in the water sign Cancer and the water calms the heat. Water represents a state of calm mind, so the mind of an Ashlesha person is usually calm unless it is provoked, the heat is buried in the water due to which their anger is hidden and can come out at any time. Snakes do not attack unless provoked, this is the way of functioning of this energy.

Ashlesha indicates the accumulation of energy, and whenever energy is accumulated it produces heat, therefore, they sweat more than others and feel thirst quickly. Their brain is sharp at recognizing a single particle in fresh water and they work to remove every little dust from the water. They work in the areas that provide fresh water, they make reservoirs, canals, channels, and security tanks for fresh water. Because they know the value of fresh water, they are very angry at the wastage of water. They give fresh water to others to quench their thirst and beat the heat. They love to swim and stay in swimming pools and bathtubs for hours.

Accumulation of energy is like the formation of a spring, when it will be ready transformation is inevitable in the life of the person.

As every spring follows a certain rule in a machine, in the same way, a person who is accumulating the energy has to follow certain principles in his life, then this coiled energy starts converting into spiritual energy. The poison is used for medicines, so they take an interest in the preparation of medicines, and work for mixing and separating drugs.

The accumulation of energy does not always mean the accumulation of positive energy, they also store negative energy. Therefore, they become a very vindictive person. They remember every hate, insult, and abuse and wait for the time to take their revenge. They are extremely egoistic people and cannot tolerate even a single word against themselves. They can't tolerate jokes, arguments, reprimands, and scolding, they store every negative energy and take revenge even years later. Every negative energy produces poison in the body and it is the work of the kidney to purify it. Hence people who always think negatively, get angry quickly and accumulate toxins in the body, their hearts and kidney are overworked and they suffer later in life.

Ashlesha is closely related to sexual energy which is biochemical energy in the body. Ashlesha is a sticky energy, so they cling to sexual desire and become highly sexual individuals. They don't know how to coil up sexual energy, so they become slaves of their lust. They are ready to bite others and suffer the sting of their lust, but the fulfillment of desire is important to them, and their pursuit of lust goes on until they experience the final lesson and that is poison.

Planets in Ashlesha indicate that such a person has to learn deep lessons in life and the sooner he learns his transformation begins. A big leap is possible only with the help of positive energy. That's why huge changes are seen in the lives of these people. Such a person leaves the old path forever in his life and moves towards a completely new direction.

They have the capability to dissolve many things, annihilate them forever, and never let them come out. They are very secretive people; they do work silently with full secrecy. They never reveal their true intention and keep everything in their mind. They can be engaged in their intense research work for years and no one can know what exactly they are doing.

A person likes to embrace or cling to the people he likes. Embracing or clinging indicates an intimate relationship, it also shows that the chemistry between two persons is matching and both are ready to accept and accommodate each other. It means that both are ready to give space to each other and also ready to accept the changes made by the other.

Hence, these people readily accept change and are not conservative individuals who stick to old beliefs for years. They want change in the system. Hence, they always support those who bring innovative ideas. They like to change many things where they work and their focus is always on safety. They always protect their family and friends and fight for their subordinates.

They are good at making connections and they work on profiles where connections are important.

They are a keen observer and quickly understand the changes in the environment. Because this energy is related to poison which is a chemical substance, so they like to study chemistry and work in pharmaceutical companies and do research on drugs. They keep deep knowledge of homeopathy and works as homeopathy doctor. They can handle dangerous chemicals as easily as a snake charmer handles snakes.

As the snake shrinks its body and one cannot identify its actual length by sight, Ashlesha individuals like to buy space-saving furniture and other such items for their homes. Their focus is always on how to use the space, so they tend to pile one thing on top of the other. At present, trains, missiles, long wires, pipes, canals, etc. are represented by Ashlesha.

Mercury as a chemical is the only liquid-state metal at room temperature and is highly toxic. Mercury atoms don't share electrons easily therefore it forms a very weak bond. It read the temperature quickly and is used to determine the temperature of the body, liquid, or gas. It has wide commercial applications in the industries. Due to potential hazards to human health, it requires strict control.

In the present world, information and communication arc the power and its ruler is Mercury. This is the age of technology which rules everywhere and plays a strong influence in our decision-making. Technology brings drastic changes in our lives and Ashlesha is a transformative energy that brings about big and drastic changes and whenever the situation calls for a drastic change, an Ashlesha person is needed. Serpents are protectors and come to the rescue in times of trouble.

Mercury indicates they are businessmen, but always keep in mind how much and with whom to keep the relationship. They are always cautious about their relationships and never make any strong bonds with anyone. Since mercury read the temperature quickly, they immediately catch the slightest change in temperature in the atmosphere or in the organization where they work. This is a very powerful energy, but Mercury should always be treated with the utmost care.

On the higher aspects, when the soul realizes that every desire burns, and that following the path to its fulfillment is only an accumulation of poison, it seeks to get rid of all poison. Hence, the positive energy starts accumulating in such a person and this energy gets stored in a coiled form at the bottom of the spine, which is known as Muladhara Chakra. Such a person is ready to accept the sting of every poison that he has given to others and is now ready to take a big leap for his next journey to the inner world.

Negative Traits: A strong desire for material happiness is seen in these people, they run at full speed to fulfill it and do not hesitate to adopt any wrong way to achieve it.

They work covertly to create chaos in the system. They never show their real face and do everything silently. They are chemical experts but use their knowledge for destructive purposes and make poisonous gases, chemical weapons, etc. They are greedy people and to save their skin, they will not hesitate to double-cross the person closest to them.

They are highly egoistic, cunning, and emotionless people. They are drunkards, manipulative and deceitful people. They mix chemicals to prepare cheap quality products for money.

Gender: This is a female nakshatra. Ashlesha's natives behave softly and politely, but jealousy and possessiveness are also seen here.

Animal Symbol: The male cat is the animal symbol of this constellation; its counterpart is Punarvasu symbolized by the female cat, and inimical to Magha and Purva Phalguni nakshatra symbolized by the rat.

Male cats cannot stay calm and are more playful than female cats. It can display some obnoxious behavior, while female cats tend to be more loyal than males. Male cats have a strong urge to scratch and claw, so they scratch trees and walls.

The male cat's desire to roam does not allow him to stay in one place for long and the desire to defend or gain territory also leads him astray. They can roam for miles in search of females and their desire to roam becomes stronger during the mating season.

Sun's Ingress: Sun enters this Nakshatra every year on the 3rd August and stays there till the 17th August. During this time many seasonal diseases start spreading among the people.

Profession: Lawyer, politician, diplomat, reporter, journalist, and editor. They work for; the media and entertainment, paint industry, chemical, pharmaceuticals, pulp and paper, and plastics industries. They work in the medical field as scientists, chemists, pharmacists, and homeopaths.

Favorable Activities: It is good for legal cases, fighting, planning for a sudden attack, gambling, pest control, doing research with chemicals and poison, and sexual activity.

Unfavorable Activities: It is not good to start any auspicious work. Not auspicious for marriage and starting a new venture.

Gana (Type): The type of the nakshatra is Rakshasa. They like to roam, are very desirous people, and are ready to do anything to achieve their aim.

Guna (Quality): The quality of the constellation is "Rajasic-Satwik-Satwik". This indicates that this is a very active nakshatra and sattva always pulls them.

Body Parts: Nails and ears are related to this nakshatra.

Tree: The tree associated with the nakshatra is Nagkesar or Nagchampa. The scientific name of the tree is 'Mesua ferrea'. It is a medium-sized evergreen plant and grows up to 13 meters in height. The root of this tree is used as an antidote to snake venom. This plant has many medicinal properties and is used in diseases like arthritis, asthma, inflammation, kidney ailments, dysentery, piles, and fungal infections.

Padas: The first pada of this asterism is 16° 40' - 20° 00' in Cancer and ruled by Jupiter (Sagittarius Navamsha). The outlook of such a person is philosophical but not necessary for spirituality. They are thinkers and their approaches are always practical. They think, write and talk about reality, discuss only the current situation, and work for places where it is always important to deal with the current situation.

The second pada of this asterism is 20° 00' – 23° 20' in Cancer and ruled by Saturn (Capricorn Navamsha). They are always ready to fight difficult situations and can control them. They are materialistic persons and work hard to fulfill their desire but do not hesitate to use unfair means to achieve their objectives.

The third pada of this asterism is 23° 20' - 26° 40' in Cancer and ruled by Saturn (Aquarius Navamsha). It is the energy of Mercury-Moon-Saturn but influenced by the traits of Aquarius. Hence, they are always equipped with all the latest technologies. They like to sit in isolated and remote places and practice the occult. But if Moon is afflicted, instead of doing positive work, they do negative work.

The fourth pada of this asterism is 26° 40' - 30° 00' in Cancer and ruled by Jupiter (Pisces Navamsha). This is Mercury-Moon-Jupiter energy but influenced by Piscean traits. If the Moon is strong, then the person is visionary and strong in imagination, otherwise hallucinations, confusion, mental disturbance, and fickle mind are seen here. They are very sensitive and receptive people but gullible too.

Chapter 10

Magha

Magha is the 10th of 27 Nakshatras and is located at 00° 00' - 13° 20' Leo. The sign Leo is represented by lion and the stars situated represent the forehead of lion.

Astronomy: Among the brightest stars in the night sky and in the constellation of Leo at a visual magnitude of 1.35, this star is known as "Regulus (Alpha Leonis)". Its declination is 11° N 51' 22.98" and right ascension is 10h 9m 34.1s. It appears to be single, but is actually a quadruple star system made up of four stars arranged in two pairs.

Deity: The deity of the nakshatra is known as "The Pitris". In Hindu culture, the Pitris are known as the spirits of the departed ancestors.

Magha people should always be aware of their roots because it is the roots that provide the strength. When a person dies, the fire burns away the physical body but the karmic deeds remain and each generation has to bear the karma of the previous generation.

The relation of ancestors with this Nakshatra indicates that the person born in Magha Nakshatra should give proper respect to his ancestors i.e., they have responsibility to follow their culture and tradition. The seeds which implanted by their ancestors, it is their responsibility to protect, which gradually take shape and a new cycle begins.

Connection with 'The Pitris', indicates that the person born in this nakshatra has ability to bear great responsibility and they have ability to complete it without fail. Magha indicates the beginning of a new journey by taking care of the seed from the ancestors.

Shakti (Power): The Shakti of the nakshatra is known as "Tyage Kshepani Shakti", it means "The power to leave the body".

The Sight of Nakshatra: It is Adhomukhi Nakshatra – Facing Downward. A downward energy has potential to create a strong pillar and create a great base where many people can take shelter. This energy has the ability to go deep and once it has made its base, such a name remains for centuries.

Nature: Ugra (Dreadful)

Element: The element of the nakshatra is "Water". Water has quality to go down and penetrate anywhere and always makes its own path.

Activity: Active

TriMurti and Behaviour: Brahma and Creation

Planetary Ruler: The planetary ruler of the nakshatra is Ketu. After every Gandanta, Ketu nakshatra starts. Ketu is the ruler of all the three nakshatras from where a new cycle begins. The headless planet indicates high intuition to these people but such a person can lose his patience and even go into a headless state of mind. Since each seed requires utmost care and not a single seed is allowed to go to waste, utmost care is required to start a new cycle.

Symbol: The symbol of the nakshatra is a "Throne". A throne is a special chair where a person attracts the attention of others while seated on it. This chair always keeps a distance from other chairs, always situated alone and never be with others. This chair situated at some elevated place so that the person situated on the chair can easily become visible to others.

The second symbol of the nakshatra is a "Palanquin". A palanquin in olden days is a big covered wooden box with a seat of a person. It is attached to poles and is carried on shoulders by two or four men. The cover of the box shows protection and safety. When it is move on the shoulders it is elevated and its movement is slow, the slow movement catch the attraction of every passerby and the curtains of the palanquin makes curious to others, who is inside.

Caste: The caste of the nakshatra is "Shudra". A shudra is a person who work hard by his legs to earn his livelihood, he has to stand up and move for work. A shudra's work rests on the strength of his knees. They do not feel tired even after standing and walking continuously. They get ready to walk again after a short rest.

In the same manner a king has to move from one place to another and observe everything for its proper functioning. Like Sun always moves and this movement gives life on earth, if Sun stays at one place then everything would be destroyed, in the same way a king can't stay at one place for long time and everything gathered momentum only by the news that the king is coming.

Characteristics: The beginning of Magha is the second Gandanta point; from there a new cycle starts which contains another set of nine tamasic nakshatras. Magha has strong connection with creation and these people have capacity to start something new in life with the help of old seeds. They have strong power to command people and good in arguments and fight. They work at the key positions of the organization and have connection with the government and the administration.

Lions live in a mountain cave, so these people prefer to live in solitude and don't like to mingle too much with others. Magha people make their own boundary and don't allow anyone to cross that. A mountain cave indicates a separate room or a separate work place where others hesitate to come.

They are very friendly but one has to deal with Magha people very carefully. They can become fierce and aggressive and unable to be controlled by anyone like a lion. They are committed person and never break their promise. They never leave anything in between and never leave any person in lurch.

They want recognition of their work and like to show their talent. The symbol of throne indicates a person wants to show his face to the world and don't like to sit behind the table. The elevated space of the throne indicates they like to be seen and attract the attention of others; due to their work, due to their clothes; due to their style. They do everything to seek attention and feel pleasure to show their work, they want to show their talent to the world. Hence, they work for media and entertainment, fashion industry, TV hosts etc. This royal sign indicates manners are their top priority and they also expect the same from others.

They are always cautious about protection and safety, and before taking any step they always ask questions related to safety. They prefer to cross check everything and take next step when the previous one is completed. Like a person sitting in a palanquin lifts the curtain a little bit, shows some of his face and hides some of his face and makes others curious. They always make others curious, keep secrets and surprise others by their acts.

They always maintain a distance with others and prefer to work alone. They don't like to take order from others and don't want hinderance of others in their work. They show their best result when they get free hand to complete a task. They prefer light jokes in their discussion and prefer to go at the places of amusement and entertainment. They want pleasant environment in their surroundings and love to listen to music.

They get motivation to do the work on money, and power related matters, otherwise remain in tamasic (inactive) state. But once they become active, their speed of completing the task becomes very high. They run here and there, finish a meeting and run for another meeting. They are magnanimous person and like to do charity and do philanthropy.

Magha means seed, the precious seed that our forefathers have gathered through their deeds, overcoming every obstacle and perfecting it, so that one day when it sprouts it will give better results. So, these people take interest in genetic engineering, seed manufacturing and work to remove barriers for good yield and improved seeds. They have a good knowledge of chain reaction and they understand the process of each chain quickly, so they work as technicians and scientists in research laboratories.

They like to study old documents, balance sheet, profit and loss account and work as an accountant. They are excellent at analyzing the past and its impact on the future, so they make good strategies and work for investment-related jobs. They always keep every memory, pictures, documents and every other important thing related to the past in a safe place and they feel attached to all those things. They can recall the events with exact date even after years.

Every new cycle is related with death, then a new life begins. To understand future, it is necessary to understand past. These people take interest in death related discussion and respect all knowledgeable persons, saints and hermits. They look for the answer of what happens after death and take interest in spiritual activities. They like to study astrology and other occult science.

On the higher aspects, this energy indicates a hermit who sits in a mountain cave, isolated from the people and indulge in deep meditation. Pitris indicates the seed, the palanquin indicates the shell of the seed and the quality of tamas indicates the darkness of the soil, which every seed has to face for its germination. Magha nakshatra people have potential to become a big tree and their ancestors have implanted that seed and have given the task to germinate it. This nakshatra has potential to create a very great personality.

Negative Traits: If it is afflicted, then they lose their patience and temper quickly, and indulge into fight with others. Due to their impatient behaviour they want to see the results of their work quickly and often loose the fruits of their hard work.

They shout and misuse their power and position to dominate others. They loose consistency in their work, become restless and show lack of manner in their behaviour. As a boss, they fire their staff without any notice, recruit another staff and next day fire them too. Rather than creating innovative ideas their mind become blank and unable to produce anything.

They are highly rigid and stubborn who don't listen the voice of any person. They take abrupt decisions and suffer from the problem of superiority complex. They lack the necessary manner and often cut abruptly the meeting or the phone calls of others without showing any courtesy.

They become highly selfish and use their power and position for their benefit. They make relation only with those people who can help them to get more money, power, and other enjoyment, etc.

Gender: The gender of the nakshatra is "Female". Women have the quality to keep things safe and secure for years. She looks to safety first and secures her creation firmly before taking the next step.

Animal Symbol: The animal symbol of the nakshatra is a "Male Rat". It is compatible with Purva Phalguni symbolized by female rat and hostile to Ashlesha and Punarvasu Nakshatra symbolized by cat.

Rats are very smart, intelligent and have good memories. They are highly sensitive to smell and are able to detect the presence of food inside the home, even if they are still outside and they love to chew it. Male rats are highly sexual animal and some species of rats die immediately after sex.

The animal symbol indicates that Magha people are very smart and intelligent. Sex means creation without sex there is no creation in the world and this nakshatra has very strong relation with creation. It is because of sex that children come into existence and children are our future. Each generation transfers its seeds to its next generation and the process goes on.

A rat is unable to stay at one place, in the same way, they get bored quickly, leave that place and seek for the other and prefer engagement of any kind. They eat like a rat, take a bite then engage in doing the work, after some time they take another bite of food and run around all day. A rat wander here and there, in the same way, they are very busy person, run for completion of work and unable to sit at one place for long time. They call a meeting provide necessary guidance take a bite of food and run for another meeting. At the end of the day, they are completely exhausted, go to bed like a rat and wake up only in the morning.

Sun's Ingress: Sun enters in this nakshatra from 17th August – 31st August every year. Along with several public occasions, the month also marks the beginning of the festive season in the country.

Profession: Family business, Politics, Leader, Actor, TV hosts, Lawyers, Judges, Head, Musicians, Defense, Historians, Archeologists, Accountants, Investment consultants, Performers, Antique dealers, Entrepreneur, Public servant, Scientists, Professor, Construction related work, Hospitability, Genetics, Occultists, Astrologers, and any other work related to the study of past and requires deep roots for the future.

Favourable Activities: Good for rewards, occasions, genealogical work, religious activities, settling disputes, charity, marriage ceremonies, following tradition, career related strategy, promotion, seeking favors from government and officials. It holds good for all functions where past activities support development for the future.

Unfavorable Activities: It is a downward energy and doesn't support anything moving in upward direction.

Gana (Type): The type classified to Magha people is Rakshasa (Demons). They are not demons by body, but it is the type that affects their demeanor. Rakshasa live in forests; these people love flowers, plants, trees and fight to protect it. These people maintain a small garden at home and like to pour water. They have natural inclination towards wild life, and like to visit remote places.

Rakshasa like to live in luxury and get angry when there is any obstacle in their enjoyment. They want money, power, and authority and make relations to only those who help them to achieve it more. To achieve their objective, they fight fiercely. They are egoistic, selfish and misuse their power for their own benefit.

Guna (Quality): The quality of the nakshatra is "Tamasic-Rajasic-Rajasic". Tamas means darkness and in darkness any activity will take shape only if there is some motivation behind it, otherwise it will remain in a dormant state for a long time, just like a seed takes shape in the darkness of the soil. The quality of the nakshatra shows that they are secretive persons and show their energy to move ahead when there is some motivation, otherwise they remain lazy for a long time.

But when they show their energy then their rajasic quality comes out and only their action is visible. In the state of tamas they are ready to work for some time without any compensation. Soon, they become highly active and the seed starts germinating. Magha people have the potential to become a big tree and their forefathers sowed that seed and gave them the task of making it sprout.

Body Parts: The body parts connected with the nakshatra are "Nose, Lips & Chin". The people of Magha Nakshatra have a protruding nose on their face which differentiates their identity from the rest of the people.

Tree: The tree associated with the nakshatra is the "Banyan tree" which is the national tree of India. It is also known as 'Bahupada' (many legs), as its roots grow downward from its branches and form additional trunks and connect the tree to the ground. The banyan tree is huge and its canopy of leaves thick enough to provide ample shade. The tree provides habitat for many species on its branches and roots. The tree has the ability to live for centuries and is worshiped in Hindu culture, its large leaves is used in many rituals. This tree has many medicinal properties and its root, leaf and bark cure many diseases. This tree is considered a symbol of immortality.

Padas: The first pada of this nakshatra is 00° 00' - 03° 20' in Leo and ruled by Mars (Aries Navamsha). The energy in this pada is influenced by 'Ketu-Sun-Mars'. They are energetic, aggressive and hard-working person. They are very bold and have strong leadership quality. They are cruel, courageous and lonely person. This Martian energy always fights to win the battle and they prefer a military job.

The second pada of this nakshatra is 03° 20' - 06° 40' in Leo and ruled by Venus (Taurus Navamsha). They are very reliable and hardworking person. They want to enjoy the pleasure of life and are not ready to compromise on that. They prefer costly items in their home and like to show off to others. Their approach is practical but they are stubborn.

The third pada of this nakshatra is 06° 40' - 10° 00' in Leo and ruled by Mercury (Gemini Navamsha). They are intelligent and versatile person. They are strong in logic and like to chat with others. But they are unable to handle critical situations and become nervous soon. They are timid, greedy and change their face immediately when circumstances turn. They are profit seeking person and make relations with those who help them to get some profit.

The fourth pada of this nakshatra is 10° 00' - 13° 20' in Leo and ruled by Moon (Cancer Navamsha). They are very soft and emotional person. They have quality of nurturing and take care of every member in the family. They have strong memory and powerful intuition. They are deep observant and notice everything but they are unable to control their emotions and cry soon in odd circumstances.

Chapter 11

Purva Phalguni

Purva Phalguni is the 11th of 27 Nakshatras and is located at 13° 20' - 26° 40' Leo. The Sanskrit word Phalguni means 'Red' or 'Reddish' and Purva means 'Earlier', 'Before', 'First', 'Prior', 'Foremost', 'Advance', 'East', or 'Being in front of'. Red is the color of love, joy, and happiness. The horizon turns red in the morning. The red color of dawn is a prior indication of a good omen. It is an indication that darkness has gone, light is about to come. Purva Purva Phalguni is the harbinger of joy, happiness and a new beginning in life.

The other translation is 'A hairy fig tree' or 'The fruit of the tree'. The association of 'A fig tree' reflects the delicate functioning of this nakshatra. This nakshatra has a strong relation with creation and every creation requires effort, 'The fruit of the tree' indicates that the person will get the fruits of his efforts.

Astronomy: In the constellation of Leo, and at magnitudes 2.56 and 3.32, two bright stars named Delta Leonis (Zosma) and Theta Leonis (Cherton) are visible in the night sky. Its declination is 20° N 24' 0.21" and 15° N 25' 46.45" and right ascension is 11h 15m 18.1s and 11h 14m 14.40s respectively.

Deity: The deity of the constellation is known as "Bhaga". The Sanskrit word Bhaga means division. He is one of the twelve Adityas, who are the gods of wealth, love, and marriage. He is the deity who ensures the distribution of goods and fortune to each person according to his merit.

Everything on Earth is created by the Sun. The energy of the Sun is divided into 12 equal parts also known as 12 Adityas. All the 12 Adityas represent different types of energies and the Sun stays one month in a sign. The movement of the Sun in all the 12 signs completes one cycle of creation. The manifestation of this creative energy is controlled by the 12 solar deities. Bhaga is the deity of Capricorn. In India, on every calendar day of 14th or 15th January, we celebrate Makar Sankranti, when Sun enters in this sign. From this day onwards, the marriage ceremony starts in India which had been on hold for the last one month.

Shakti (Power): The Shakti associated with the nakshatra is known as "Prajanana Shakti". Prajanana means Birth, Delivery, Production, Procreation, Generation, or Conception. The process of 'Prajanana' involves male and female genital organs, without which birth is impossible. So, the power of asterism is known as the 'Power of Production', 'Power of Creation', and 'The Power to Give Birth'. It is that energy which forced to conceive and it is controlled by nature.

Prajanana Shakti can't work alone, to give birth one requires the support of opposite energy and conception means the union of masculine and feminine energy. In chronology, the number of Purva Phalguni is '11', birth is not possible by only '1', it requires support of another '1' and that is reflected by its number.

The Sight of Nakshatra: It is an Urdhvamukhi Nakshatra i.e., Facing Upward.

Nature: Ugra (Fierce)

Element: The element associated with the nakshatra is 'Water', which is the most important element for any creation.

Activity: The activity of the nakshatra is 'Balanced'. Nature keeps balancing everything in this world. If there is any creation then it must be balanced otherwise it cannot take birth or can't survive for long.

Trimurti and Behaviour: Vishnu and Maintenance

Planetary Ruler: The lord of the Nakshatra is Venus who is the lord of the reproductive organs in the body. It is the sexual energy that compels a person to have children. Children are our creation and without sexual energy it is not possible. The lordship of Venus indicates that Purva Phalguni person has the best quality to create something new.

On the lower aspect, they are always in search of a new partner to fulfill their desire, but on the higher aspect, this energy can give birth to new and innovative things in life.

Symbol: The symbol of the nakshatra is "The front leg of the bed". A person uses a bed to relax his physical body. The front part of the bed is used to put the head and the lower part is used to put the leg. When a person takes rest on the bed his body rejuvenates and when he leaves the bed, he is full with the energy. Bed represents that the functioning of the nakshatra is related with the source of the creative energy.

Bed indicates a place of rest where a person can do anything for his pleasure. The person is the master of his bed and does anything to get enjoyment and relaxation. The placement of head at the front part indicates that the person will take initiative to fulfill his desires. Hence, Purva Phalguni person take initiative for creation, pleasure and enjoyment. When they want something then they are ready to pay any price for their pleasure. They are the one who buy the costliest item for their enjoyment and never hesitate to pay for that. The fierce nature of the nakshatra shows that they become very angry and violent if someone tries to interrupt them to get pleasure in bed.

The second symbol of the nakshatra is a 'Hammock'. It is a swinging bed, made of rope and suspended between two trees or pillars. The hammock provides the freedom of space while you lay your head for rest. It provides a space to take some rest on uneven ground. The symbol of the hammock indicates that this energy serves to provide relaxation after a busy day. Rest is necessary to rejuvenate the body and the mind, after some rest the person is ready to work again. When a person takes a little rest, this creative energy works quietly in his body and gives peace to the mind. Every night we take rest and nature works silently in our body. This energy silently involves in the process of creation.

Caste: The caste of the asterism is 'Brahmin'. It means that a person uses brain in his work. Hence, they are involved in activities where the brain is required for functioning.

Human mind plays an important role while taking rest on the bed, at that time functioning of mind continues, body is taking rest but brain is working. People solve many problems; new and innovative ideas emerge in the mind when they are taking rest on the bed.

Characteristics: Association of red colour with this nakshatra indicates enthusiasm. Before the Sun rises in the east, the horizon turns red. When a person feels happiness and his body feels rejoice redness is visible. Red is the colour of joy and happiness and the first thing Purva Phalguni natives ask before taking any step is that whether enjoyment is there or not. They are joyful in nature but very sensitive and can catch the subtle differences in the behaviour. They love music and dance and can catch on minor nuances.

Red is also the color of caution; Heat is red, anger is red, danger is red. The fierce nature of the nakshatra indicates that the colour of joy immediately turns into the colour of heat, if any obstacles come into their enjoyment. Therefore, the red color should be handled with extreme caution.

Purva Phalguni person are very attractive, generous, well-mannered and fun-loving. They are loyal and kind towards the people they love and are very social. They are talented and very creative but often lazy.

They are entertainment seeking person. They do what makes their mind and body happy. They spend a lot of money for their luxury, in fact they never think of spending money for their comfort. They have expensive hobbies. The front foot of the bed indicates that they are the initiator. They take the initiative for their pleasure. They like gatherings and take initiative for parties and like to intimate every person. They are very romantic person and like to sing songs in parties. They say jokes in gathering and make everyone laugh.

With a free mind they love to create something new in life. They keep on searching new and innovative ideas. They whole heartedly involve in marriage ceremony and love to arrange it.

This energy helps to support the union of two opposite energy, they work as a counselor or negotiator. They make agreement for the two opposition parties and bring the person on the table of settlement.

The best outcome is possible when the body and the mind is fully relaxed. Purva Phalguni people tend to be very carefree and relaxed. They are the person of their own will and don't like any pressure on fulfillment of the work. They don't like interference of any other person. The best creation is possible when the person is completely free from any pressure. An artist can do better if he performs without any pressure, a singer can perform best when there is no pressure on his head.

The natural quality of creation comes in front and shine when the flower bloom without any pressure. A slightest pressure can destroy the natural inclination and outcome is not pleasant. When everything is done without any pressure and with extreme care then everyone feels rejoice to see the outcome, like dawn in the sky. A good artist practice and hone their skills always in the morning. When the Sun is about to come and the horizon turns into red, it is the time to hone the skills.

A beautiful creation is possible only when the mind is completely relaxed and the body follows the direction given by the mind. A weak mind and a tired body cannot create anything. Hence, the energy of the Nakshatra compels the person to rejuvenate and the best creation in the world is seen when the person is completely relaxed and calm. Every moment the whole existence is giving a new birth, reproduction is going on incessantly.

As indicated by the power associated with it, this nakshatra has a strong connection with the genitals. To give birth, the help of the reproductive organs is needed, only then conception is possible. When masculine sexual energy meets feminine energy, a new birth takes place. It is creation for the outside world.

Every human body is made with these two energies but in the physical body only one is manifested and the other is hidden. Everyone is searching for the hidden half and the search for that half continues in the outside world, so everyone feels lonely. When the direction of this search moves inward, the energy starts harmonizing and it moves in the upward direction.

On a higher aspect, this reproductive power symbolizes the union of the masculine and feminine energies within and the birth of a new soul. The energy indicates the union of Shiva and Shakti and the birth of an enlightened soul. In Hindu culture this union is represented in a figure half Shiva and half Shakti, called Ardhanarishvara.

Negative Traits: Purva Phalguni person misuses the power of sexual energy. They may indulge more in sexual activities and become sex addicts. They become furious for the fulfillment of their lust and can go to any extent for the fulfillment of this desire. Sex is the only thing left in their life and they can become a sexual pervert. They have many companions and are always on the lookout for new ones. They do not hesitate to take their step forward for sex. They do everything that gives some sensual pleasure. They only waste their subtle energy which has immense potential to create something new in life. The power which can move upwards starts moving downwards and fulfillment of sense-pleasure becomes the goal of their life.

They procrastinate everything and become a very lazy person. They lack enthusiasm and seek their comfort before doing anything and without it, they are not ready to move an inch. They want everything highly comfortable; Chair, bed, couch, etc. They always seek comfort in travel and become very angry when their comfort is disturbed.

To fulfill their expensive desires, they need money at any cost. Right or wrong doesn't matter to them; the source of earnings doesn't matter. They are very extravagant and are always in debt. They are not motivated to do any work or activity if they do not enjoy doing such work. They like to stay on the bed, eat on the bed, sleep on the bed, and everything on the bed.

Gender: The gender of the nakshatra is 'Female', indicates its soft nature.

Animal Symbol: The animal associated with the nakshatra is the "Female Rat". It is in pair with the previous nakshatra "Magha" whose symbol is "Male Rat", and inimical to Ashlesha and Punarvasu symbolized by the cat. Creation is possible when male and female co-exist under one roof. These two Nakshatras simultaneously exist in the sign of Leo.

Rats are intelligent, social, curious, and tend to move around. Purva Phalguni person are masters of their own will and like to roam around, they attract attention with their skill and cheerful nature. Female rats are very active and like to be busy exploring. Purva Phalguni natives are very active and very busy people. The feminine side is visible in their personality and they have soft qualities. They are always pleasure-seeking people and that is their priority.

Sun's Ingress: Sun enters this Nakshatra every year on 31st August and stays till 14th September. A 10-day Ganesh festival is celebrated in Maharashtra (India) during this period. The famous Indian festival 'Holi' is celebrated after Holika Dahan on the full moon day of Phalgun month.

Profession: Work related to film and entertainment, female products, fashion, cosmetics, beauticians, make-up artists, professional singers, and musicians. Work that requires delicate handling of products, decorations and event management, photography, etc.

Favourable Activities: Romance, marriage, sex or other activity to get pleasure. This energy supports anything to do creative and constructive in life, painting, dancing, singing, or any activity which provide pleasure.

Unfavorable Activities: This delicate energy is not to do any aggressive activity. It is not good for treatment and cure.

Gana (Type): The type of the nakshatra is Manushya (Humans). Humans are social animals; they do not live in isolation. Purva Phalguni people like to mingle with others.

Guna (Quality): The quality of the Nakshatra is "Tamasik-Rajasik-Tamasik". This indicates that they need some motivation to act otherwise they remain inactive for long periods. Tamas is essential for creation; great creations keep taking shape in total darkness. In the mother's womb, the embryo is in complete darkness, and nature quietly does its work. Purva Phalguni persons work quietly for the creation and they prefer to work in the night.

Body Parts: Right Hand

Tree: The tree associated with the nakshatra is Palash. It is called the Flame of the Forest. It has another colloquial name - Parrot Tree. It is a very attractive and beautiful medicinal plant. Its flowers have five petals with a beak-shaped spike. Its flowers grow in clusters on leafless branches; it is widely used as a symbol of the arrival of spring and the color of love.

Padas: The first pada of this nakshatra is 13° 20' - 16° 40' in Leo and ruled by Sun (Leo Navamsha). The Venusian energy of the nakshatra is highly influenced by the Sun. They are an egoistic, kind-hearted, and very creative person. They have leadership qualities and lead themselves as a role model. They are ambitious and take the initiatives to fulfill their desires. They are dignified people, hate to get their hands dirty and prefer to get others to do the work for them.

The second pada of this nakshatra is 16° 40' - 20° 00' in Leo and ruled by Mercury (Virgo Navamsha). Due to the influence of Mercury, they are an intelligent and diplomatic person. They are good at speaking and expressing their thoughts effectively. They have good retention power and are always aware of the latest news and information. They use tactics to stay ahead in life.

The third pada of this nakshatra is 20° 00' - 23° 20' in Leo and ruled by Venus (Libra Navamsha). The force of energy in this pada works as Venus Sun-Venus. The creative force is highly influenced by Venusian energy. They are soft-spoken and pleasure-seeking people. They work as an expert in their field. They are good in relationships and draw attention due to their skills and their charming personality.

The fourth pada of this nakshatra is 23° 20' - 26° 40' in Leo and ruled by Mars (Scorpio Navamsha). The force of energy in this pada works as Venus-Sun-Mars. They are arrogant, stubborn, and do not care about criticism. They have a strong fighting spirit and are not ready to compromise easily. They prefer to work on those activities where physical movement is required; like dance, sports, etc. They never compromise with their will and work very hard to achieve their goal.

Chapter 12

Uttara Phalguni

Uttara Phalguni is the 12th of 27 Nakshatras and is located at 26° 40' Leo - 10° 00' Virgo. The word Uttara means next, latter, subsequent, and remaining. It also means north direction, higher, superior, and excellent. The stars in this nakshatra constitute the remaining part of the Phalguni nakshatra. Another meaning of the nakshatra is "The latter red one".

Astronomy: Two stars named Denebola (Beta Leonis) and 93 Leonis appear at the end of the constellation Leo at magnitudes 2.14 and 4.52. Its declination is 14°N 26' 46.3" and 20°N 13' 08.15". Its right ascension is 11h 50m 12.4s and 11h 47m 59.135s respectively. A high magnitude indicates that the star looks faint to see in the night sky.

Deity: The deity of the nakshatra is known as "Aryama". The Sanskrit word Aryama means a noble-minded and creative person. Aryama is the demigod in charge of Pitrloka. Lord Krishna says (BG 10.29), "Amongst the departed ancestors, I am Aryama".

Sun is the supreme benefactor and the twelve Adityas represent different forms of his boons. Aryama is the presiding deity of Taurus which is the most fertile sign of the zodiac. He is one of the twelve Adityas who are the gods of marriage, union, and friendship. Lord Shiva and Shakti got married in this Nakshatra.

Shakti (Power): The shakti associated with the nakshatra is known as "Chayani Shakti". The word "Chayan" means "The act of choosing or selecting". This energy provides the ability to choose the best which is helpful in development and growth. Thus "Chayani Shakti" works to provide prosperity through selection or union.

Goddess Lakshmi appeared during the churning of the ocean and chose Lord Vishnu. The energy of the Nakshatra is related to the power of choice and bestows prosperity.

The Sight of Nakshatra: It is Adhomukhi Nakshatra – Facing Downward.

Nature: The nature of the Nakshatra is Dhruva (fixed). Under the influence of this Nakshatra, it is good to start those works where the person wants stability, like moving to a new house, etc.

Element: The element associated with the nakshatra is "Fire". The flame of the fire always rises up, it illuminates and shows visibility. Fire helps in cooking and transforming things.

Activity: The activity of the nakshatra is "Balanced", which means, when a person takes the next step, he should also take the previous step forward. If he focusses only on the next step in life, imbalance is created and one is sure to fall from the chosen path.

Uttara Phalguni natives maintain a proper balance in each and every activity of life. They take proper care of every step and never leave anything in between. They never leave their intimate ones in trouble and always keep their promises.

TriMurti and Behaviour: Shiva and Dissolution

Planetary Ruler: The lordship of this nakshatra is given to the Sun, who is the supreme creator. Lord Sun bestows the native with courage and the quality of showing light to others. Hence, these individuals are very courageous and have leadership quality.

Symbol: The symbol of the nakshatra is "Rear legs of the bed". When a person completes rest on the bed, it is his legs that provide the support to get out of bed and get back to work. Hence, Uttara Phalguni natives do not take initiative to fulfill their desires, they believe in hard work, maintain patience and like to wait for their time.

"A full-grown fig tree" is also associated with this Nakshatra, indicating that this energy bestows the fruits of one's hard work.

The difference between the back leg of funeral cot of Uttara Bhadrapada nakshatra, and the back leg of bed of Uttara Phalguni nakshatra is; The funeral cot people carry from one place to another place but bed remains at the same place. So, behaviour of Uttara Phalguni people are very stubborn and they don't like to change their decisions. They are very laborious person and have strong ability to sit at one place for long hours.

Caste: The caste assigned to the Nakshatra is "Kshatriya" (warrior).

1. Warriors are those whose ultimate aim is to win the battle. They don't settle for less than victory.

2. Warriors are belligerent, they have a strong ability to survive in difficult times. Once decided a warrior never deviate from the chosen path.

3. Warriors are ready to bear any pain to achieve the objective, mission is always important to them.

4. Warriors are completely dedicated to their goal, they never retrace their steps and find their own way to continue their journey towards achievement of the goal.

Characteristics: Uttara Phalguni first pada begins in Leo and the remaining three padas fall in Virgo. The lordship of the Sun indicates creation and the lordship of Mercury indicates intelligence. Uttara Phalguni people use their intelligence in creative works. These people are very good in making unions and friendships. The first part (Purva Phalguni) indicates beginning of something and the last part (Uttara Phalguni) indicates ending, conclusion or finalizing things. This indicates that the interference of Uttara Phalguni brings the dispute to the table of settlement; hence they work as a mediator.

Purva Phalguni gives birth to the creation and the energy of Uttara Phalguni shows that creation to the world. When a child takes birth (Purva Phalguni), it is the legs (Uttara Phalguni) that support it to walk. But without linkage with its predecessor star, Uttara Phalguni can't utilize its intellectuality. So, its first pada falls in Leo, and rest three falls in Virgo, here creation is related to intelligence.

Sun always moves in one direction and never retrograde. Sun has a deep effect on these people and they have many qualities of the Sun Uttara Phalguni people prefer independence in life and work as an entrepreneur, counselor, or engage in some other independent profession. Sun also indicates government, so they work for the government.

They always take firm decisions and dislike the fickle behavior of others. They are very solid people and committed to their words. They don't give heed to gossip and they don't like to listen to hot and spicy news. They are dignified people and others respect their knowledge and wisdom. They work as a leader and they are an expert in their field.

Uttara Phalguni is called "The star of Patronage". These people are benevolent, compassionate, charitable, and helpful person. They have strong willpower and can cross any hurdle for the achievement of their goal. They dream big and don't like to waste their time and energy in any dispute. Their behavior is friendly but they are very stubborn in their decisions. They are self-dependent and don't prefer to take anyone's help to uplift their career.

Under the influence of this nakshatra, people are thirsty for knowledge and truth. They are ready to travel anywhere for attaining such knowledge. They prefer to live in luxury but they don't feel an attachment to material things. They do not demand for their comfort, they are down-to-earth people and adjust themselves as per the circumstances.

With the Uttara Phalguni person, the story of King Janaka giving a lamp to a monk and asking him to roam around his palace without extinguishing the lamp fits perfectly, as the monk asked how he could live as an ascetic in this luxurious palace. When the monk had gone around the palace, King Janaka asked what he had seen in the palace. The monk replied that he had not seen anything as his attention was always on the lamp. Janaka said that this is the way to live in a luxurious palace.

Uttara Phalguni means "The latter reddish one" and red is the color of Phalgun (Joy and Happiness). Red is the color of sweet and blue is salty. The word 'latter reddish' means these people will get the fruits of success after very hard work. There is "No rose without thorns", this proverb fits perfectly on these people. They never get disheartened by difficulties and always believe in working hard in life. Their legs are always ready to complete the difficult task and they never show their back. They never run from the circumstances and never weep about the scarcity of resources. In any adverse situation, you find that these people never complain to anyone, they believe in doing their work and they find their own ways to complete the work. They are the perfect "Karma Yogi".

Lord Krishna says, "You have the right only in doing your work, not in its fruits. Because the result is in the hands of God. That's why it is not right to run away from karma, nor is it right to expect the fruits of karma". The great warrior of Mahabharata Arjuna was born in Uttara Phalguni Nakshatra.

Uttara Phalguni people believe in doing their hard work without expecting the result, and one day, the red color blossoms and success comes in their hands in the form of a blooming rose. The color red indicates caution and when it takes time for something to turn red, it can only happen if someone doesn't shy away from putting in the effort. It is only possible with due consideration and the person keeps patience with their fruits. Such a person takes utmost care to complete the work and leave the rest in the hands of God. Uttara Phalguni indicates that the fruits will come when the person keeps patience.

Uttara Phalguni people are choosy in nature, they spend hours to select the best. They work on multiple options and chose the best which is suitable as per the circumstances. Without options, it is difficult for them to take a decision, either in the matter of clothes or work. Once they have decided they remain firm on their decision. They have a collection of various unique things at their home and they like to collect those items which are rarely available. They can spot a diamond among pebbles and they rarely do any mistake in their selection.

Due to the influence of Mercury in the 2nd, 3rd & 4th pada, they are intelligent and sharp minded while the effect of the Sun is seen on the 1st pada. They dare to walk the unknown path alone. They take a keen interest in exploration and love to use their mind to solve mysteries. They read books related to secret and occult knowledge and spend a lot of time-solving the mysteries of nature. They accumulate knowledge that has become obsolete over time.

They are warriors and show leadership ability. They always encourage their companions and participate in every activity that requires determination to win. On the higher aspects, when creative sexual energy begins to enter the chakras, its ultimate goal is to conquer the sex drive and reach the crown chakra. It is the path of a warrior and winning this battle is their ultimate aim.

Negative Traits: If it is afflicted, then they can become greedy for prosperity and can do anything for money. Money can become the only motivator for them and they make relationships only with those people by which they can satisfy their greed. They can be extremely stubborn and do not like to give any importance to another person's opinion. They can become an egoistic person and highly arrogant in behaviour. They are dogmatic people and always keep their voices up in a meeting. They can cheat others to satisfy their greed.

They always want multiple options and are unable to take a decision. They always remain in confusion, about what to decide and what to leave. They are unable to take any decisions and waste their time and energy. Their behaviour delays various important things but they are not bothered about trouble faced by others. They have a misconception that they always take the right decision. Sometimes, they are too picky and take wrong decisions for their selection. They indulge in making many relations, contracts, and associations and face many problems. They prefer to run away from the situation instead of facing the problem.

Gender: The gender of the nakshatra is "Female". It shows that the planets in this Nakshatra display feminine qualities. So, an aggressive planet in this Nakshatra shows only its benevolent qualities.

Animal Symbol: The animal associated with the constellation is Vrishabha (bull). Its counterpart is Uttar Bhadrapada whose animal is cow and it is the inimical of Vishakha and Chitra Nakshatra whose animal symbol is tiger.

Bulls are known for his masculine energy and fertility. They are very hard-working animal but stubborn. They are ferocious and need to be cautiously dealt with. They are aggressive and violent and can fiercely attack or even kill the handler. The above quality of the bull is present in the personality of Uttara Phalguni natives. People of this nakshatra play an important role in cultural events like bull taming and bullfighting.

Sun's Ingress: Sun enters this Nakshatra every year on 14th September and stays there till 27th September. This period is known as Pitru Paksha in India. It is a period when Hindus pay homage to their ancestors (Pitrs), especially through rituals of prayer and food offerings.

Profession: They have strong ability to show light and provide guidance to others. They work as Professor, Teacher, Trainer, Business advisor, Counselor, Sports-coach. They are good in research, discovery, astronomy and other jobs where findings are important after long search.

Favourable Activities: It is auspicious for marriage, ceremonies and other benevolent activities. It is good for inauguration, moving into a new home. This energy supports growth in a harmonious manner, so it is good for investments and all those activities where a person is looking for stability and growth. This downward energy favors digging, mining and laying of foundation stones for long term stability.

Unfavorable Activities: This modest energy is not good for quarrel, combat, and harsh decisions. It is not good for aggression and retaliation.

Gana (Type): The gana assigned to the nakshatra is Manushya (human). Humans can't live in isolation; they work hard to achieve their goal in life. Humans get encouraged when they get reward of their hard work. Uttara Phalguni are very laborious and they are motivated to achieve big success in life.

Guna (Quality): The quality of this nakshatra is "Tamasic-Rajasic-Satwic". For creation Tamas is required, for movement Rajas is required. Every movement of a person is pulled by some desire and destination, if that desire is wrong then the person can fall from the chosen path or wrongly utilize its energy (Rajas). So, after Rajas, 'Satwa' is required for right direction. The highest quality of this energy moves as, "Creation - Movement in right direction - Attainment of enlightenment".

Body Parts: Left Hand

Tree: The tree associated with the nakshatra is 'Badari Tree' which is also known as the Ber or Jujube tree. Scientifically it is known as *'Ziziphus Mauritiana'*. It is a fast-growing tree and reaches a height of 10-15 m. Jujube trees are found in abundance as they can grow naturally in harsh weather conditions. They have small shiny leaves and tolerate extreme heat, drought and winter temperatures.

The tree is strong and survives even if cut at the base. This fast-growing tree starts bearing fruits within three years. Its fruits are soft, juicy and have a pleasant aroma. The whole tree has immense medicinal properties. It is a good source of antioxidants, it is used to cure sunburn, dryness of the skin, wrinkles, various facial and skin related problems. It rejuvenates the cells of the body, and cures liver and kidney dysfunctions. It provides good protection against cough and cold. The famous pilgrimage of Badrinath is named after Badri trees.

Padas: The first pada of this nakshatra is 26° 40' - 30° 00' in Leo and ruled by Jupiter (Sagittarius Navamsha). The energy works for this pada as, "Sun-Sun-Jupiter". The autocratic and dogmatic nature of Sun is visible here. They are very courageous and independent person and show leadership quality. Due to influence of Jupiter they are very learned and wise person. They show ethics, follow rules and possess good advisory capacity.

The second pada of this nakshatra is 0° 00' - 3° 20' in Virgo and ruled by Saturn (Capricorn Navamsha). The energy in this pada works as, "Sun-Mercury-Saturn". They are very practical, hard-working and disciplined person. They are very good in administration and know how to utilize the available resources. They are down to earth person and never blame about scarcity of things.

The third pada of this nakshatra is 3° 20' - 6° 40' in Virgo and ruled by Saturn (Aquarius Navamsha). In this pada influence of Saturn exists as earlier but its approach is towards humanitarian. They prefer innovative and progressive thoughts, take interest in science and technology and have philanthropic approach.

The fourth pada of this nakshatra is 6° 40' - 10° 00' in Virgo and ruled by Jupiter (Pisces Navamsha). In this pada the energy of Jupiter works towards search of knowledge and wisdom. They take interest in occult science and learn astrology and tantra-mantra. The energy of Jupiter works in search for salvation, so they take deep interest to find out the mystery of sex and how to transform this energy.

Chapter 13

Hasta

Hasta is the 13th of 27 Nakshatras and is located at 10° 00' - 23° 20' Virgo. The sign Virgo is ruled by Mercury, so Hasta natives have a strong influence by Mercury. The Sanskrit word Hasta means hand, so it has a strong relation with the hands.

Astronomy: Four bright stars, namely Gamma, Delta, Epsilon and Beta Corvi, are visible in the night sky in the southern hemisphere and in the constellation of Corvus. They form a four-sided polygon and the next star, Alpha Corvi, the fifth-brightest star in the constellation, appears slightly below the polygon. Of these, Gamma Corvi is the brightest star in this constellation with a magnitude of 2.59. Its declination is 17° S 32' 30" and right ascension is 12h 15m 48s.

Deity: The deity of the nakshatra is known as "Savitr". The Sun before sunrise is called Savitr. He is a solar deity and one of the

Adityas. He is believed to have divine influence and vitalizing power of the Sun. He is represented as golden arms, beautiful hand and pleasant tongue.

The Sun is visible to us about two minutes before the actual sunrise and the first ray is visible on the horizon in a golden colour. That is the time when visibility is totally clear and darkness is removed. The deity of the nakshatra bestows all these qualities on the native. He has the power to remove all the darkness and show a new horizon to the person.

Shakti (Power): The Shakti of the nakshatra is known as "Hasta Sthapaniya Agama Shakti", i.e., the power to gain what one seeks and to place it in hand.

The Sight of Nakshatra: Tiryanga-mukha (Sideways)

Nature: Kshipra (Swift)

Element: Fire

Activity: Passive

TriMurti and Behaviour: Brahma and Creation

Planetary Ruler: The ruler of the nakshatra is Moon. It is a feminine planet and rules our minds and emotions. The Moon has no light and is always dependent on sunlight, Sun shows independence and moonlight means support from the Sun. The deity of the nakshatra reflects soft rays which mean an extremely soft and polite nature of the person, who never want to indulge in any type of quarrel.

Symbol: The symbol of Hasta nakshatra is "The Hand". For proper functioning of a hand, it requires all five fingers with a palm; it indicates a perfect grip that means full control. All fingers work simultaneously to achieve one objective, it indicates unity, strength, and cooperation. An open hand indicates receptivity and acceptance. With an open hand, a person welcomes another person and shows cordial behaviour.

Caste: The caste of Nakshatra is Vaishya. These people are businessmen and are quick to analyze profit and loss in business. Where there is no profit, they do not take any interest. To attract money, they know how to play their cards.

To get money, they can spread their hands very far, which mean they can go to any extent to get money. Such a person makes an excellent finance or marketing executive as they have a quick eye for the movement of money and know how to do business. Therefore, they prefer to associate with those people where there is a possibility of any business.

Characteristics: Moon is a receptive planet and makes people kind and benevolent. Hasta Nakshatra people are highly intelligent individuals, listen patiently to the views of others, and prefer to walk by consensus. They are very humble people, good at logic, and ready to admit their mistakes. This Nakshatra bestows a person with many qualities which are necessary to become dexterous. They are excellent at communication and know how to use the right words to get maximum results. Such a person is good in writing, speaking and expressing their thoughts deeply.

The hand plays an important role in expression. When a person wants to give something to others, he needs an open hand. This indicates that Hasta people are big-hearted, they always think broadly and reject any kind of orthodox and narrow thinking. Such a person believes in giving and is always ready to help others.

Each person's hand is represented by special lines that belong to palmistry and contain hidden signs that require special knowledge to read. Similarly, the people of Hasta like to talk in symbols and quickly understand the hidden meaning of the sentence. Their brain works to identify the meaning of codes and they can write complex codes, so they work as a computer programmer. They can read hidden treasure maps because their brain works fast to read message related to money. It does not mean that they are palmists, but it means that they understand signals of money quickly, so they are successful businessmen.

A businessman always maintains cordial relations with others and such a person never wants any trouble that hinders the operation of his business, so they never quarrel or fight with others. This energy works for balance, they can balance difficult situations with their intelligence and fix things optimally to get good results.

The quality of earning money is amazing in them, that's why they are sure of the tongue. But if the wind of money has changed, then their nature also changes and they take interest in the direction where the money is flowing. This makes them selfish and always thinks about their own benefits.

The hand is used to provide direction to others. Hence Hasta people provide proper direction and being kind in nature they provide all necessary help. They are loyal to their friends and also help financially when needed. Their network is very good and spread far and wide and they use this kind of relationship for successful running of their business.

A person uses his hand to make the proper shape of an object. Hasta people have dexterous hands and can give a neat shape to a disorganized thing. They are skilled in arts and make good sculptures, paintings and other things even from waste products. Their mind works instantly to convert the disorganized into the organized, so they always work in a structured manner and keep everything in its place. They never get discouraged by any complication and use their intelligence to find a solution.

They always believe in cooperation and make good relations with the people of Sun-ruled Nakshatras as Sun is the source of light for the Moon. The darkness dispels with the first rays of the sun, it is a divine time used for prayer. The deity of the Nakshatra signifies that the rising Sun can dispel all the darkness and the person who worships the Sun can never go on any wrong path in life. Such a person uses his potential only for the betterment of humanity because this potential is unique.

Negative Traits: They negatively use their sleight of hand and become pickpockets, thieves, and robbers. They can create replicas of original documents, currency, and passports and indulge in various criminal activities where money is easily available because being merchant caste money is always on their mind. If the Moon is under the influence of malefic planets, such a person can easily lose his way and use his skills to harm others.

Their thrust of money may be so much that they do not care for relationships and engage in fraudulent activities. They are greedy people, entice others with their words for negative purposes, and never trust anyone. They always suspect others and always hide every piece of information related to money.

They never give a single penny to anyone free of cost and if they are donating to the temple then they aim to bribe God that their business should not suffer.

Gender: Its gender is Male. They take initiative to fulfill their desire.

Animal Symbol: The associated animal is the 'Female Buffalo'. Its counterpart is Swati nakshatra whose animal is the male buffalo and it is inimical to Ashwini and Shatabhisha nakshatra whose animal symbol is horse.

The milk of female buffalo is condensed and represents nutrition, but it has a commercial purpose. They are very docile, lazy animals, can stand in the water for hours, and they are good swimmers. Buffaloes are gregarious and live in mixed herds; they have an excellent sense of smell and use this sense to find food or to detect nearby danger and predators.

Sun's Ingress: Sun enters this Nakshatra every year on the 27th of September and stays there till the 11th of October. Many festivals are celebrated during this period in India.

Profession: They work in those professions where dexterity of hand is required; Artists, Craftsmen, Painters, Performers, Writers, Comedians, and Dancers who use their hands in their arts. They work as; Stockbrokers, Bankers, Cleaners, Housekeepers, Gardeners, Farmers, Agriculturists, Typists. Such a person makes good shape of food and works with food production. They work as Barbers, Sculptors, Calligraphy, Tailors, and any job where the movement of fingers is important. They perform better in those sports where hands are important.

Favourable Activities: It is auspicious for marriage and celebration. It is good for all activities related to art and craft and all those activities where active response is expected.

Unfavorable Activities: Procrastination, overindulgence, and aggression are not good.

Gana (Type): It is a Dev Nakshatra. It indicates a dignified person who is inclined to do religious work.

Guna (Quality): The quality of the nakshatra is "Tamasic-Tamasic-Rajasic". It means a long period of tamas, where such a person is deeply involved in isolated and underground activities and comes out only when his inner work is done.

Body Parts: Fingers of the hand

Tree: The Juhi plant is associated with this Nakshatra, which is also known as 'Jasmine Auriculatum'. It is easy to grow and tolerates both sun and shade, dry and moist conditions. It is mainly used for ornamental purposes as a fragrant flower. These flowers create intimate relationships; they enhance our connection with family and friends. Fresh bulbs of jasmine floating on water are placed at the entrance of many public areas and commercial areas. The cosmetic industry uses these flowers in large quantities for the manufacture of perfumes and hair oils.

Padas: The first pada of this asterism is 10° 00' - 13° 20' in Virgo and ruled by Mars (Aries Navamsha). Energy levels are high and such individuals prefer a secluded place for their work. When they spot an opportunity, they move forward with confidence against all odds. They are passionate about their goals but impatient.

The second pada of this asterism is 13° 20' - 16° 40' in Virgo and ruled by Venus (Taurus Navamsha). Such a person is honest and a man of his word. They are very productive and responsible people. They are fun-loving and have a strong sense of humor. They have strong business acumen but their pace is slow. They are good at arranging disorderly things but avoid taking any kind of risk. Here Mercury is exalted at 15 degrees.

The third pada of this asterism is 16° 40' - 20° 00' in Virgo and ruled by Mercury (Gemini Navamsha). A high level of intellectualism is seen here along with a strong sense of business. They are a very skilled and versatile person, have strong negotiation skills, and always believe in cooperation. A poorly placed Moon can make a person fearful and nervous.

The fourth pada of this asterism is 20° 00' - 23° 20' in Virgo and ruled by Moon (Cancer Navamsha). They are a very sensitive and emotional person. They are very kind and loving people but also moody and irritable. They are mysterious people who are not ready to open up easily. They have nurturing qualities and like to help others. They are always looking for a safe environment and avoid taking any kind of risk.

Chapter 14

Chitra

Chitra is the 14th of 27 Nakshatras and is located at 23° 20' Virgo – 06° 40' Libra. The Sanskrit word Chitra means, "Beautiful", "Brilliant", "Shinning", "Attractive", "Illustrious", "Painting", "Picture" or "Amazing". These words themselves indicate the features of this nakshatra. This energy works to make things excellent and beyond comparison to anyone, so it becomes very attractive and immediately draws attention.

Astronomy: In the constellation of Virgo and at a magnitude of 0.98, Chitra is represented by a single bright star named "Spica (Alpha Virginis)". Its declination is 11° S 16' 41.07" and right ascension is 13h 26m 22.9s. It is one of the 15th brightest star in the whole sky which appears as a single blue-white star.

Deity: The deity of the nakshatra is "Tvastar" also known as "Vishwakarma". He is the celestial architect who designed and created many attractive and beautiful things. He created a mighty weapon for Indra known as 'Vajra' or 'Thunderbolt'. In the story of Mahabharata, he created a palace for Pandava's; he created many things that are very useful and friendly to the Gods.

Shakti (Power): The Shakti of the nakshatra is "Punya Cayani Shakti", means "Force of Virtue" or "Power of Virtue" i.e. the ability to accumulate merit in life.

The Sight of Nakshatra: Tiryanga-mukha (Sideways)

Nature: Its nature is Mridu (soft)

Element: Its element is "Fire", it indicates vigor and energy to achieve the objective.

Activity: Active

TriMurti and Behaviour: Vishnu and Maintenance

Planetary Ruler: The lord of this Nakshatra is Mars. The lordship of Mars indicates that this energy works for protection and keeps away every bad and evil thing. Whosoever is looking for protection, Chitra is always ready to help. Mars means tamas and desire. It doesn't have only one meaning, that desire for material pleasure, tamas also means darkness and seclusion.

The desire to accomplish goals and excel requires constant energy; such a person is not easily discouraged and never sits idly by. They are not satisfied with simple things and are not ready to give up their will; they believe in hard work and have the ability to do more than others. Mars does not indicate a quarrelsome person, but it shows the fighting spirit against all odds to achieve the goal.

Symbol: The symbol of the nakshatra is the "Multifaceted Jewel", which means a gem that has many aspects or sides. A jewel is usually cut to be faceted to increase its ability to reflect light. A gemstone has great potential to attract attention, but when it is multifaceted it dazzles more and its luster immediately catches the eye, it becomes more precious than a normal gemstone.

Each distinct cut creates a new shape and imparts a special charm to the jewel, thereby increasing its value. Chitra person is a multi-talented person who has many abilities. Like shining gems, they immediately attract attention.

Its secondary symbol is the "Pearl". Most precious metals and gems are found buried in the earth, whereas pearls are the result of a biological process, and are found inside a living creature. Unlike other gems found on the earth, natural pearls do not require polishing or other intervention to increase their value.

The symbol of the pearl describes the way this energy works, it works hard away from others and comes to the fore only when it is ready to shine.

Caste: The caste of Nakshatra is Farmer or Servant. The main quality of a farmer is to produce, so Chitra people are very creative people and their focus is always on increasing production. The servant indicates that they run for the work of others. Be it a farmer's job or a servant, feet always play an important role. Hence Chitra natives have very strong legs and they like to run for work. Such people do not like to sit at one place for a long time, they like to travel, they like short term meetings where they can generate their creative ideas and run for another meeting.

Characteristics: Chitra natives are beautiful in appearance, social, and well-mannered. They are very dynamic, energetic, and ambitious individuals. They are very creative and can make even the worst of things into good shape. They are very hardworking people and do not allow their efforts to go to waste at any cost. They are very happy when their efforts are recognized and rewarded. They do not take the share of others but fight fiercely for their pie.

Mars indicates protection and Vishwakarma is for creation. Chitra people have the ability to do a creation that can become a shield of protection. They are very protective in nature and always keep a backup plan for an emergency. They work in those filed which provide a protective shield in life, like insurance. They can easily describe the benefit of the protective shield, so they are a good salesperson or can create a plan for protection and work as an actuary. They work as a programmer or a software designer who create such shields or a firewall to protect computers from viruses. They create a complex molecule in the laboratory that provides protection to the human body against serious viruses.

Vishwakarma created a thunderbolt from the bones of sage Dadhichi. Chitra people work in the weapon industry and design a powerful weapon like a thunderbolt that work as a shield for the protection of the country. They work as a blacksmith who works continuously in front of the fire and prepares a weapon. These people make things or work in those fields where they create a masterpiece and later it is replicated by others. It is a highly protective energy, but on the downside, they become extremely fearful and look for protection in every aspect of life.

In modern days refrigerators, air conditioners, and shock absorbers are used to protect food, heat, and accidents. Chitra persons work in all those areas and immediately put food and drink item in the fridge for safety. They prepare delicious food and work long hours for its preparation.

They make sophisticated gadgets that can be beneficial to many people. They are never disheartened at the sight of scattered things; their mind immediately works out how to organize them. They make a useful thing out of disparate and disorganized things. They know how to use things in a highly efficient manner, so they are able to make the best out of waste. They are a very good manager who knows the worth of each and every member of their team.

They work as a successful business people who buy an unorganized company that is completely useless in the eyes of others, but these people have the ability to make it a profitable company. They are brilliant at visual presentation, and the manifestation of their work is important to them, so they open their YouTube channel and work hard to upload a beautiful video.

Being a social person, they like to mingle with people and Chitra indicates a very soft-spoken demeanor. This indicates the quality of a businessman who does not like to get involved in useless arguments because deep down they know that it is not good for their business.

Chitra natives love to participate in the competition and when the competition becomes cut throat their energy also goes high, they never back down, once they have decided they will go to any lengths to achieve it. They like to participate in office competition, sports where they show their skills, win trophies and get admired by the public. They want to be the center of attraction; hence they love photography and are always cautious about their looks. They are skilled photographers who know how to adjust lighting for a perfect picture, they are selfie experts.

Chitra is related to aesthetics, arts, and crafts. These natives have a strong sense of colors to design a beautiful painting, which requires the power of imagination and a sense of excellence, as one wrong stroke can ruin their hard work. So, they think about all the pros and cons before taking any action and prefer to wait patiently for the right time to act.

To create fine art, they prefer to go to a secluded place where no one knows what they are doing and they will not reveal their work until it is finished. Excellence comes after a lot of practice and shine comes after a lot of rubbing. Chitra natives love to honc their skills and never hesitate to work hard to excel in their field. They have an inherent desire to shine and they do everything that they can do, on the downside, negatives too.

This energy falls in two asterisms – its first two pada fall in Virgo and its next two pada falls in Libra. In Virgo, its focus is on intelligence, practicality, improvement, and problem-solving. On the Libra side, the focus is on taste, show, presentation, and outward appearance. We can understand these differences with the help of making an ornament. At first, a goldsmith takes a piccc of gold and gives various pressure and cuts, he uses his intelligence to make a masterpiece, but till the jewelry is in the hands of a goldsmith it is not in the limelight, this is Virgo's part. Virgo is a sign of virginity; it means that such a person does not let anyone touch his work.

When the jewelry is ready, it enters a showroom where everyone's eyes are dazzled by its glitter. Everyone is interested in seeing that multifaceted gem, every pressure and cut has increased its price and now everyone is realizing its value. This is part of Libra where presentation, admiration, beauty, looks, glamour, ostentation, and market value are strong.

Every cut on jewelry is made with a purpose, that enhances its appearance and outer beauty, and every pressure on jewelry adds to its sturdiness and complexity. Diamond is one of the most complex substances known and as the quality of the cut improves, so does its cost. Chitra people are like this only. Just like a jewel bears the burden and pressure of being cut but each cut adds to its value, similarly, Chitra people are very hard-working people and are ready to face any pressure to make themselves a shining star.

They can engage themselves in work for long hours and completely forget their food and drink; they are highly alert for their work. Because shining is important to them, it also means no mistakes, so they double-check their documents or other work before finalizing and one cannot find even a single mistake in their work, they are perfectionists.

They do everything very well and like to handle things very carefully. They are suitable for professions where delicate handling is required, so they work as midwives, babysitters, cosmetologists, musicians, broadcasters, etc., and for all those jobs where the situation needs to be handled very delicately and in a refined manner.

They do everything excellently and want the best of everything in life. They are very conscious about their appearance and always prefer to wear branded and expensive clothes. They never compromise with quality and are quick to reject anything that forces them to compromise. Hence, they never go to places where they find the quality lacking. Such a person prefers not to do any work where he sees people compromising on quality.

They want fair value for talent and don't like those who don't respect their talent. They do not like to have any relationship with such people, they leave the place forever without saying a word and keeping their mouth shut.

They are silent observers and immediately recognize quality levels and deficiencies. They seek perfection and know that there is no shinning without rubbing, so they work diligently. They work as; Craftsmen, furniture makers, artistry, and for all work that requires rubbing and polishing.

Recall the story of the Mahabharata, the Pandava's palace built by Vishwakarma. Chitra people can create illusions that seem real to others. They work for an industry where creating confusion is a part of the business, so their work areas are; Video gaming, cinema, advertising, media and entertainment, magicians, plastic surgeons, and all work where the creation of false is necessary to look like truth. They can create a replica of the truth like a copy machine, but if it is influenced by malefic then they negatively use their skills.

At a higher level they find the answer to this worldly illusion, which is called Maya. The Virgo part indicates curiosity and a thirst for answers, and the Libra part indicates that the person has the answers and is ready to face the world. Such individuals prefer to go into deep isolation where they completely withdraw from the activities of the outside world and return only when they are ready to shine. Chitra is the builder, when a mason adds a few bricks every day, a great construction becomes possible. When a person does good deeds every day and walks on the path of spirituality then he shines like a diamond, he becomes a unique gem and shines in the sky forever.

Negative Traits: Its negative quality is overindulgence, achieving one's desire, and hiding every development from everyone. They pay more attention to appearances and less to work. They just become show people and are more interested in showing off their things, and wealth and their discussion gets limited to money only. They become highly selfish people who always think about how much profit they will get. They do not hesitate to use unethical means to fulfill their desires and like to spend a lot on their luxuries and comforts. They do not want to work hard and get easily discouraged, go into a state of depression, and withdraw themselves from every activity.

In the corporate world, such people know that the people at the top of the organization shine and many people know them. They become extremely greedy and selfish individuals who use every unfair means to earn money and reach the top. Morality has no value for such a person, they want to reach the top at any cost and are ready to do anything to achieve their objective. They want to enjoy the luxuries of life and in search of quick money, they indulge in creating fake documents, printing fake money and doing all those things where their fake work looks real. That's why their every move is hidden and no one knows what their next move is.

Gender: The gender of the nakshatra is "Female". Women are more interested in preserving than finding things. Women have a maternal instinct, which keeps them always alert for the safety of their children. Similarly, female gender constellations are also very alert for safety. They do not like to take risks and their focus is always on security and strengthening it.

Animal Symbol: Its associated animal is "female tiger". Its counterpart is Vishakha Nakshatra whose symbol is the male tiger. It is inimical for Uttara Phalguni and Uttara Bhadrapada whose animal symbol is cow.

Tigers are known for their intelligence; they adopt strategies while hunting, are unusually calm on sight, and wait for the right moment to attack. It never chases its prey in a disorderly manner and can remain motionless for long periods. They always use the right time and method to kill their prey. Tigresses are more protective and careful about their cubs because male tigers do not help. If a tiger is often seen fighting, it is probably a male.

Sun's Ingress: Sun enters this Nakshatra every year on the 11th of October and stays there till the 24th of October. It is a time for celebration and festivals in the country as the heat subsides and the weather becomes more pleasant.

Professions: Fashion designers, Jewellery designers, Cosmetic surgeons, Architects, Builders, Interior designers, City and Highway planners, Insurance agents, Software designers, and Weapon Manufacturers. They love beauty and making things beautiful, so they work as; Embroiderers, Frame makers, Photographers, Make-up artists, and Cosmetologists. They love to design gadgets and work as Technicians, and Design engineers. They are business people and experts in their field. They can handle things with extreme care and work as: Midwives, Gynecologists, Pediatricians, Surgeons, Tailors, etc., and all those professions in which not a single wrong cut is allowed.

Favourable Activities: Every maintenance activity, construction or entry into a new house, purchase of a vehicle, wearing new clothes, and art & craft related activities are good. It is auspicious for business expansion and starting new ventures.

Unfavorable Activities: It is not good to do any harsh activity.

Gana (Type): Among three types – Dev, Manushya (Human), and Rakshasa (Demon), the type of Chitra is Rakshasa. While understanding the personalities, one should not take the literal meaning of Rakshasa. Chitra natives are highly aspiring individuals, they cannot give up their desires easily and work hard to fulfill them. They have a very strong hold on their things, their attitude is – "It's mine and no one can touch it without my permission." They fight fiercely for their rights and are never afraid to confront anyone, and can cause serious trouble for a mischievous person.

Rakshasa prefer to live in forest, in present days such a person take deep interest in gardening and keep lots of flowers and plants in their home. They are not easily satisfied and this dissatisfaction drives them towards "more and more". They prefer to visit places that are largely isolated from the public and where they can enjoy their solitude.

Guna (Quality): The quality of the nakshatra is "Tamasic-Tamasic-Tamasic". It is the most tamasic among all the 27 nakshatras. Every development begins in a state of tamas (darkness), a seed remains in the soil in darkness for some time before germination, a child in the mother's womb is in a state of total darkness. The three level of tamas means everything is hidden and every development is underneath.

For instance; a lot of work has to be done to make a piece of jewellery valuable and all that development happens beyond the eyes of others. A carbon turns into a diamond but before that it has seen the face of deep darkness. Such a person never opens their heart to anyone and keeps everything in secret.

Body Parts: Forehead and Neck

Tree: The related tree is the Bilva or Bel, also known as 'Aegle marmelos'. It is a medium sized tree up to 8-10 meters in height. It is considered a sacred tree and its leaves, flowers, and fruits are used for worship. It is very useful for dysentery and irritable bowel syndrome. It has many other medicinal benefits and helps in curing many diseases.

Padas: The first pada of this asterism is 23° 20' - 26° 40' in Virgo and ruled by Sun (Leo Navamsha). They are very intelligent, brave individuals and have the ability to lead. They are very determined and positive people and never take their steps back. They are ambitious person who work hard to achieve their goals. They are independent person with the ability to organize things quickly.

The second pada is 26° 40' - 30° 00' in Virgo and ruled by Mercury (Virgo Navamsha). They are good in cooperation and negotiations and possess strong analytical mind. They are very practical, careful, and meticulous person and good to organize a disorganize things. They are good in critics and like to find answers to difficult questions. They are very responsible person and have perfection in their field.

The third pada is 00° 00' - 03° 20' in Libra and ruled by Venus (Libra Navamsha). They have a charming personality, seek harmony and are very cooperative people. They are very social persons who are ready to help others. They always avoid any kind of quarrel in life and do not like to get into any controversy. They are good counselors and always weigh all the pros and cons of a situation before taking any step.

The fourth pada is 03° 20' - 06° 40' in Libra and ruled by Mars (Scorpio Navamsha). This pada reflects a strong power of intuition, secrecy, and an eye for every detail. They check everything before sending or signing any document and can easily remember all the facts related to the work. All their actions are done in deep silence and they like to give surprises. They are never in a hurry and always have patience to work.

Chapter 15

Swati

Swati is the 15th of 27 Nakshatras and is located at 06° 40' - 20° 00' Libra. The word "Swati" is derived from two Hindi words; 'Su' and 'Ati'. Su is a suffix attached before some words giving the meaning of 'Good', 'Beautiful', 'Auspicious', 'Pure' and 'Proper'. Ati means 'Excess', 'Abundance', or 'Exaggeration'.

Hence, the word Swati means 'Goodness in excessiveness', 'Excessive beautiful' or 'Purity in abundance'. Swati represents balance and it comes in the middle of the sequence of 27 Nakshatras. Saraswati, the goddess of knowledge, music, art, wisdom, and learning is associated with this bright star.

Astronomy: In the northern constellation of Bootes, Swati is represented by a single bright star named Arcturus or Alpha Bootes. It is the third brightest star in the sky with a visual magnitude of -0.04. When binary stars are included it is said to be the fourth brightest star in the night sky after Alpha Centauri. Its declination is 19°N 3' 58.07" and right ascension is 14h 16m 41.3s.

Deity: The associated deity of this nakshatra is known as Vayu, the Lord of Wind. Vayu is known as Prana (Breath) and do act of balancing. When such balance gets disturbed or an air gap is created, the surrounded wind flow immediately to fill that gap, which create gusty wind and storms. These strong winds don't follow any rule to fill such gap, there is only rule, fill the gap immediately, this universe does not accept any vacuum anywhere and it is wind that forces all the nearby things to fill such gap.

This technique is used in pranayama, create the gap and universe will fill you. Various breathing exercises of pranayama are an act of creating balance of air in the body. Swati is related to air and other related activities.

Shakti (Power): The power associated with the Nakshatra is known as "Pradhvamsa Shakti". Pradhvamsa means destruction, it is a very strong destructive force that creates great disturbances and has a strong ability to annihilate. This energy wipes off the face of the earth.

As strong winds cause significant changes, destroying everything in their path, causing great havoc. After a gusty wind the form of the earth does not remain as it was earlier.

The Sight of Nakshatra: Tiryanga-mukha (Sideways)

Nature: The nature of the nakshatra is Chara (Movable)

Element: The element of the nakshatra is "Fire"

Activity: The activity of this nakshatra is "Passive". Passive energy remains calm until it gets some stimulus or inspiration to act.

TriMurti and Behaviour: Shiva and Dissolution

Planetary Ruler: The ruler of the nakshatra is Rahu. The existence of Rahu indicates the desire for the material world and the finest things in life. Rahu indicates chaos and disorder, and the association of wind indicates a gusty storm.

This energy works to get the purest things, but it is not easy. To become a master or a perfectionist, one has to learn many things and correct mistakes. It is very difficult to recognize the impurities of our mind, then work hard to remove it, for this strong willpower is required. When a person is in the process of getting rid of all the impurities that are causing obstruction, no order is needed to remove them. Hence, Rahu, the planet of disorder compels such a person to seek perfection and he uses all means to achieve his objective.

The planets in Swati Nakshatra indicate that the life of such a person is not normal. They have to go through many disturbances till they become perfectionists.

Symbol: The main symbol of this nakshatra is "A very delicate and tender plant shoot blowing in the wind". A tender plant moves in the direction where the wind flows and has a strong potential to convert into a big tree.

Swati people are peace-loving people and never do any harm to anyone. They always aspire to achieve big in life, but as a delicate plant needs protection, they have to nurture their potential. They are easily influenced by the outside wind and flow in the same direction. When they see anything attractive they immediately get influenced. They are like small children who are unable to differentiate between the good and the bad.

The second symbol of Swati is a "Blade" or "Sword". A blade or sword is a sharp object and is used to create discrimination. Swati plant is delicate and tender but it is sharp, so proper care is required to handle it. The sword also symbolizes achievement through conquering, indicating that the Swati people have a strong fighting spirit and do not give up until they have achieved it. This tender plant is razor sharp, indicating the sharpness of their personality and they do not hesitate to cut those things immediately which create obstacles towards their achievement

Its third symbol is "Coral." It is associated with Mars, the planet of energy, indicating the high energy level of this star. Coral is an animal although looks like a colorful plant. The bright colors of the coral are different types of algae, due to photosynthesis these algae use the waste products of the coral and the plant makes its food. This indicates the highly independent nature of this Nakshatra.

The by-products of photosynthesis include oxygen and carbohydrates, which are used by corals to build reefs. Coral reefs are among the most complex and fascinating marine ecosystems in the ocean. It provides a habitat for fish and other organisms. The reefs attract tourists and help local economies. Coral reefs also protect people and land from storms, acting as a barrier that reduces the impact of large waves on the coast.

The symbol of coral indicates how this energy functions, how it helps and supports, and creates balance. Therefore, in this nakshatra "Saturn - The Lord of Balance" gets exalted at 20 degrees.

Caste: The caste associated with the Nakshatra is "Butcher." A butcher is a person who ruthlessly destroys things. He shows no mercy while destroying and acts in a very harsh manner. Swati indicates a tendency to destroy brutally and such people do those things which others refrain from doing.

Characteristics: The word Swati signifies the utmost level of purity, hence the energy of this Nakshatra churns and works to achieve the supreme. They look for perfection and believe in honing their skills. They are a passionate person and want to enjoy the luxuries of life. They don't like anything deshaped and ruthlessly cut those things which are making hindrances in coming to a beautiful shape. Even they don't like to eat anything deshaped and when the shape of food gets distorted they prefer not to eat. They are highly sensitive people and planets in this nakshatra indicate a perfectionist in their field.

It is said that a special bird named Chatak (Jacobin Cuckoo) drinks only the rainwater that falls in Swati Nakshatra. Even if the bird is thirsty, it does not open its beak to any other water, it never drinks water from lakes, ponds, or rivers and quenches its thirst only when it rains.

In the same way, people of this nakshatra believe in purity at any cost, and they keep patience for the outcome. As long as there is a minor fault or impurity, they will not accept it and will pass the work to another process. They are the finest artists who continuously work for their masterpiece and as Chatak bird waits for years, they are ready to wait but never agree with anything sub-standard or lower in quality. Such excellence is difficult and they have to see many ups and downs in life because they are not ready to compromise with their masterpiece and when it is ready it shines like one of the brightest stars in the sky.

Such purity comes after a lot of churning, it is like pure ghee and the process of making pure ghee from milk is not easy. The milk has to go through various processes and after that only the finest part of the milk remains, gradually all the excess goes away and then the aroma of pure ghee spreads all around.

Swati Nakshatra people never back down and never give up trying. They are not afraid of disturbances; deep down they know they have the potential to shine and would have to go through such a process without any complaint. They know that purity does not come easily and they have to work very hard. They have infinite patience like the Chatak bird that constantly looks up to the sky for rain but will settle for nothing less than the finest drop.

This Nakshatra has the potential to produce great musicians who can capture subtle differences of waves. Their senses are sufficiently trained to catch even the tiniest mistake and they never tolerate it.

Swati nakshatra people are passionate to achieve the excellence, they are ready to destroy anything which comes on their path of achievement, they annihilate every obstacle forcefully and make their own way in life. To get the purity at utmost level processing from multiple dimensions is necessary, this is the key theme for this nakshatra.

They are sophisticated individuals and like the finest things in life. They prefer processed foods like cheese, and butter to raw foods. They like to drink expensive wine, wear diamonds and collect not easily available items. They work in places where multiple processing is required to get the final result.

They are very good in communication, speak very clearly and take full care of the chosen words. They are kind and skilled in trade and commerce. All four padas of Swati fall in Libra, which is a semi-fruitful, masculine and odd sign. Libra represents a busy town or marketplace, which indicates they are very busy people, moving around for business is their top priority. Business without relations is not possible, so they are a soft-spoken person and quick to identify business opportunities. Swati people work as entrepreneurs and leading business people. They have a strong ability to channelize the resources to get the optimum results.

The quality of air is roaming and it never stays in a place, if the air does not move, it becomes stale. This energy compels one to move and such a person cannot sit at one place for long. They prefer to move and are very adaptable with the changing circumstances. They like to visit large and open space, surrounded by fresh air where they can move easily. They feel fresh and energetic when they roam.

Air is very sensitive and influence quickly by subtle waves. It is easily affected by the surrounding atmosphere, and anything spread in the air quickly. In the same way, they get easily hurt by the loud voice of others, they can quickly identify the differences in flavors and catch the changes in emotions and behaviour without saying anything.

Due to the presence of air, they are a very active, nimble, and unrestrained person. They are a good mediator and bring calm to a tense situation. Air spreads rapidly and due to effective communication skills; they give a good speech and soon become popular. Following are some points that describe the quality of air and the characteristics of Swati people;

1. Air indicates flexibility and continuity. It indicates Swati nakshatra people are very flexible and believe in continuity, they don't like anything stagnant in life.

2. Air is quickly adaptable to the changing circumstances. These people quickly change themselves as circumstances changes and adapt themselves to any type of situation.

3. To hear the sound of the air is difficult, until it starts roaring and turn into a strong wind. The behaviour of Swati people is like the same. They are very silent person, but when they get angry it is like a storm.

4. The air moves freely everywhere without any boundaries. In the same way, these people do not want any kind of bondage and always prefer their independence. They get irritated by asking questions about their roaming. Swati people perform better when they get free hand to finish a work.

5. Without any discrepancy air is available to everyone. Swati people are magnanimous person and believe in giving to others. The exaltation of Saturn shows that they believe in justice and always behave justly with others.

6. Due to effect of air, the energy of this nakshatra is scattered. But when it is channelized it becomes very powerful.

7. Air spreads far and far quickly. Due to presence of Rahu suddenly they become very famous person.

8. Air is quickly affected by heat and starts spreading from there. Swati natives do not like arrogant people and wherever they see signs of arrogance (heat in behaviour), they immediately leave from there.

It is said that when Sun is in Swati Nakshatra, an oyster waits to catch a drop of rain. Then it goes into the deep ocean and turns that drop into a priceless pearl. No one knows where the shell has gone after getting that drop, but it continues to function internally and away from the activities of the outside world.

On a higher aspect, the story indicates that a single drop of wisdom from the Guru is sufficient for a disciple to become an enlightened person. When the pearl is ready, the oyster does not keep it in the mouth and gives it to the world. In the same way, now such an enlightened disciple is ready to distribute his knowledge with the world.

Negative Traits: They always feel the need to talk and they discuss pointless things and raise any issue without any meaning. They have an inherent desire to spread the fame and if good work is not possible, they do bad things. Notoriety also makes one known. They always exaggerate their words and take pride in their exaggerated stories.

They get distracted easily and forget their objective. They are easily influenced by what they see and immediately demand it. But they never stay, the value of the thing ends as soon as it comes into their hands and they immediately demand the other.

They are a very stubborn, adamant, and arrogant person. They are not ready to listen to anyone and feel that what they think is always right. They are uncertain about taking decisions and their decision is influenced by pomp and show. They are restless persons and feel uncomfortable in clothes within a few hours and like to change them immediately.

When this energy is channelized in one direction it becomes extremely forceful. To overcome such negativities a person should avoid indulgence in any type of argument.

Gender: The gender of the nakshatra is "Female". They are receptive person and ready to learn quickly.

Animal Symbol: The animal associated with the nakshatra is 'male buffalo', its counterpart is Hasta nakshatra whose animal symbol is female buffalo and it is inimical to Ashwini and Shatabhisha whose animal symbol is horse.

Buffalos are big, strong but lazy animals. They are used to pull the cart indicates strength of the legs. They are moody and tough to move from their place. They love water and hours standing in the river. They are very fertile animals. Buffaloes always try to live in herds and are successful in defending to a great extent, even if faced with a lion. They are very brave and do not hesitate to attack and kill lions. The above mentioned qualities are found in these people. As a group they can defeat even a more powerful enemy.

Sun's Ingress: Sun enters this Nakshatra every year on 24th October and stays there till 7th November. In India, during this period the condition of weather is calm and pleasant.

Profession: Pilots, Airhostess, Diplomats, Lawyers, Hosts, Musicians, Artists, PR professionals, Salesman, Yoga teacher, Aerobics and dance trainer, Diplomats, Entrepreneur, Businessmen, Experts in some field, Business of sound, Travel and tourism industry, Balloonists, Cleaning through vacuum cleaner, and any work where flow of air involves.

Favourable Activities: All activities related with communication, business and trade, start a marketing campaign, travel or to move anything, to organize an event, transaction of money, agreements, learning, performing social activities, breathing exercises.

Unfavorable Activities: It is not a fierce energy, so any type of aggression is not good.

Gana (Type): Swati belongs to "Dev" gana. It indicates a righteous person with sophisticated behaviour and surrounded by highly refined and finest things.

Guna (Quality): The quality of the nakshatra is "Tamasic-Tamasic-Satwik." They prefer to work in isolation where no one can see them. They close the door and allow no one to see their work. They never say their sufferings to anyone. They have to see a state of darkness before they shine. Just like an oyster taking a drop and goes into the deep ocean, the first two levels of Tamas indicate that they engage deeply until they achieve their goal, and return only when they have created their masterpiece.

Body Parts: The body parts related with this nakshatra is "Chest", which is related with air and breath.

Tree: The tree associated with the nakshatra is "Arjuna", also known as *'Terminalia arjuna'*. It attains a height of up to 25-30 metres. The tree has various medicinal properties and it helps reduce the risk of heart diseases. It helps to reduce high blood pressure, useful in skin disorder, control diarrhea, asthma and cough. It balances the Kapha and Pitta doshas in the body.

Padas: The first pada of this nakshatra is 6° 40' - 10° 00' in Libra and ruled by Jupiter (Sagittarius Navamsha). They are inclined to learn religious texts and love long distance travel. This is Rahu-Venus-Jupiter energy; they are attractive, knowledgeable person and good speakers. They are good negotiators, not money-minded person and like to follow ethics.

The second pada of this nakshatra is 10° 00' - 13° 20' in Libra and ruled by Saturn (Capricorn Navamsha). They are much disciplined person and have strong quality to organize things. They do everything in a structured manner; they utilize things efficiently and always try to save things. They have own set of rules and always follow them with strictness.

The third pada of this nakshatra is 13° 20' - 16° 40' in Libra and ruled by Saturn (Aquarius Navamsha). They are very intellectual person and keep strong knowledge on information technology. They are very technical person and always equipped with latest gadgets. Their approach is always humanitarian and likes to assist underprivileged of the society. If Moon is weak and influenced by malefics then they can misuse their skills.

The fourth pada of this nakshatra is 16° 40' - 20° 00' in Libra and ruled by Jupiter (Pisces Navamsha). They are very emotional person and keep everything in secret. They are social and flexible person and ready to adapt with the changing situation. They are very imaginative and creative person.

Chapter 16

Vishakha

Vishakha is the 16th of 27 nakshatras and situated at 20° Libra – 3° 20' Scorpio. The Sanskrit word Vishakha has come from two words – the first is "Vi" which means "Divided" and "Shakha" which means "Branch". It means a branch that is forked or divided into two parts. It also means a two-way path is merged into a single path and indicates one point or one direction. It is known as "The Star of Purpose". It's another name is "Radha".

This is the only nakshatra in which one planet (Saturn) is exalted and the other (Moon) is debilitated. Fair division is needed to properly divide an object into two parts and only an impartial person can do that. Justice means balance, hence, the lord of justice – Saturn, find this place perfectly fit as per his disposition and exalted at 20°, at the onset of this nakshatra.

The last pada of this nakshatra comes under the sign of Scorpio, which is the darkest, most poisonous, and most dangerous part of the zodiac. Moon, the planet of emotions, feels extremely uncomfortable at this place and becomes debilitated at 3°.

Astronomy: In the constellation of Libra four bright stars known as Alpha Librae (Zuben El Genubi), Beta Librae, Gamma Librae, and Iota Librae create this nakshatra. Alpha and Beta are the two brightest stars in this constellation and appear at magnitudes 2.7 and 2.6, respectively. Its declination is, 16° S 8' 2.39" and 09° S 22' 58"; right ascension is, 14h 52m 7.6s and 15h 17m 00s.

Deity: The two-branched Nakshatra is ruled by two deities "Indra" and "Agni". According to some scriptures, it has only one deity known as "Indragni". Indra is known as the king of the gods and Agni is known as the god of fire. Indra represents the materialistic desire of a person who is ready to do anything to fulfill his wish as according to mythology Indra did many evil deeds to fulfill his desire.

Hence, they are power-hungry people and always looking for higher positions in the organization and they are ready to do anything to achieve it, like Indra. They are jealous and possessive and use unfair means to achieve their target. On the other hand, Agni represents purification and inner awareness. Indra and Agni arc also related to agriculture and harvesting. Therefore, this makes this nakshatra a strong association with agriculture.

Shakti (Power): It relates to "Vyapana Shakti", the power to manifest and achieve the goal. Especially, the first three padas which come under libra represent the strong power of manifestation and the fourth pada indicates focused energy with penetrating insight.

The Sight of Nakshatra: It is Adhomukhi Nakshatra – Facing Downward. It means the energy of this nakshatra supports underground activities. It supports research and investigation, drilling, digging, trenching, sowing, and agriculture-related activities.

Nature: The nature of the nakshatra is Mixed i.e., sharp and soft. Krittika is another nakshatra in which nature is mixed. They indulge in more than one assignment at a time, focus always on goal and don't bother about criticism. They are people with high intelligence, sharp vision and achieve what they want.

Element: Fire

Activity: They are a highly active person. Planets placed in this nakshatra indicate that the person will utilize such energy to fulfill his desire. Fiery planets like Sun and Mars make the person arrogant and aggressive.

TriMurti and Behaviour: Brahma and Creation

Planetary Ruler: This is the place where the energy level is very high and such energy should always be in the right hands. Dealing with such energy requires both wisdom and benevolence. Even poison becomes medicine in the hands of a worthy person. High energy and great knowledge can harm the hands of the wrong person. Therefore, Jupiter is the ruler of this Nakshatra.

Symbol: Its symbol is a "Triumphal Gate" decorated with leaves or a "Potter's Wheel". A decorated gate in India used in marriage ceremonies indicates success and achievement and the potter's wheel is a symbol of patience. Vishakha people are endurance, they keep patience to achieve their desired goal. They do not easily leave the battle and want to be victorious at any cost and they are ready to fight for years. When others are losing their patience, they take full caution in their move to achieve success. On a higher aspect, it indicates a person who will do tough penance on the spiritual path and will not lose his patience.

Its second symbol potter's wheel indicates a transformation in life. But the transformation from clay to a beautiful pot is not easy. The clay has to go through a process and it has to become soft before putting it on the wheel and then the transformation begins. Then it has to face the whirl of the pot and during that process, it starts taking a beautiful shape.

Hence, Vishakha nakshatra people's life is full of turmoil. They have to leave their ego and have to become a humble person. They have to see both faces of life only then a perfect balance is possible. It also means that the higher the ego the higher the turmoil would come in their life, because it is the exaltation star of Saturn, and surrender of ego is the only key.

Caste: The caste of the nakshatra is Mleccha (Outcaste). Outcastes are those who do not live within society due to their eating habits, clothes, general behavior, etc. They do not bother about such things in life and do not give any heed to others or their social affairs. They like to do something strange which is not prevalent in society.

Characteristics: Vishakha Nakshatra people are highly focused on their objective. They are very determined person and become ruthless to achieve their desires. They are goal-oriented people, play gimmicks, always tense, and want to finish the task within the limited time frame. Hence, they often use the word "target" and "deadline" in their discussion. They are always conscious about their image, so they always dress elegantly and believe that success requires an impressive outfit. They like to give direction and demand attention from others.

They are passionate, clever, daring, and fearless people, and are known for their courage. They are intelligent, attractive, and good-looking people and females of Vishakha look very beautiful and charming. They are hard-working people and love adventure. They are very confident people and sometimes they take wrong decisions due to overconfidence. They are always suspicious on others and find it hard to trust anyone.

They have little regard for the rules and regulations that restrain their free-spirited nature. They are impulsive, lively, and dynamic and want to be the center of attention at social gatherings. One moment they look furious and the next they become calm and emotional. It is very difficult to predict their movement and a person never knows what their next move is going to be.

The exaltation of one planet and the debilitation of another planet in this sign indicate that in one aspect of life they reach the pinnacle and in the other aspect their life touches the abyss. There is another meaning of this exaltation and debilitation; There is a time their life touches the bottom and no one pays any attention to them, then when time changes and their life touches the pinnacle, everyone likes them.

They show complete integrity in doing their work and like to do things efficiently and accurately. They prefer proper documentation of every work and keep every file at its proper place. They do not believe on verbal commitment and like everything in black and white.

They have a strong throat and can speak for hours. So, they have the quality to become good orators and speakers. They are great motivators and have a strong capacity to bring passion and enthusiasm among team members.

Due to their strong vocal power, they dislike small discussions and want to speak more in a meeting. They have superiority complex and repeat the same sentence many times. They do not like to listen to others and for them others are there only to listen to them. They are highly professional and maintain a high standard in business dealings. They have a bossy attitude and always want to give order. They keep an eye on every development and never miss any minuscule detail. They are best in those jobs where sharp instincts are required, such as lawyers, investigators, spokespersons, etc.

Vishakha means a branch that is divided into two, hence, they believe in diversification and at a time they indulge in many projects. But underneath of all they have single-mindedness and use the power of aggression to achieve their target. They are highly dedicated to their aim and wait patiently to achieve the outcome. To fulfill their desire, they can wait for years without intimating anyone.

The Mleccha (Outcaste) caste of this nakshatra indicates, on the lower aspect, they take interest in underworld activities and those acts which are not generally done by the common people.

On the higher aspect, they take interest in occult science and like to do various occult practices in remote places. It represents a bandit and a hermit, both are opposite to each other, but both cannot live in society. A bandit is one whose energy is high but the direction is wrong and a hermit is one whose energy is high in the right direction and exactly the lordship of Jupiter of this nakshatra represents this. They have the potential to go high if they chose the right direction in life.

As per Hindu mythology, the character of Valmiki perfectly fits with this nakshatra. The two branches of Vishakha indicate that one has to see the dark phase of life before one can see the light or become a hermit. When a person can control the negative energy then it transforms and moves in the upward direction and that direction is provided by Jupiter (Guru), as after getting the direction from sage Narada a robber Ratnakar turned into sage Valmiki.

Negative Traits: They are very talkative people, like to gossip and pry into other people's affairs. They don't like boundaries and restrictions and are ready to cross them to fulfill their desire. They often lose their close friends due to their adamant behaviour. They are always in a hurry and show that they are very busy.

They often say "fast-fast" with their colleagues and co-workers in the organization. They don't trust anyone and prefer to work alone. They don't like to take advice from others, they are stingy and ready to take revenge. They are greedy and ready to manipulate things for their benefit.

They are fond of material pleasure. They are sex obsessed and want to enjoy finer things in life. They make promises but never bother about its fulfillment. They are always looking for profits and when the situation is not in their favour they easily take U-turn regardless of the loss of others and hesitate to fulfill their obligations.

They are party lovers and prone to drugs and alcohols. They are not blessed with love from family. They fail in relationships because they say one thing and do the exact opposite. Their marital life also gets disturbed and break-up is possible as they never give importance to their spouse as both Indra and Agni, the deities of this Nakshatra, wooed other wives.

Gender: The gender of this nakshatra is female. Such persons remain silent for a long time and patiently wait for the result.

Animal Symbol: Its animal symbol is a 'Male Tiger', its counterpart is Chitra nakshatra whose symbol is 'Female Tiger' and inimical to Uttara Phalguni and Uttara Bhadrapada whose symbol is bull / cow.

Tigers usually attack their prey from behind. So, the people of Vishakha attack suddenly and in arguments they can surprise the opponents with facts and figures. Once the stomach is full, the tiger will not eat even a single morsel. They can preserve it by burying it to come back to it the next day. That's why the people of Vishakha Nakshatra often stop eating when their stomach is full. They don't take a single bite more and prefer to keep it in the fridge for the next day. Along with eating, they also like to do business discussion and can leave the whole meal after eating a few bites.

Sun's Ingress: The Sun enters Vishakha nakshatra from 7th – 20th of November. In India, the sunlight at this time is not scorching and the weather is pleasant. The energy is high, people like to participate in competitions and win prizes. This energy favors to do struggle and people work hard to fulfill their ambition.

Profession: Lawyers, Entrepreneurs, Public Speakers, Professors, Priest, Preacher, Speech pathologists, Psychotherapist, Fashion models, Actresses, TV anchors, Broadcasters, Spokesperson, Mafia lords, Prostitutes, Revolutionists, Mountain climbers, Bartenders, Sportsperson, Soldiers, Guards. They like to do unusual professions and tough assignments.

Favorable Activities: War and aggression, argument and execution, goal-oriented and focused task, competition, ceremonies, parties, resolving, ornamentation, getting dressed up, digging, sowing, harvesting, fighting, penance.

Unfavorable Activities: Marriage, travel, new corporate initiation, new initiation for peaceful activities, etc.

Gana (Type): It comes under the category of Rakshasa nakshatra. Rakshasa lives in the forest and is fond of luxury. Hence, they love nature and work as a protectionist of the environment. They immediately grab those items which are available free. They like to go to hotels and pubs and eat luxurious foods and costly wines. They want a fancy environment with their surroundings.

Guna (Quality): The three combined qualities of the constellation are 'Tamasic-Satwic-Rajasic'. It shows all three tendencies. Sometimes, they are lazy, work in the dark, have secretive tendencies, have spiritual tendencies, are very active, and work hard to fulfill their desires.

Body Parts: The breast is related to this nakshatra.

Tree: Naagkeshar (Ironwood) and Bael (Wood Apple) Tree are related to it. Naagkeshar is an evergreen ornamental tree and is beneficial in relieving colds and cough as it removes excess mucus from the lungs. Wood apple is a sacred fruit cultivated in the country and has various healing properties. It boosts immunity and improves digestion. The association of trees with high medicinal value indicates how powerful is the energy of this Nakshatra for healing.

Padas: The first pada falls in 20° - 23° 20' Libra and its lord is Mars (Aries Navamsha). This is the point of perfect balance where Saturn is exalted. Hence, the energy is very focused. It indicates passion, dominance, and the ability to lead. At the point of balance, there is no leniency; therefore, they are ruthless and adamant with no mercy. They are ready to make great sacrifices in the name of justice.

The second pada falls in 23°20' - 26° 40' Libra and lord is Venus (Taurus Navamsha). They are creative and good at planning. They are highly materialistic person and work with utmost perfection. Venusian energy tends to push towards public persona, they love luxury and do well in the media and entertainment industry.

The third pada falls in 26°40' - 30° Libra and lord is Mercury (Gemini Navamsha). They are good teachers and do well in commercial enterprises. They are strong in communication and make money in different and unusual ways.

The fourth pada falls in 0°0' - 3° 20' Scorpio and lord is Moon (Canccr Navamsha). It is a fierce and dangerous sign of the zodiac. A planet situated here indicates the highly vindictive nature of the person. To satisfy their greed and lust they take undue advantage of their position and power and do not hesitate to betray their most trusted person. At the lower level, the person does not hesitate to commit heinous crimes and can fall into the deep abyss of human life.

It is the point of transformation. On a higher aspect, they help people to transform. They use such power for the benefit of others and develop a penetrating insight that can find the roots of the problem. They dig deep to find the information. Doctors, surgeons who provide shock therapy, trauma therapy, and occult counselors who transform people through thcir unusual nurturing methods come under this pada.

Chapter 17

Anuradha

Anuradha is the 17th of 27 nakshatras and is located at 3° 20' - 16° 40' Scorpio. The word Anuradha is divided into two parts, the first word "Anu" means; 'After', 'Behind', 'Repeatedly', 'Secondary' or 'An attitude that leads to the attainment of something'. This constellation has a close association with the previous star Vishakha of which alternate name is Radha. Hence, another meaning of this nakshatra is 'After Radha', 'Subsequent Success' or 'Success after perseverance'.

One more meaning of Anuradha is "After the shock". Because transformation in Vishakha is very sharp and severe. After the shock of Vishakha, the phase of recovery starts in Anuradha.

Astronomy: Located in the southern constellation of Scorpius, three stars known as Beta, Delta and Pi-Scorpii, form this nakshatra. These stars appear at a combined apparent magnitude of 2.5 to 2.9, it can be easily seen with the naked eye in the night sky. The declination of Delta Scorpii is 22° S 41' 2.31" and right ascension is 16h 1m 40.1s, others stars are also visible in the same vicinity.

Deity: The deity of this constellation is "Mitra". The meaning of Mitra is a friend and he is one of the twelve Adityas (solar deities). The deity of the constellation bestows the person the quality of friendship, compassion, cooperation and warmth.

Shakti (Power): The shakti of this nakshatra is known as 'Aradhana Shakti - The Power of Worship'. This energy is closely related to its previous energy but its mode of action is different. Vishakha achieves success by focusing its energies, while Anuradha achieves success through collaboration.

The Sight of Nakshatra: Tiryanga-mukha (Sideways)

Nature: Mridu (Soft)

Element: Fire

Activity: Passive

TriMurti and Behaviour: Vishnu and Maintenance

Planetary Ruler: The Lord of patience 'Saturn' is the ruler of this nakshatra. Slow moving planet Saturn indicates that success is not easy in their life, they achieve their objective but after a lot of struggle and it requires immense patience.

Symbol: Its first symbol is a Staff or a Danda. The bamboo wood is used to prepare a good staff. The wooden staff is very hard; it is an ideal weapon for fighting and self-defense. A staff provides strength and support for struggle and fight. It is capable of taking great force and providing punishment. A staff is useful for carrying loads and crossing rough terrain. A simple wooden staff is useful to overcome fear and focus on learning techniques to fight to emerge victorious. In many culture people always keep a staff and learn fighting skills. Such skills develop agility of the mind and they are always prepared for any unforeseen situations and never feel panicked.

The symbol of staff represents that Anuradha people mind is always active and they never feel panic in any situation in life. Their mind is always ready to find the way to get away from the problem. They believe in fighting and with a simple wooden staff (less resource) they challenge the circumstances. When no one believes in his victory, doubts his ability and leaves him, he fights alone and emerges victorious.

The second symbol of this nakshatra is "Lotus flower". Lotus is the only flower which shows its beauty just above the surface of the mud. The lotus plant has a hollow and spongy stem that is filled with air. This makes them light and helps them float on water. This indicates that even the mud has the potential to produce such a flower if one harnesses its energy in a proper way. It also indicates that such a person will achieve ultimate success and be victorious, but their path is full of struggle. Many a times, they get defeated, but their hard work pays off one day. The lotus flower (success) emerges from the mud after much patience and the beauty of such a flower (achievement) is beyond comparison.

Its third symbol is a "Triumphal Gate" decorated with leaves same as Vishakha. It indicates success and achievement, and like Vishakha people, Anuradha people also never give up a struggle or fight in between and emerge victorious one day.

Caste: To walk alone on a muddy path with the support of a staff requires strong legs. Therefore, the caste assigned to this nakshatra by the ancient sages is 'Shudra'.

Characteristics: Anuradha people believe that the path to loneliness is tough and things become easier when we are together and support each other. This energy favors cooperation to make things easier and believes that cooperation is the only way one can cross muddy waters. A flower can bloom with the help of a long stem that throws a bud out of water. The lotus flower has immense potential to collect energy from the mud. Similarly, difficulties in life make them stronger.

The natives of this Nakshatra have to face a lot of obstacles in life but they always have a positive outlook and emerge stronger when life knocks them down. When no one is ready to support them, they resort to a staff and this is enough for them to fight against all odds. They do not expect huge resources and they go on with their staff on the belief that one day the lotus flower will bloom but it takes time.

Their behavior is very friendly and they are always ready to help everyone. They are soft-spoken and bring out the best when the situation challenges their skills. They never harm anyone but never forgive those who harm them. They become vengeful and take up their staff to teach the culprit a good lesson.

They are very responsible, sincere and hard-working person and never let anyone down in fulfilling his duties. They struggle hard in the early part of their life and lack the support of their parents and siblings. In fact, they do not have good relations with other family members in the house. They provide them all their support but get nothing in return not even moral support. It is very difficult for them to live in the house of their birth due to not having good relations, but they are also evicted from the house which they had built with their hard work. They are sociable, soft-spoken and tending to cooperate with others, but their siblings do not allow them to live in their own built house due to bitter relations.

Sign of Scorpio indicates transformation but none of the transformation is easy. Such a person has to cross various difficult phases of life and every phase make them stronger. They have tremendous potential to take everything positive in life and they keep moving on with their staff. Like the stem of the flower find its own ways no matter how muddy the water is, their optimism is always alive which shows to find ways in difficult times and become victorious.

Being ruled by Saturn, they have inherent quality to maintain balance. They can balance their legs with the help of a staff. While they don't get support at their home, they get a lot of support outside because of their cordial nature. Friends are their great supporters and they always stand with them.

Anuradha nakshatra people have a strong ability to survive in difficult circumstances. They are persistent and determined to achieve their objectives. They like to follow rules and regulations and expect others to do the same. They are good leaders, mentors and masters who provide proper guidance and support to others.

They believe in logic and are good at reasoning and mathematics. If Mercury is in this Nakshatra, then the power of reasoning prevails in such a person. They like to learn hidden and other esoteric sciences, if their birth chart supports them, they learn quickly. In pursuit of knowledge, they are ready to travel anywhere and like to visit religious places. They are quick to learn the meaning of hidden messages and often use shortcuts and code words in their messages.

They like to socialize with people, and prefer to be involved in gatherings and discussions. They are very talkative especially females. They are very honest but are always in dilemma and cannot stick to their decisions. They are adept at collaborating, forming alliances and signing agreements. They are very good at building connections and have a strong network of people.

They work as a bridge between two extremes. They befriend first and later pull the person on the table to sign the deal. They work as a clever salesman who likes to discuss first and sell their product later. They have sharp and penetrating eyes who keep watching everything without knowing anyone. They work as a negotiator between a company management and workers, they work between two people to resolve the issue, they work between an immature and a mature person and fill the gap with their understanding. As a staff is used to balance two objects, their whole energy is for balance and cooperation. They are the first who break the ice and bring calmness to a heated situation.

Although they are very cordial but these natives can face sudden break up in relationships. Such a person has to face struggle and many changes in their life and also with their beliefs and thoughts. They like to discuss when the things are pleasant, but when circumstances changes, they remain silent and do not say a word to anyone; everything is hidden in the deep ocean of their mind. Once a young chatterbox converts into a taciturn and a silent person.

This nakshatra falls completely in the sign of Scorpio which is all about uncertainty, changes, and transformation. Due to the effect of Saturn, they try to maintain balance for a long time, but one day Mars suddenly cuts off all those relationships. They resist change and the stem remain in the mud and no one knows what a great opportunity is hidden here. But Saturn teaches them a tough lesson without which the lotus flower cannot blossom.

Anuradha is next to Vishakha, so, readers will find many qualities carry forward from the previous constellation with some additions and deletions;

1. Vishakha has seen the abyss where there is no one and the soul is all alone. Whereas in Anuradha the soul wants to come out of that abyss, so they always believe in cooperation.

2. Vishakha has seen the bottom, therefore, the power of penetration and investigation is much higher in Vishakha than in Anuradha people.

3. Vishakha people are goal-oriented people, always under stress, and want to complete the task within limited time frame; While Anuradha people prefer comfort and freedom and they hate stressful environment. They want to finish the work in a peaceful manner.

4. Vishakha people fight across; but Anuradha people look for some soft way.

5. Vishakha people are patient and wait for the right time to come out; but Anuradha people believe in persistence and unnecessarily they don't like to hurt anyone.

6. Anuradha doesn't like harsh behaviour of Vishakha. They respect others' feelings and never put anyone down; their staff or danda is always ready to assist.

7. Vishakha prefer to solve the matter using diplomacy; Anuradha prefer to solve the matter using cooperation.

Vishakha energy is sharp, with a mix of soft; While Anuradha energy is only soft. Both the constellations symbol is a "Triumphal Gate", and both will enter the gate after winning. Vishakha people will enter the gate after winning it by force, Anuradha people will enter the gate after winning by their cordial behaviour and cooperation.

On a higher aspect, deep down they know that if they have to cross the muddy waters of this material world, they cannot do so without support, and the ultimate support is the support of the universe, the support of God.

They are not afraid to venture into the unknown and believe that the universe always supports them. They often say, go ahead on your faith, when no one supports then God supports. They know that perseverance and devotion are the keys, and surrender to God is the only way to get rid of this muddy path of life and death. This energy has the tremendous potential to create great devotees of God.

Negative Traits: They like to keep everything secret and are afraid to reveal anything. A weak Moon shows unpredictable mood swings. They are jealous and demanding and tend to panic over a small problem very quickly. They start losing control of their mind and start crying and screaming. They prefer to exercise caution before extending any kind of cooperation and tend to be narrow minded individuals who suspect everyone.

The staff which is used for support and protection may lose its direction and they may use it for selfish purposes. They indulge in wrong activities, work silently and when everything is cooked underneath, they show their true motive. Instead of devotion to God, they become devotee of their seniors and bosses who blindly follow the orders and misuse their staff. The soft-spoken person converts into flatterers and sycophants and the transformation which has potential to touch the sky, can touch the bottom.

Gender: The gender on the constellation is 'Male'. This energy believes in persistence and is not ready to give up until it achieves its goal.

Animal Symbol: The symbol of this nakshatra is 'Female deer'. Its counterpart is Jyestha Nakshatra whose animal symbol is male deer. It is the enemy of Mula and Ardra Nakshatra, whose symbol is dog.

Deer is beautiful, delicate, elusive, flexible, shy and inconsistent. Deer are known for their agile mind and their agile body makes them vulnerable. Deer is very sensitive and attentive to small things and likes to live in quiet environment.

Anuradha people reflect the above qualities of a deer in their personality with a tendency to hide every pain from their life.

Sun's Ingress: Sun enters Anuradha Nakshatra from 20th November – 03rd December every year. This is the time to increase struggle and positivity. Many important exams take place and aspirants work hard to fulfill their dreams.

Profession: They are very good in those activities which require cooperation, like group activities of dancing, music, counselling, construction, travel agents, property brokers, factory workers, emergency related services, safety services, cleaning related services. Occultists, Numerologists, Statisticians and other activities which require understanding of high level of mathematical calculations. Agricultural activities, Team leaders, Surgeons, Mechanical Engineers, Damage control services, Patrolling services, and all other services which requires sideways movement in a group.

Favourable Activities: This energy works for all lawful activities, safety activities, damage control activities. Anuradha native never feel panic in tough situations, so they can best deal with the situation like emergency and risk. They can handle better the dangerous situation with peaceful mind because this energy always looks for a way how to get rid of this problematic (muddy) situation.

Unfavorable Activities: This energy is good not for those work which requires sharp action. It is not good for those works where initiation is involved and action of a single man is required, the work that requires tough and harsh activity. It is not good to start or inaugurate a new work, marriage, etc.

Gana: The 'Deva' gana of the Nakshatra represent that they are always doing something for the benefit of others and when asked for help, they are ready to help in any situation.

Guna: The category of three Guna of this nakshatra is "Tamasic-Satwic-Tamasic". They like to remain at dormant state for a long time, never do anything to harm anyone and silently bear everything in their life. But every birth takes shape in deep dark, in the same way the tamasic Guna of the constellation help them to take shape of a Lotus Flower.

Body Parts: Breasts and stomach are related to it.

Tree: The tree associated with the nakshatra is Bakula, which is a very beautiful and evergreen tree with a dense canopy of small shiny leaves. Its flowers are small whose fragrance pervades the air. People like to collect its flowers as they retain their odors for many days. The tree has many medicinal properties and its decoction is used to treat diseases of the gums and teeth. Bakula tree is also known as Vajradhanthi Plant.

Padas: The first pada of this nakshatra is 3° 20' - 6° 40' in Scorpio and ruled by Sun (Leo Navamsha). The focus of energy in this pada is on courage and dignity. They are a noble, generous and magnanimous person. They are a self-expressive, outspoken, egotistical, and prideful person. They are mysterious and take interest in the hidden things of life.

The second pada of this nakshatra is 6° 40' - 10° 00' in Scorpio and ruled by Mercury (Virgo Navamsha). They are intellectual, learned, and have strong communication skills. They find logic before accepting anything. They often ask riddle-related questions and like to solve deep riddles. They have a practical approach and do strategic planning. They are an active person in conferences and administration.

The third pada of this nakshatra is 10° 00' - 13° 20' in Scorpio and ruled by Venus (Libra Navamsha). They are very kind, happy, and creative people. They love to enjoy materialism in life but also take interest in occult sciences. The depth of a matter attracts them and they can deal with deep and complex matters easily. The colour 'black' influences them and they like to wear bright black colour clothes.

The fourth pada of this nakshatra is 13° 20' - 16° 40' in Scorpio and ruled by Mars (Scorpio Navamsha). They are very hard-working people and put their whole energy into fulfilling their obligation. They are passionate, extremists, and revengeful people. They struggle and face various ups and downs in life but never get discouraged. They are always ready to help others. They are very eager to ask but very secretive. Due to the strong Martian energy, they like to go deep and are good at investigation and research.

Chapter 18

Jyeshtha

Jyeshtha is the 18th of 27 Nakshatras and is located at 16° 40' - 30° 00" Scorpio. The Sanskrit word Jyeshtha means the eldest. It means first, main, major, highest or the most senior. The name reflects the quality of the nakshatra and it is related with authority, power and leadership abilities.

Astronomy: In the constellation of Scorpius, three stars known as Alpha Scorpii (Antares), Sigma Scorpii and Tau Scorpii form this nakshatra. Among them Antares is the brightest and slightly red star in the heart of the Scorpio constellation with a visual magnitude of 0.9 to 1.8. Its declination is 26° S 28' 48" and right ascension is 16h 30m 47.4s.

Deity: The deity of the nakshatra is Indra, who is known as the king of the gods. There are many legends which say that Indra was always in fear of losing his throne and did not hesitate to take any step to protect it. Fulfillment of desire was always important to Indra and he adopted many wrong ways for this. Several times he lost his throne but regained it. In his hands is a mighty weapon known as Vajra (thunderbolt).

Shakti (Power): The Shakti of the nakshatra is known as 'Arohana Shakti', i.e., the power to ascend and rise. It indicates the power of ascension or progress through a ladder or ride.

The Sight of Nakshatra: Tiryanga-mukha (Sideways)

Nature: Tikshna (Sharp)

Element: Air

Activity: Active

TriMurti and Behaviour: Shiva and dissolution

Planetary Ruler: The ruler of the nakshatra is Mercury. It rules our intelligence, reasoning, memory and power of speech. It represents all financial activities, trade and commerce. Jyeshtha signifies progress and rise which is possible only through intelligence. Mercury is exalted in Virgo which is a virgin sign, indicating that a person can make his Mercury strong by following the path of celibacy and with that strong intelligence he gains inner strength.

Mercury is the prince of the solar system and represents childhood stage. Children are jealous with each other because they are immature, when they see their value being threatened, they feel insecure, become possessive and demand attention. One should always follow the right path and stay away from jealousy and cunningness as these are negative qualities of Mercury.

Symbol: The main symbol of the constellation is 'Umbrella'. It is used to protect against rain and heat. When it is opened, its round shape disperses the rain and protects the person from getting wet. When something comes in the middle of a round shape it becomes completely safe and secure. This indicates that this energy works to secure things to protect them from any unforeseen event. In ancient times, the king never went outside without a royal canopy, they always used to travel with their round-shaped protection.

Rainy days indicates difficult times in the life of an individual or the life of an institution or the life of a country. In these difficult times, there is a need for Jyeshtha person to protect everyone, it shows the leadership quality of the person and Jyeshtha makes a strong leader who protects everyone with his big umbrella.

An alternative symbol is the round talisman or circular earring. The round talisman signifies protection from mystic forces. In ancient times, royal persons used to wear circular earrings. Hoop earrings show identity, strength, and unity by being circular and demanding attention.

Jyeshtha people first secure their position before acting for the next step. They protect their family, friends, and subordinates. This umbrella is ready to provide protection to all who are willing to come under it without any discrimination.

Caste: The caste of Nakshatra is Servant. Like a servant runs whole day to fulfill his master's wish and does not get tired of running with the sound of the bell. Similarly, these people run from place to place to fulfill their obligations. When one of his meetings is over, he immediately rushes to another without taking a break. They are servants and their job is to run. Just as a servant runs to the call of his master and leaves his other work in the middle, sometimes these people rush to complete the work and leave their half-eaten food in the middle.

Ears and legs play an important role for these people as these two body parts are important for a servant. They can hear sounds from a distance even if it is indistinct, and their legs are strong. Jyestha person can walk more than others without getting tired. A servant never waits for the eleventh hour and prepares everything in advance to fulfill the wishes of his master. Similarly, Jyeshtha people never do any work in haste and haphazard manner, they prepare everything in a perfect way.

It is an active nakshatra and they never like to sit idle. A servant quickly understands the requirements of his master and plan everything accordingly. These people understand what the situation demands only by their observation and do necessary planning.

Characteristics: Jyestha people are authoritative in nature and like to control everything. They want to achieve supremacy, so they take more interest in showing their work and getting appreciation. Their aim is always to attain a higher position in the organization, therefore, their every step is to move a step more on the ladder of hierarchy. They don't trust others easily, being a secretive person, they keep their every move hidden and prefer to work alone. They are known for quick decision making and excellent management skills. They are hardworking individuals and determined to overcome obstacles to achieve their goals.

They are intelligent person, have strong analytical skills and always believe in logic. When they are not satisfied with the logic of something, they are not ready to accept it. Hence, in the early years of life they are atheists and do not like to follow the traditional rules and order as they look for logic everywhere and most of the time they are not satisfied with the prevailing logics. They are inquisitive people and always interested in asking questions. They don't want to hurt others, but they refuse to follow that, which logic doesn't satisfy their mind.

To achieve their goals, they do not hesitate to take strange steps in life and present out-of-the-box ideas. Jyestha people have complex personalities, so they can understand the complex matter easily and have excellent problem-solving skills. Hence, they like any kind of innovation and provide their necessary support. They prefer to take a unique and innovative approach to solve complex issues.

They want to win at any cost, so they don't give up easily, once they fail, they come back to the battle with full preparation. They are courageous person and work as a leader. They become merciless when the matter of achieving the target is concerned. Their only objective is to overcome the obstacles and defeat the enemy. They create illusions, use latest technology and employ all possible means to fool and defeat the enemy.

Due to influence of Mercury they know where to bow and when the tide turns they prefer to wait before taking the next step. Due to strong hold on speech, they speak well and impress others with their emphatic words. As a leader, they deliver great speech and provide enthusiasm to their followers and supporters.

It is possible that the person born in Jyeshtha Nakshatra may be the elder among siblings. Because of their feeling of being the eldest, they are always conscious about their image and make every possible effort to impress others. They don't do those acts which create any harm to their image, so they always talks about the great works done by them. They respect senior members, always care about etiquette, do charity and have a kind and benevolent approach with a focus on image building.

The characteristics of Indra indicates that Jyeshtha natives are always interested in attaining high position and are always afraid of losing it, so they hold on to it tightly and do not want to do anything that may create a problem for their position. They always keep good relations with those in power, due to which they always keep themselves safe. They fight fiercely to win and resist all forces that hinder them from achieving their objective.

Jyeshtha falls in the sign of Scorpio. Scorpions are tough, fierce, and ruthless hunters. They survive even in the harshest climate and environment and are ready to face any challenge or danger. They are persistent and determined to achieve the desired object. Therefore, dark, secret and hidden things naturally attract them and they don't want to reveal much about themselves. Due to lack of trust they do not have much friends in life.

Scorpio is the darkest of all the constellations, so no one can anticipate the next move of these people. They are extremists, work hard with intense dedication, and often become workaholics.

Jyeshtha is the end of Scorpio sign. Here the second Gandanta exists where water sign ends and fire sign begins and there is no relation between these two signs. This is the second border of the zodiac where there is no bridge and to cross such a border it requires plenty of courage and accumulation of energy.

The strength that these people look for is actually the inner strength that they look for in the outer world. According to legend, sage Gautama cursed Indra to have a thousand vaginas on his body for having an illicit relationship with his wife Ahalya. In order to nullify the curse Indra goes to Lord Shiva for severe penance and with his blessings all the marks on the body turn into eyes. It indicates the vision of seeing the futility of desires.

This story tells that one day the life of these people changes and they repent for every wrong deed they have done to fulfill their wish like Indra did. Their life begin to change when their hands get burned and they become interested in mysticism.

Jyestha is a transformative energy. On the higher aspects, the accumulation of power signifies inner transformation. As Indra transformed himself through rigorous penance, every step of power is a step of inner transformation and one day he sees with his thousand eyes the illusory nature of the material world.

Negative Traits: They are power-hungry people who are ready to do anything to gain power. They are corrupt officials, politicians, bureaucrats, corporate executives, etc. who want to enjoy power at any cost and are not ready to leave the chair under any circumstances. They are a revengeful person and quick in temper.

Jyestha people keep full control over financial matters because it provides them power over others. They are cunning people, seduce others, and adopt wrongful methods to achieve their objectives. They are stubborn and rigid about their beliefs and thoughts. They look for security at every step in their life and without taking care of security, they are not ready to move even an inch.

Gender: It is a female gender nakshatra. It indicates the caring nature of the person. They are sensitive and intuitive people and keep a generous approach towards those who demand their help.

Animal Symbol: The animal symbol of the nakshatra is a Male Deer or Hare. Its counterpart is Anuradha nakshatra of which animal symbol is a female deer and it is inimical towards Mula and Ardra nakshatra whose animal symbol is dog. .

Male deer also known as Buck, and Stag is used for a larger male deer. They are calm and gentle animals and have an excellent sense of smell. They are herbivores and eat only plants and grasses and can jump up to 10 feet high and as far as 30 feet. They are timid and shy animals and are under constant threat from carnivores. They are quick to sense danger and react quickly to sudden movements or sounds. They are fast runners and great swimmers and protect themselves from predators by running.

Sun's Ingress: Sun enters this Nakshatra every year on the 3rd December and stays there till the 16th December. Jyeshta indicates the end of the previous cycle.

Profession: Politician, Leader, Philosopher, Corporate Executive, Chief, Head, Detective, Government Official, Military Leader, Entrepreneur, Sportsman, etc.

Favourable Activities: Administration, acting for security, taking charge of an official position, taking control of a situation, holding a meeting for a critical situation and other business meetings, and planning.

Unfavorable Activities: Speculation and over-indulgence should be avoided, it is not auspicious for marriage.

Gana (Type): The gana of the nakshatra is Rakshasa. They want to enjoy luxuries in life and do not bother if they have to borrow money to fulfill their desire. They spend their hefty salary quickly and for the rest of the month they live on borrowed money, they are always in debt, no matter how much they are earning. They always prefer to go to the costliest place and want to enjoy the costliest food and drink. They believe that life is only for enjoyment.

Guna (Quality): The guna of the nakshatra is "Tamasic-Satwik-Satwik". The tamasic quality indicates that such a person will show no interest in doing work without gain. But once they accept it, they move forward to achieve the higher objective.

Body Parts: The related body parts are the neck and upper hips.

Tree: The associated tree of the Nakshatra is 'Shalmali' tree which is also known as the Silk Cotton Tree. Its botanical name is *"Salmalia malabarica"* and in hindi it is known as Semal. It is a large tree with trunk thorns and large red flowers. The wood of the tree is used for matchbox and plywood and the cotton is used for quilts and pillows. It has various medicinal properties and is used for smallpox, rheumatism etc.

Padas: The first pada of this asterism is 16° 40' - 20° 00' in Scorpio and ruled by Jupiter (Sagittarius Navamsha). They are energetic, ambitious and a man of their principles. They are philosophers and explorers. They fight for justice and don't hesitate to speak harsh truth in front of others.

The second pada of this asterism is 20° 00' - 23° 20' in Scorpio and ruled by Saturn (Capricorn Navamsha). They are very hardworking and determined to achieve their goals. Safety is always the top priority for them and avoids taking any kind of risk. They are strict followers of the rules and know how to use every available resource. They do not make friends easily and do not want to move from their place.

The third pada of this asterism is 23° 20' - 26° 40' in Scorpio and ruled by Saturn (Aquarius Navamsha). They are silent workers and reserved in nature. They believe in making persistent efforts to achieve success. They do research before taking any action and always work with the latest technology.

The fourth pada of this asterism is 26° 40' - 30° 00' in Scorpio and ruled by Jupiter (Pisces Navamsha). They are sensitive and receptive person. They are moody persons and live in their fantasies and dreams. They like to secure things first before taking the next step to move. They act as a mediator and are good at giving advice. They are passionate about achieving goals and know when and where to bow down and show their humility. They keep matters secret and always hide information from everyone. They are always worried about their financial security and keep everything in secret.

Chapter 19

Mula

Mula is the 19th of 27 Nakshatras and is located at 00° 00' - 13° 20' Sagittarius. In Sanskrit Mula means, "Root", "Base", or "Foundation". The root is the first essential thing that creates a base for a large tree. There is no stability without roots, if there are no roots things become fragile and quickly lose their existence. Any new beginning requires a strong foundation, so a new set of nine satwic nakshatra starts from here. This nakshatra is placed at one of the three Gandanta positions in the zodiac, so it is called Gandmoola Nakshatra.

Mula represents the beginning and is related to the foundation. The roots of spirituality become strong when one gets tired of material desires and then the search for the unknown begins. The roots start getting deeper and now such a person is ready for the inner journey to the spiritual world. It is forming the foundation of supreme knowledge and is known as 'The Foundation Star'.

Astronomy: A bunch of stars in the tail of the Scorpius constellation, located in the southern celestial hemisphere, forms this constellation. These stars form a J-shaped pattern and resemble the curved tail of a scorpion. At its end, two stars named Lambda Scorpii (Schaula) and Upsilon Scorpii (Lesath) are located and represent the stinger stars of Scorpion. They appear close together, at magnitudes 1.63 and 2.70. The declination of Schaula is 37° S 7' 4.69" and right ascension is 17h 35m 8.3s.

Deity: The presiding deity of Mula is known as "Nirriti". Our ancient scriptures have described that Nirriti is the bringer of loss, poverty, disease and is known as the "Goddess of Misfortune". Nirriti is also known as Alakshmi, the elder sister of Goddess Lakshmi. The Goddess Nirriti looks dark and is associated with the Goddess of destruction and death, "Mahakali".

Strangely, the deity of the nakshatra is known to bring bad luck, so the people get afraid of this nakshatra. According to the author, there are some subtle meanings hidden behind this and without knowledge, people interpret it wrongly.

This universe records our every action from our millions of births. A person can't go ahead on the path of spirituality with the heavy baggage of unclosed accounts. The balance sheet of our karmic assets and liabilities should be equal before starting a new journey. The soul which has taken birth in Mula nakshatra is spiritually evolved but can't go ahead on that path with unfulfilled obligations. First it has to equalize its karma balance sheet.

The deity of the nakshatra destroys those things in life which create hurdles towards the path of spirituality and if necessary it gives death, but the deity has to cut and close all pending accounts that prohibit the spiritual growth of the person. The planets situated in this Nakshatra indicate to balance the karmic imbalance.

Hence, any negative event in the life of Mula natives becomes a positive event, as the soul is now freed from that debt and is slowly getting ready to fly in the sky. So, Mula natives can't be materialistic people. They have seen the worthless of the material world in their past lives and now the time has come to make stronger the roots of spirituality. The time has come for Mula natives to go deep into the spiritual world and raise their consciousness level.

Goddess Mahakali grants the utmost courage to the native to fight against the demons of darkness. She has infinite power to destroy all the demons of darkness within seconds. This sharp nakshatra has immense potential to remove all the darkness of ignorance. Hence, Mula people take very much interest in the occult and meditation.

Shakti (Power): The shakti associated with asterism is known as "Bharana Shakti". The word "Bharana" means "fill in", "settle down", "not remaining vacant" or "the process of paying off a debt". It means to pour something into an empty space inside a vessel.

The power of the nakshatra indicates that Mula natives have to pay off all his pending karmic debts. This soul is now an evolved soul which has the experience that everything in this world is burning, so making efforts to the collection of those fragile things is futile but old baggage doesn't allow it to go ahead. So, he has to settle down all his debts.

The Sight of Nakshatra: It is an Adhomukhi Nakshatra – Facing Downward.

Nature: The nature of the Nakshatra is Tikshna (Sharp). It is not a benevolent energy which works for cooperation and settlement. Hence, Mula natives are sharp and straightforward person and they prefer to take immediate action.

Sometimes, in life it is necessary to take immediate action and medical person understand better that to save the life of a person it is necessary to cut some rotten parts otherwise the person can die. Mula people take immediate action and they never think twice. Such a person has ferocious anger and lacks the quality of melody.

Element: The element of the nakshatra is "Air". It indicates they are highly intelligent and have a strong capacity to think deeply. Air cannot stay in one place, so, they are changeable and like to move around. They are very courageous people and can cross any boundary.

Activity: It is an "Active" nakshatra. Mula people are very active person and their mind always requires some engagement. They prefer to handle difficult tasks. If Sun or Mars is placed in this nakshatra then the activity of such a person is very high and he may forget day and night to complete the work.

TriMurti and Behaviour: Brahma and Creation

Planetary Ruler: The ruler of the nakshatra is Ketu. From where the Mula starts, the watery sign ends and fiery signs begin and there is no relation between water and fire. Hence, Ketu, the planet of separation is the lord of this Nakshatra.

Following are the differences between the nakshatras of Ketu;

• **Ashwini** – A new beginning with courage

• **Magha** – A new beginning from seeds collected in the past

• **Mula** - A new beginning by strengthening the roots

Symbol: The main symbol of the nakshatra is a "Bunch of roots tied together". It's another symbol is the "Lion's tail".

The roots are the most essential part of a tree. Its direction is downward and is not visible from the surface but a tree cannot stand without them. These roots help the tree in its nutrition and growth. They are deeply intertwined with each other and every small root supports the main root which ultimately supports the tree. The strength of a tree does not depend on its branches but on its roots. No construction can take place without roots; it provides the vital source of energy which decides the strength of any structure.

Caste: The caste assigned to the constellation is "Butcher". A butcher deals with flesh and blood and has a strong understanding of the quality of meat, cuts, and preparation. He can use sharp objects, knives, and hand tools, lift meat by hand, and work in a cold environment. A medical surgeon falls into the butcher caste and uses his skills to save lives.

Characteristics: Mula natives are very intelligent and sharp mind person. They have very penetrating eyes and they silently watch every development. They are a very passionate person and possess strong skills in research and investigation. They are very good at mathematics and crunching numbers. They tend to go deep into the matter and are not satisfied until they find the root cause of the problem. They are detectives and are never satisfied with superficial information given by others. They do their search and sometimes they travel thousands of miles to find the truth.

It is a self-destructive energy and in deep anger they do those acts which they regret later. They throw their watches, dinner plate or break other objects on the floor and regret it later. Being highly straightforward people, they lack the quality of diplomacy but always abide by their words. They are highly inquisitive people, have philosophical attitudes, and like to study religious texts.

Mula natives do not hesitate to destroy old beliefs and thoughts. As a butcher cuts the flesh without any mercy, Mula people cuts immediately those things which have become irrelevant but others are carrying it in the name of tradition. They have penetrating eyes, that thing have become rotten or outdated, they cut them immediately. They always come up with new thoughts which are relevant to society. They take an interest in innovation and always support new and revolutionary ideas. They are the rebels against the old beliefs and systems. They like to plant new seeds, hence, they have a strong interest in agriculture, horticulture, and gardening-related activities.

They are a very honest person and it is sure that if they earn money in any wrong way, it will never be fruitful for them. They never support any wrong doing nor do anything wrong under any pressure.

As roots provide support to the tree, Mula people provide their help and support in the form of money or their physical presence for the growth of others, but they don't take an interest in beating the drum of these activities. This energy creates a vital source for making a base on which a new structure can take its shape.

They create a solid foundation so that others can easily create a beautiful structure. They never take interest in show-off their benevolence and believe in silently doing their work as roots grow underneath the surface silently.

To understand the energy of this nakshatra, it is necessary to understand the quality of the roots;

1. Roots are associated with medicines, so these people possess strong knowledge of medicines.

2. Roots are not visible from the surface so they take interest in the unseen and unknown. Mystery always fascinates them, so they love watching movies that involve mystery and exploration.

3. The bunch of roots indicates they have a strong ability to solve complex matter and to find the root of the beginning of the problem. They never forget their focus, grasp things quickly, and are excellent at navigation.

4. Roots always grow in a downward direction and are not visible to anyone. Hence, their mind is full of complexity and it is difficult for others to read them.

5. Roots do not spread in the limitations. Mula natives don't prefer limitations in life. They like to wander here and there without any purpose and they get important clues in these wandering.

6. Roots make their way. They are explorers and make their way. They love to travel and make their way out even in extremely difficult circumstances in life.

7. The development of roots requires soil and water. Hence, Mula native keeps a strong relationship with these two things. They take a deep interest in plantations and never hesitate to apply soil to their hands.

In complete darkness, roots start taking hold. The path of spirituality is strong when roots are strong without roots no one can enter this regime. Planets in this nakshatra indicate roots of true spirituality are taking place. When the roots are strong such a person can never do anything wrong in life.

This soul has had some great spiritual experience and is not ready to enter again into the idiocy of the material world. The unknown world of mysticism is pulling him in but past-due karmic payments are fettering his feet. At times their life shakes them, but they are strong human beings and stand up again with full confidence.

This nakshatra falls in Sagittarius, a sign ruled by Jupiter. It is the sign of religion, if the roots are not strong then it cannot hold its ground, but when the roots are strong the castle of religion never falls and such a person ultimately attains the supreme wisdom.

The symbol of Sagittarius is half animal and half human. It indicates transformation is inevitable in their lives. It is possible that a staunch non-vegetarian may suddenly change and decide not to eat non-veg food ever. They take alcohol or drugs and one day decide not to touch it again in life. This sign indicates transformation from animal to human and it is not possible unless a person sees tough lessons in life.

Therefore, the life of the Mula people is not stable. In the childhood phase, they can be accompanied by the wrong friends. So, Mula natives require the utmost care and guidance at this stage of life. If the energy is channelized properly it can give great results because this type of energy is not present anywhere else, which can understand the complexity quickly and find the solution easily.

When they accept all happenings in their life without complaining to anyone, then the knots of their karmas start opening and this energy starts working wisely. With the heavy burden of past karmic debt, the soul feels guilty; hence, they straightforwardly deny doing anything wrong. They are ready to fight with anyone if someone forces them to do so. They say, "No, I can't do that, it would be better if I suffer in life but I will not support any wrong".

Such persons refuse to commit any wrongdoing, if someone force then they prefer to leave that place because deep down they do not want to create any further karmic imbalance in life. Their whole efforts are that how to open the karmic knots, hence, they possess the strong skill to open the tight knots. They take an interest is solving puzzles because their mind can understand the complexities and they are responsible to create such complexities in life. Now, the soul has awakened and is eager to solve all the complexities. Therefore, they are skilled in mathematics, like to solve complex mathematical problems and can easily perform mental calculations of large numbers. A strong horoscope suggests that such a person can easily pass difficult mathematics exams.

Hence, it is a very powerful nakshatra. The association of Goddess Kali indicates this energy has a strong potential to remove the demons of darkness immediately as Goddess Kali kills the demons on the battlefield and they run here and there to save their lives. When Kali appears immediately the demons disappear and only victory remains. She quickly cuts and destroys any obstacle that blocks Her path.

In the same manner, Mula people cut every irrelevant thing and always focus on their main objective. They always want point discussion in the meeting. They are a very good editor who cut anything irrelevant and always use very precise words.

Deep in their mind, they regret those past deeds that they did in deep darkness, therefore, they worship "Goddess Mahakali" to remove darkness. Repentance is the only remedy for the Mula people. Ketu is a planet of separation, when the Mula natives' previous unpaid dues are paid then that karmic account is closed and Ketu separates the person from that place.

This soul has to ascend to the spiritual world, but the bondage of past deeds does not let it go. First, they have to clear the outstanding dues; only then the knots will open. It is like a balloon filled with helium gas and is ready to go high in the sky but when it is tied with knots then it can't go. So, every loss and suffering are in fact opening of their knots, if he accepts it without making any complain.

An evolved soul has no grudge with anyone, neither with any human nor with the God. Everything is accepted because he knows that some higher power is continuously watching him.

Although, they are very strong person in outside world. Very active, sharp and highly intelligent but they cry when alone. Like a small child cries in its mother's arms, they cry and seek forgiveness from Goddess Kali. Their tears of repentance wash away all their sins.

It is said in Buddhist scriptures that on the day of his last journey when Angulimala went to a village and the villagers started throwing stones at him and his body started bleeding, he still had no grudges or complaints against anyone. He was only weeping and tears of repentance were coming out of his eyes and he died soon.

When the monks asked Lord Buddha where Angulimala's soul had gone, the Buddha replied, "That soul has attained Nirvana", the tears of repentance having washed away all his sins.

Negative Traits: The direction of their search can forget the path and these people involve in search of worthless matters and unnecessarily create issues. They create mess and complexities and prefer to keep busy themselves on all these activities. They can be highly manipulative, indecisive and lack the skills of taking concrete decisions.

They become highly egoistical and rather than closing the unpaid karmic debts they open new karmic debts and become victim of a vicious circle.

They can misuse their intelligence and knowledge, they lack the necessary skill to channelize the energy and create chaos. They never keep things in organized manner and always shout when the things are not there as its place.

They always blame others for their situation and always make a complain for what they have not achieved in life. They are cruel people and engage in aggression, torture, murder, and other illegal activities. They do brutal things, they are cold blooded killers and they are mass murderers. They never feel remorse for committing any crime.

Gender: The gender of the nakshatra is "Neutral", and indicates harsh nature of this nakshatra.

Animal Symbol: The animal symbol associated with the nakshatra is "Male Dog". Its counterpart is Ardra nakshatra and it is inimical to Jyestha and Anuradha nakshatra whose animal symbol is deer.

They are dominant, attentive, very active and independent; any breed of dogs is aggressive. With proper training and care dogs become obedient, faithful, and become like a family member. Dogs have extraordinary sense of smell and can detect odors from at a very low level. Dogs have better hearing quality than humans. They are very good in running and to find the lost things, one simple clue is enough for a dog and they return with the solution. Mula natives possess all the aforesaid qualities of a dog.

Sun's Ingress: Every year on December 16, Sun enters in this constellation and stays there till 28 December. This period is considered inauspicious for any ceremony or festival.

Profession: Mula people are suitable for research and investigation-related jobs. They work as medical surgeons, pharmacists, healers, and social workers. They are suitable for the legal profession, journalism, and politics. They work as the seller of Agri products, flowers, and fruits, etc. They take a deep interest in spirituality and work as a spiritual speaker and a priest. They quickly learn astrology, palmistry, and other occult science and advise others.

Favourable Activities: This energy supports research and findings. It is good for laying foundation, construction and moving into a new house. This energy helps to go deep into the matter and helps to solve complex matters, investigation and meditation. It supports agriculture, gardening and plantation related activities.

Unfavorable Activities: It is not good for conducting marital events, conducting financial transactions, diplomacy, tact, or taking initiation for material activities.

Gana (Type): Among the three types of Dev, Manushya, and Rakshasa, Mula people are Rakshasa-type people. It doesn't mean they are demons but it means they take interest in wildlife activities. They take interest in forests and like to spend their time among trees than in busy market places. They work as protectionists of trees and participate in activities related to agriculture, horticulture, and other plantation activities.

Guna (Quality): The quality of this nakshatra is "Sattwic-Rajasic-Rajasic". Under the category of Sattwic, this energy works for purification and the rest two rajasic quality indicates activity level is very high. Hence, it is very fierce and sharp and do not hesitate to cut anything which goes wrong. They look for purity up to the utmost level and are never ready to compromise below standard. Hence, they look for standard and often use the word standard in the general conversation.

Body Parts: The body parts associated with the nakshatra is "Feet". Such a person can take big responsibility on their shoulder as the feet take weight of the whole body.

Tree: The tree associated with the Mula is known as "Sal Tree" or "*Shorea robusta*". It is a large tree that can grow up to 40 metres in height. The resins of the tree are useful in pain in nerves, abnormal discharge from the body, diarrhea, bleeding piles and many other diseases. Its oil is used for ear troubles, and skin diseases. Its wood is strong, durable, and resistant to fire. This tree is native to the Indian subcontinent and is considered a sacred tree in Hindu culture.

Padas: The first pada of this asterism is 0° 00' - 3° 20' in Sagittarius and ruled by Mars (Aries Navamsha). They are a very active person and take quick decisions. They are an independent, courageous, competitive, and aggressive person. They are a hard-working person and love to travel. They are egoistic and don't like suppression from anyone.

The second pada of this asterism is 3° 20' - 6° 40' in Sagittarius and ruled by Venus (Taurus Navamsha). They are a very loyal and diligent person. They work hard for material pleasure but never take others' money. They are a very honest, kind-hearted, and trustworthy person. They prefer to eat fine food, love arts, music, and have an inclination toward other Venusian pursuits.

The third pada of this asterism is 6° 40' - 10° 00' in Sagittarius and ruled by Mercury (Gemini Navamsha). Due to the influence of Mercury, they are strong in communication and making relations. They possess strong business sense and can identify the loopholes in the accounts quickly. Where others fail to identify the root cause of the problem in the business they quickly identify it. If Mercury is afflicted then these traits turn negatively and they can become manipulators of accounts. Due to the influence of Rahu, they can become scammers and fraudsters.

The fourth pada of this asterism is 10° 00' - 13° 20' in Sagittarius and ruled by Moon (Cancer Navamsha). The strength of the Moon must be strong to create positive results in this pada. The energy of Ketu-Jupiter-Moon produces positive results and such a person is very intelligent, honest, and has a quality of nurturing. They possess strong medical knowledge and heal others. They are a very emotional person and wet their eyes easily.

Chapter 20

Purva Ashadha

Purva Ashadha is the 20th of 27 Nakshatras and is located at 13° 20' - 26° 40' Sagittarius. It is a combination of two words "Purva" and 'Ashadha'. The Sanskrit word 'Purva' means 'First' or 'Foremost' and the word 'Ashadha' means 'Invincible' or 'Unconquerable'. The word Purva Ashadha means 'Undefeated' or 'Not to be overcome'. This star is related to war or a declaration of war.

Astronomy: In the southern constellation of Sagittarius, three bright stars known as Lambda Sagittarii (Kaus Borealis), Epsilon Sagittarii (Kaus Australis), and Delta Sagittarii (Kaus Media) form this nakshatra. The apparent visual magnitude of these stars is 2.82, 1.85, and 2.70 respectively. These stars are easily visible in the night sky with the naked eye. Lambda Sagittarii marks the tip of the Archer's bow and Epsilon Sagittarii is the brightest star in this constellation. The declination of Kaus Borealis is 25° S 25' 18.1" and right ascension is 18h 27m 58.2s.

Deity: The ruling deity of the nakshatra is "Apas" also known as "Goddess of Cosmic Waters". This nakshatra has a very deep relationship with water. At the time of the beginning of life on earth, there was only water and the first life evolved in sea water which contains all the essential elements which were necessary for the origin of the first life, then life on earth expanded. Water has strong healing properties and when it starts raining, optimism for life starts among the people.

Purva Ashadha people provide optimism in a dire negative condition; they never lose their hope and believe that the expansion of life never ends. Following are some of the properties of water and these properties are visible in Purva Ashadha people;

1. Water has strong nurturing quality.

2. It provides coolness to our minds.

3. It cures diseases and purifies our bodies.

4. Water is life and life get expansion in water.

5. The cool splash of water brings joy to our faces and turns a sad face into a smiling face.

6. Everything is visible in clear water. The tears of repentance wash away all sins, and the soul becomes clean and pure again.

People in India say that "all sins are washed away by taking a bath in the Ganges River". It means that when a soul becomes completely pure and holy like the river Ganga then all its sins are washed away.

Those who understand this secret always provide their little help in the vast universal activities of expansion, then their expansion of soul begins and it cannot be defeated by anyone, it is invincible. But such a person's old habits and karma do not allow them to win easily. They want to keep them in their prison, they want that slavery will continue forever. They want to keep them in their shackles and want that such a person always follows their order.

Then the battle erupts, this is not a battle in the outside world. It begins with oneself, either going on the path of expansion of one's soul or following the course of one's old habits which one has followed for many lives. Purva Ashadha is an undefeated star, those who have taken their first step towards the path of ultimate truth, ultimately, will win this battle.

Shakti (Power): The Shakti of the nakshatra is Varchograna Shakti (Power to invigorate).

The Sight of Nakshatra: It is Adhomukhi Nakshatra – Facing Downward.

Nature: Ugra (Fierce)

Element: Its element is 'Air', which signifies intellectualism and the expression of thoughts in a profound manner.

Activity: Balanced

Planetary Ruler: The lordship of the nakshatra is given to 'Venus' which represents fresh drinking water that energizes us and boosts our body functions. The water of Purva Ashadha is not like the Ardra water which wreaks havoc, it is the sweet water of the rain that people enjoy. This water gets stored in various reservoirs which are used by the people throughout the year. This water gives us life, this water gives freshness to our face, and is used to wash away dirt and clean everything. Venus is an attractive planet, when the dirt is removed, things become clean and attractive.

Venus is a gentle and non-aggressive feminine energy. There are differences in all three Venusian energies;

- **Bharani** - This energy is to nourish and protect

- **Purva Phalguni** – This energy is for creation with joy

- **Purva Ashadha** - This is the energy for rejuvenation

Symbol: Elephant's tusk is the symbol associated with this nakshatra. Elephant is a symbol of strength and wisdom. It uses its tusk for a whole range of activities, to dig roots and water, strip bark from trees, fight with other elephants to determine dominance, and protect themselves from predators. These tusks are deep-rooted rodents that have nerve endings and elephants feel extreme pain if someone cuts off their tusks. Killing an elephant for its ivory is a crime.

The symbol reflects the fighting spirit of the Purva Ashadha people but they are not aggressive. Since tusk is an inherent part and an elephant uses only against predators, the Purva Ashadha people never fight over trifles and use their weapons when someone attacks them. Due to the lordship of Venus, they never initiate fights.

Purva Ashadha person feel immense pain like cutting of tusk from an elephant, when they are unable to fight with the circumstances. When fighting remove from their life they prefer to die than to surrender.

An elephant always protects its family, in the same way Purva Ashadha people are always ready to protect their family, subordinates and helpless people. They are very calm person but when someone challenges them, they become very fierce like an elephant.

There is a story in the Mahabharata that Lord Ganesha broke his tusk in order to write this great epic told by Maharishi Ved Vyasa. So, the symbol of tusk shows the writing skills of these natives.

A 'Hand held fan' is another symbol of this nakshatra. These fans were almost everywhere before the advent of air conditioning, showing decorative fans as a sign of wealth. In those days, a stylish fan fits into a tight-fitting dress and was easy to carry to any place.

When we feel hot, the cool air from a hand fan can reduce the feeling of breathlessness. The coolness on the face immediately sends a message to the brain that there is no need to worry about the heat. The symbol of the hand fan represents wealth and this energy works to rejuvenate things. It provides new energy in a murky and gloomy situation in life. These symbols indicate that Purvashadha provides new energy in depressing situations in life.

Purva Ashadha person is always full of energy and never feels frustrated under any circumstances in life. It is the Nakshatra of Venus that represents fresh water, when all hope is lost they still believe that a drop of water will come and save their lives. They are always optimistic and believe in fighting, they never drop their sword. Venus also represents women, so the people of Purva Ashadha always respect every woman and are ready to fight to protect her.

This Nakshatra is called 'Ajeya' Nakshatra and the truth is invincible, it cannot be defeated by anyone. So, they are always ready to fight for the truth and become very fierce, they cannot accept anything wrong because all the four padas of this nakshatra fall in Sagittarius which signifies purity and religion.

Due to the influence of Jupiter, they are very trustworthy people and never break their promises. When they are unable to fulfill their promises due to some adverse situation, they feel very sad, but they never forget to fulfill them.

The third symbol of the nakshatra is a 'Winnowing Basket', which is used to separate the grain from its husk. It removes the husk with the help of air.

This symbol reinforces the working of this Nakshatra that it removes everything unwanted and brings happiness to the face. Just like a farmer uses a winnowing basket and removes all the mild debris and gives happiness to people, these grains give us energy and make people alive. In the same way, this energy always works to revive and restore things.

Caste: It is a 'Brahmin' caste nakshatra. Brahmin is a person who works with his mind first, so such a person thinks about all aspects before doing any work. If the wind is not favorable at that time then they prefer to keep silence but their mind is always engaged in planning the strategy but they execute it only when the wind is favorable.

Characteristics: Purva Ashadha people are honest, intelligent and philosophical. They are very adventurous and ambitious people and are always on the lookout for opportunities out of the box. They look very cheerful like a child and agile like a monkey. It is not possible for them to sit in one place for a long time, so they change their jobs, places and are engaged in more than one project at a time. They have a very sharp mind, pays attention to every move and investigates everything deeply. They are highly determined individuals who believe in their skills to achieve their goal but do not take help from others.

Planets in Purva Ashadha show that such a person never gets discouraged and always inspires others to fight against bad situations. They find a way out of every problem just like water finds its way. Just as people feel empowered by being filled with water in a reservoir, Purva Ashadha bestows strength on the battlefield. This energy works to bring balance and they have the power to convert defeat into victory. Planets in Purva Ashadha indicate that such persons like to see war movies and when Mahadasha or Antardasha of such a planet starts their engagement is high.

If any chaff remains, the farmer uses the basket again until only pure grain remains. In the same way, this energy compels the individual to hone his skills until he becomes a master. Purva Ashadha throws away everything that is hindering the skill to come out. They support people to remove any unwanted things and hone their skills. They act as an instructor, guru, master who teaches the students and the process goes on till the students become fully proficient.

Such persons focus only on high skill and if there is anything left they always pick out the mistake (husk) and repeat the process again. Being the auxiliary element of air, this energy works to shed everything in order to reveal the brilliance. They work on those places where extract is important after many processes. While reading a report they prefer to read at the extract first. So, they hate worthless discussion because their eyes are always looking for the outcome. Before entering in a process, they prepare ground for the outcome. That's why, many times common people do not understand their actions.

They know how to take support from the wind and they can quickly identify wind flow and changes in the environment. Only the person who can identify the change in the wind much earlier than others can make the best strategy otherwise everyone knows how to go with the flow. Their thoughts are far beyond the reach of others, because they catch the changing direction of the wind very early. Hence, they are the best strategy makers. They are never afraid to take risks. Because their thinking is far ahead of others, their opinion does not match with others. That's why many people laugh at their ideas because at that time nothing is visible related to that matter, but they always stick to their decision and is proved right when the time comes.

Sagittarius is a sign of wisdom; planets in Purva Ashadha indicate such a person to have knowledge in various fields. They have strong oratory skills and use optimistic, motivational and enthusiastic words in their speech, so they influence people with their speech.

With the influence of Jupiter, they are expansionist, make big plans and always think of doing big things in life. Their vision is always clear about their goal without any ambiguity and every day they take a step towards achieving it. Others find the way impossible but they never get discouraged. They always work to improve and strengthen the situation in life, hence work on multiple facets and never believe the reliability of only one.

Purva Ashadha people are philanthropic people. As water is available to all, similarly they do such works which are for the benefit of humanity. They have a keen eye for throwing away the unnecessary and keeping only the essence, so they are good at analysis. The planets in this Nakshatra indicate that such a person possesses the kind of knowledge that sets him apart from the masses. Therefore, they take keen interest in higher education and learn complex software. This work is similar to a winnowing basket which contains only the grain and removes all the chaff i.e. only the best remains and the useless is removed.

Purva Ashadha is about achieving higher things in life. Ambition, big plans, mastery of skills, higher knowledge, public speaking, changing jobs and getting varied experiences etc. All these qualities set them apart from others. While developing all these rejuvenating energy is required which provides support from the roots, only then higher things in life can be achieved. Hence, the energy associated with the constellation is a downward energy as it provides the necessary water from the roots.

Negative Traits: They are highly egoistic person, never care about the opinion of others and think that they are supreme and always take right decisions. They do not want to lose under any circumstances and take wrong decisions because of exaggerating their power and strength. They become very furious, make futile arguments, go to any extent and use any means to win a fight.

They use their speaking power in a wrong way and persuade others to do wrong things. They are manipulators and strategize for their own benefit, don't care about morality, can commit any sin because winning is important to them. Their ambition and can't-give-up attitude can go awry and result in fierce battles, takeovers of other businesses or countries. The attitude of, "I have higher knowledge" and "I will not listen to others" can put many enterprises and lives in jeopardy.

Gender: The gender of the nakshatra is 'Female'. Female planets give good results here and male planets show only feminine qualities like compassion, caring etc.

Animal Symbol: The related animal of Purvashadha is 'male monkey'. Its counterpart is Shravan Nakshatra whose animal symbol is female monkey. It is the enemy of Pushya and Krittika Nakshatra, whose animal symbol is goat.

Monkeys are known for their intelligence, they are flexible animals, always carefree and full of energy. They never sit on a tree for a long time and after a while they jump to another tree. They are never afraid of anything new, like to try it once and never afraid of falling from a height.

Purva Ashadha people are also like the same. They are flexible person, always full of energy. They work on various profiles but never stay at a place for a long time. They are adventurous person and never afraid of going alone. They never feel any kind of depression even if their life throws them at the bottom; they are monkeys and know how to jump.

Sun's Ingress: Sun enters this Nakshatra every year on 29th December and stays there till 11th January. There is no festival or celebration in India during this time.

Profession: Consultants, strategists, advisors, motivational speakers, research and investigation, and administrative jobs. They work as writers, editors, and all those jobs that require a high level of skill. They work for; Jobs related to filtration and air-related work, jobs that require debris removal, raw material processing, refinery, and product manufacturing where it is necessary to move raw materials through various processes to achieve a result. They deal with shipping and water utilities.

Favourable Activities: Strategy making, planning, to overcome a difficult situation, declaration of war, make an inspirational or public statement. Good for digging; Wells, water tanks, ponds etc. It's good for refreshments, perk up, fortifications, and anything related to adventure. It is good for paying off debt and removing any encumbrances that may be hindering growth. It is highly suitable for setting high goals in life.

Unfavorable Activities: It is not auspicious for marriage and doing delicate acts.

Gana (Type): Out of the three types of Dev, Manushya and Rakshasa, the type of Purva Ashadha is 'Manushya'. According to Hindu scriptures human life is difficult and it is attained only when a soul passes through 84 lakh yonis (births). It shows the value of human life. Manushya has immense potential to go either up or down, he can become a God or a demon. The immense potential of this energy and association of human indicates that the choice is in the hand of human, how they utilize this energy.

Guna (Quality): The guna of the nakshatra is 'Satwik-Rajasic-Tamasic'. Every great creation take place in deep tamas, this benevolent energy becomes very active when some cause is present; otherwise they remain in a state of tamas (darkness). For example;

1. When a company is in danger, the Purvashadha person saves it with his strategies and plans.

2. When danger approaches a kingdom, a great warrior comes out of the mountain and protects the kingdom with his prowess.

Body Parts: This nakshatra is related to the 'Back part' of the body. The back of the body is used to hold weapons.

Tree: With this Nakshatra 'Ashoka tree' is associated, which is also known as '*Saraca asoca*'. It is an evergreen tree with beautiful flowers and reaches a height of 35-40 feet. The word Ashoka means without sorrow, so it is believed that this tree reduces all sorrows and bestows good fortune. It has many medicinal benefits; Its products increase intelligence, it is used to relieve pain, reduce fever, lower blood sugar, purify the blood, and treat skin disorders.

Padas: The first pada of this asterism is 13° 20' - 16° 40' in Sagittarius and ruled by Sun (Leo Navamsha). They are very creative person and shows leadership qualities. They are egoistic and never take help from anyone. They are courageous, bold and generous people make big plans and never do narrow things.

The second pada of this asterism is 16° 40' - 20° 00' in Sagittarius and ruled by Mercury (Virgo Navamsha). Here the intellect moves towards religion, philosophy and spiritual pursuit. They are good at communication and have strong oratory skills. They are practical but impulsive, lack consistency, believe in change and unable to stay at one place for long time. They focus on alternative resources, make good strategies and engage themselves in more than one project at a time.

The third pada of this asterism is 20° 00' - 23° 20' in Sagittarius and ruled by Venus (Libra Navamsha). It is the strong energy of Venus that inclines towards achieving the finer things in life. If even a single husk remains, they start the whole process again to clean the grain completely. They never accept anything, less than perfection. They review the situation frequently, handle difficult situations and make proper plans to overcome them.

The fourth pada of this asterism is 23° 20' - 26° 40' in Sagittarius and ruled by Mars (Scorpio Navamsha). The research and investigation power are high in this pada. They are mysterious person, try to hide everything and work behind the scene. They do their work underneath the surface and their strike is sudden. They take interest in occult science, want to go deep in that field and prefer isolation.

Chapter 21

Uttara Ashadha

Uttara Ashadha is the 21st of 27 Nakshatras and is located at 26° 40' Sagittarius - 10° 00' Capricorn. The word Uttara means "Subsequent", "Rejoinder", or "Answer". It also means "High", "Excellent" or "Superior". It is the remaining part of Ashadha star and it has the same meaning "Invincible" or "Unconquerable". Hence, the word Uttara Ashadha means "Later Invincible", "Final Victory" or "The victory that is immortal".

Astronomy: In the southern constellation of Sagittarius, four stars known as Phi Sagittarii, Sigma Sagittarii (Nunki), Tau Sagittarii, and Zeta Sagittarii form this nakshatra. They appear in the night sky with visual magnitudes of 3.17, 2.05, 3.30, and 2.59, respectively. The lower magnitude of stars indicates more brightness in the sky.

Deity: The deity of the asterism is 'Vishwadevas', also known as 'Ten Universal Gods'. There are 10 Ganadevatas who sustain the world and all their qualities are present in this Nakshatra. Ten is a symbol of duality, the letters up to 9 alone but to write 10 requires '1' and '0'. It signifies a collective force to achieve higher things in life.

This energy produces its best results when it mobilizes resources toward the achievement of a common goal. Indian philosophy considers 10 Indriyas (senses) in our body which are the means of a person's direct perception of the external world. The first five are known as jnanendriyas (entrance senses); eyes, ear, nose, tongue, and skin. The other five are known as karmendriyas (exit senses); mouth, hands, feet, genitals, and rectum. By controlling these senses with the help of yogic techniques, a person can bring awareness to the unconscious process and discover the hidden truth of life.

Shakti (Power): The associated Shakti on this nakshatra is known as "Apradhrisya shakti" (a victory that can't be challenged by anyone).

The Sight of Nakshatra: It is an Urdhvamukhi Nakshatra i.e., Facing Upward.

Nature: The nature of the Nakshatra is Dhruva (fixed). Under its influence, people do those acts which are fixed forever.

Element: Air

Activity: Balanced

Planetary Ruler: The lordship of this nakshatra is given to the Sun. The focus of the Ashadha star is always on victory, and only an enlightened person can be victorious forever. Worshiping the Sun dispels all the darkness of a person and only light remains. The Sun indicates an adventurous person who is never afraid to go it alone. It also indicates a committed and conscientious person. Uttara Ashadha indicates a charismatic personality, once they accept a task they never leave it before its completion.

Following are the differences between the nakshatras of the Sun;

• **Krittika** - Both sharp and soft qualities are present here, but only one comes to the surface at a time.

• **Uttara Phalguni** - This energy works for development and growth through hard work. This nakshatra represents the quality of action.

• **Uttara Ashadha** - This energy works to become victorious at any cost.

Symbol: The tusk of an elephant is the main symbol of this asterism, like Purva Ashadha. It is always in pair, so many astrologers believe that the left tusk belongs to Purva Ashadha and the right tusk belongs to Uttara Ashadha. The elephant is associated with Lord Ganesha and his idol has a broken left tusk.

Purva Ashadha is a concentrated energy that works to achieve maximum output by rejuvenating and removing, Uttara Ashadha signifies ultimate victory and emphasizes completion, utilization, and attainment of the ultimate goal.

Caste: The caste of the nakshatra is 'Kshatriya' (Warrior). Warrior never hesitates to sacrifice their lives on the battlefield. It is their duty to obey orders and have only one goal - to win. They know very well how to play with dangerous weapons and always keep them under their control. Planets in Uttara Ashadha indicate that such a person has all the qualities of a warrior; they fight very fiercely till they win and wait for the right moment for each attack.

Characteristics: This nakshatra bestows the person with many qualities. The 10 Universal Gods indicates 10 major qualities of the person and their focus is always on achievement. With all the combined energy these people have the potential to achieve higher things in life. They are intelligent and truthful persons who work without any partiality. They are able to see all the pros and cons of a situation, they never get scared and never run away from reality. They are ambitious persons who hold senior administrative positions.

People of all the three Sun nakshatra are very dignified people. They are not flatterers who lose their esteem in order to gain something. They are very firm and determined person who boldly face any situation and take decisions. Uttara Ashadha person never take any conclusion in hurry and it come from after thinking all aspects, as it is related to 10 devas.

Both Ashadha nakshatra are highly influenced by the characteristics of elephant. Lord Ganesha got his head back in the form of an elephant's head. Getting back indicates this nakshatra has strong potential to bring back the lost things. When Lord Ganesha got his head back, Lord Shiva gave him the status of being foremost among the gods. He has become invincible, the giver of victory and the lord of wisdom. The word Uttara Ashadha means 'Later Victory' clearly signifies the above story, when such a person gets his power back he becomes invincible.

Lord Ganesha lost his first head because of his ego and for only following his mother's orders. To show his arrogance, he hurt many deities because of his immense power, such an arrogant head cannot be where Lord Shiva resides. So, Lord Shiva cut off that head and again attached it to the elephant's head.

This story has great significance with the Uttara Ashadha people. They have many qualities which make them far ahead of other people. But due to such qualities, ego also makes a home in their mind. That subtle ego may be invisible to others but not invisible to God and without removing that ego such a person cannot be victorious.

Without removing that egoistic head, Lord Ganesha could not become the first God and be worshiped by all. The head that ego has gone can't be the same head as earlier. The replacement of head indicates that earlier head with arrogance will never return, that has gone forever. By removing that subtle ego, He has now become entitled to become the 'First God'.

In the same way, without removing that arrogance, Uttara Ashadha person can't become a victorious person and this star is an ultimate victorious star. So, loss is necessary in their life to remove that arrogance, it is a part of lesson and they have to learn that and remove the arrogance of being supreme.

When that subtle ego is gone, such a person's qualities shine like a bright star and he is now loved by all, he has attained the position of ultimate victory. As Goddess Parvati wanted her son back at any cost and became extremely angry, in the same way many people do not want to lose the Uttara Ashadha person, as they are priceless people. They provide all possible help to regain his power. Just like Lord Ganesha got back his head, such a person gets everything back and is respected by all. Uttara Ashadha is an unstoppable star who got a late victory, but now it will shine forever.

Lord Shiva is the presiding deity of Saturn. Uttara Ashadha first pada falls in Sagittarius and the next three pada falls in Capricorn, whose ruler is Saturn. The festival of Makar Sankranti is celebrated in India every year when the Sun enters the Capricorn sign. Before this day every festival closes a month before and people eagerly wait for the day of Makar Sankranti. It also means that when the people of Uttara Ashadha get their power back, they only bring happiness in people's lives. They are the leaders who show light in many lives like the Sun.

Such a person regains his wealth, business or power after losing it once. Now, he is a completely changed person without any ego and is loved by millions, and then his name becomes immortal because of his great deeds. Now, he has achieved that victory that is unconquerable.

Negative Traits: They are obstinate and oppressive person who want result at any cost do not bother about sufferings of others. They are highly disciplined individuals, but cannot tolerate any disobedience and give severe punishment. They follow strict rules and force others to follow the same. They are ruthless and keep everything and everyone in their grip and don't let anyone escape.

They make everything an issue in the organization, write useless e-mails and they have the answer for everything. They argue at length over trivial matters, talk incessantly, and are quick to fight and they have ability to fight for hours. They pick up a fight with a stranger on the road over some trivial matter and winning even in that becomes a matter of self-respect for them. They drag minor matters into court cases and feel the joy of victory to suppress others.

They are extremely vindictive individuals and seek revenge at any cost, no matter how small the matter is. They are unable to tolerate any kind of harm or negative word. If the Sun or Mars is placed in the sixth house in the Uttarashadha nakshatra then it indicates a very quarrelsome person.

They have superiority complex and when someone asks for some improvement, they retaliate very fiercely. The energy of regaining and reactivating works in a negative direction and such a person can reorganize terrorist, racist group or army to seek revenge. They have subtle arrogance of their wisdom and power; never accept their mistake and this is the reason of sorrows in their life.

Gender: The gender of the constellation is 'Female'. A feminine personality is a receptive personality, a woman can be patient for a long time but it is difficult for a man. Only a woman can give birth, and to become supremely victorious, the birth of egolessness is necessary.

Animal Symbol: The animal associated with the constellation is a 'Male Mongoose', also known as Nakula. This nakshatra has no partner in the zodiac. It is inimical to Rohini and Mrigashira whose animal symbol is serpent.

The mongoose is considered the vehicle of 'Kuber', the god of wealth. They are omnivorous, adept hunters and capable of killing dangerous predators that are much larger or more aggressive than themselves. They are known for their skill in killing snakes using special techniques. They are extremely fast and agile and fight with the snake for hours. They are patient and wait for the right time to attack. They use speed to lure the snake and tire it with several strikes, effectively dodging the snake's attacks and killing it with a bite to the neck or head when the snake is tired.

The combative nature of Uttara Ashadha person is also the same. They make strategies, keep patience for the right time to attack because winning the battle is important for them. They can defeat an enemy bigger than themselves, so they are never afraid of any enmity. I dare to challenge; it is inherent in his personality.

Mongooses often live in burrows but rarely dig their own burrows. Rather they choose to move into empty burrows left by other animals. It indicates Uttara Ashadha person do not take interest in making their own home. In astrology, there is no 'Female Mongoose', assigned to this nakshatra, so they are always on the lookout for their partner. Either they face problems in getting married or it is completely denied, their married life is not successful.

Mongoose indicates friendship with Muslims or foreigners. When the dasha or antardasha of the planets situated in Uttarashadha comes, friendship with Muslims or foreigners is possible and they come to provide good support in their life.

Sun's Ingress: Sun enters this Nakshatra every year on 11th January and stays there till 24th January. During this, the season of festivals and celebrations starts again in India.

Profession: Finance, Teaching, Real estate, Military, Administration, Leader, Commander, Bureaucrat, Entrepreneur, Social Worker, Scientific research, Priest, etc.

Favourable Activities: It is the star of beginning and support new and auspicious things. It is good for starting a new venture, construction of any tall structure, building, walls, etc. It is auspicious for marriage and celebrations, business affairs and signing contracts.

Unfavorable Activities: It does not support any impulsive and egoistic activity.

Gana (Type): Among the three kinds of nakshatras, the type of this nakshatra is Manushya (Human). Like its predecessor, this star has the same potential for extreme ups or downs in life.

Guna (Quality): The quality of the nakshatra is 'Satwik-Rajasic-Satwik'. They fight for a noble cause, are driven to do noble deeds and do everything for the achievement.

Body Parts: The body part related to this nakshatra is 'Waist'. Warriors carry their weapons at their waist which can be deployed quickly.

Tree: Jackfruit Tree is associated with this nakshatra, also known as '*Artocarpus heterophyllus*'. The tree is 50-70 feet in height and the length of its fruit is 2 feet. This tree needs full sunlight to grow well and produce fruit. Its unripe fruit is cooked and eaten and the ripe fruit is used as a sweet. The tree has many medicinal benefits; it is rich in iron, high in vitamin C and antioxidants, its consumption is useful for lowering blood pressure and reducing the risk of heart diseases.

Padas: The first pada of this asterism is 26° 40' - 30° 00' in Sagittarius and ruled by Jupiter (Sagittarius Navamsha). They are ambitious, enthusiastic and highly skilled person. Due to influence of Jupiter their approach is religious and philosophical. They are explorers always inclined towards higher knowledge. They speak harsh truth, stick with their principles and fight for justice.

The second pada of this asterism is 00° 00' - 3° 20' in Capricorn and ruled by Saturn (Capricorn Navamsha). Sun gets directional strength in the 10th house and it is the highest point of the zodiac also known as Midheaven and Sun touches this point every day at noon. This shows that the qualities of the planets are most visible in the 10th house (Capricorn). They are determined, disciplined and very focused person. They are tough and forceful people and know how to use every available resource.

The third pada of this asterism is 3° 20' - 6° 40' in Capricorn and ruled by Saturn (Aquarius Navamsha). They are very helpful person and always try to bring harmony among people. They are scientific minded person and skilled in technology. They love friendship and teamwork and are excellent problem-solvers. They have a strong ability to sit at one place for hours and can become true seekers of truth.

The fourth pada of this asterism is 6° 40' - 10° 00' in Capricorn and ruled by Jupiter (Pisces Navamsha). They are very knowledgeable, wise and humble person. They are visionary person with a charismatic personality. In this pada, along with discipline, the quality of creation is more. They are inclination towards occult and mysticism.

Chapter 22

Shravana

Shravana is the 22nd of 27 Nakshatras and is located at 10° 00' - 23° 00' Capricorn. The word Shravana comes from the Sanskrit word 'Shrava' which means hearing. Therefore, Shravana means the act of hearing or that which is heard. Hearing related to the ears and that is an essential part of learning. So, it is related with acquiring knowledge and study. Goddess Saraswati is related to this nakshatra, which shows the interest of these people towards literature and art.

Astronomy: In the constellation of Aquila, the main star of this nakshatra is known as Altair (Alpha Aquilae). With an apparent magnitude of 0.77, it is the 12th brightest star in the sky. Its declination is 8° N 55' 45.28" and right ascension is 19h 51m 52.8s.

Deity: The deity of the nakshatra is "Lord Vishnu". When one thing collides with another, sound is produced, that is, two are needed to produce sound and this world is the sound of two. The energy of this Nakshatra pulls all the sound towards itself. If any sound is produced by collision, then Shravan hears it immediately. That's why the deity of this Nakshatra is Lord Vishnu, in whose ears every sound reaches. That's why Hindu philosophy says that Lord hears everything.

Shakti (Power): The Shakti of the nakshatra is known as "Samhanana Shakti", the power of connection. Connection means from one to the other and on a higher aspect it means the connection to the divine, and ears are the path, and when a person seeks that path this energy functions. This Shakti indicates everything is connected in the universe and control of that connection is in the hands of Lord Vishnu.

The Sight of Nakshatra: It is an Urdhvamukhi Nakshatra i.e., Facing Upward.

Nature: Dhruva (Fixed)

Element: Air

Activity: Passive

TriMurti and Behaviour: Brahma and Creation

Planetary Ruler: The lord of the nakshatra is the Moon. Moon is a non-aggressive planet, and it is not good to take any initiative in all three Nakshatras ruled by the Moon. The differences between the three lunar constellations are as follows;

- **Rohini** – Creation through love

- **Hasta** - Creation by intellect and hand

- **Shravana** – Creation through receptivity

Symbol: Its first symbol is the "Ear". The ear is connected to the brain and a proper shape of the ear is a sign of intelligence. All species whose ears are outside of their body are more intelligent than those species whose ears are inside. Planets in this nakshatra indicate such a person will take an interest in intellectual activities.

Shravana comes under the sign of Capricorn, it is a sign that put discipline on everything and doesn't allow moving anything worthless. Due to the effect of Saturn's strict control is visible here, what comes inside it is difficult to go outside. Our ears do the same thing; vibrations come in through this door and never go out.

There is only one way that when the vibration wants to go out, it has to change its path and use the other senses. In other words, ears are the master of all our senses, because what goes inside has the power to influence our mind. Hence, the supreme master of all the senses "Lord Vishnu" is the deity of this nakshatra.

Its second symbol is "three footprints". There is a mythological story of Lord Vishnu's Vamana avatar where a demon king Bali conquered the whole world. The story goes that the Lord incarnated as Vamana to liberate the world and asked the king for a gift of three steps of land. In the first step, he measured the Pataal Lok and the earth, in the second step he took heaven, and then asked Bali where to put the third step. King Bali bowed down before the Lord and bowed his head and said, 'Here'. Then Lord Vishnu very pleased with such behavior blessed the king. He gave heaven to the gods, earth to humans and Bali went to the Pataal Lok.

The significance of this legend is that the accomplishment of any task requires energy from three directions. A geometric triangle is bounded by three straight lines. Three is considered a sacred number and the entire universe is governed by the three energies of God; Brahma, Vishnu and Mahesh. Three is also the number of time - past, present and future. It is also considered the number of harmony, wisdom and understanding. In numerology, three is related to self-expression, balance, joy, optimism and creativity. It is the number of unity and represents the union of mind, body and soul. In mathematics, the symbol $\exists$ (there exists) is used to express the existence of a variable. "Three is the number of existence" in various cultural and philosophical interpretations.

The first step of Vaman indicates to go deep in listening, the second step indicates to introspect one's mind and expand the soul, and the third step is, be a humble person and surrender to God, such a person always gets 'His Blessings'.

Its third symbol is the "Trident". It has three sharp edges and is a very powerful energy that gives serious effects. It represents power and authority. It indicates a highly focused person whose penetration is very deep.

Caste: It is a Mlechha (Outcaste) Nakshatra. The ears are highly receptive and it immediately catches every vibration which cannot be avoided and it creates an impact. So, one should always avoid all useless sounds and listen only to that which is useful for one's life, because all these useless vibrations create hindrances in hearing the voice of God.

The voice of nature speaks of its divinity but not the voice of the market place. Therefore, to hear this divine voice, ones must avoid all worthless voices. That makes the caste of this constellation Mleccha.

Characteristics: Shravana nakshatra people are always take interest in knowledge, information and present days every medium of communication. They are eloquent speaker and keep various information in their mind. They are very talented and wise person and never satisfied from acquiring knowledge, they are always in thrust of getting more and ready to travel anywhere to enhance their knowledge. They are master of many skills and mainly there is work related with arts and literature.

These people have very sharp ears and they recognize the subtle difference of sound, so they work in the sound industry. They spend a lot of time learning, developing many skills. Once the word is heard, the mind reacts to it. That's why it is necessary to assimilate things before speaking, the knowledge that is not digested only spreads stench. Only a mature mind can share their knowledge. These people share knowledge with others and work as professor, trainer, mentor, speaker. They succeed with their skills and get fame.

Shravana natives have attractive personality. They have the ability to attract any voice towards themselves and they listen carefully to other's words, that's why people like them. They are very famous in the college and are popularly known as Romeo. They work for the entertainment industry as an actor or model.

They don't like to stay at one place for long time, they are free spirited person, roaming is inherent in their personality. Because their mind demands more and more sound (knowledge), so they prefer the job of counselor, advisor or some independent profession. They move around to get new experiences, build relationships and start a new journey all over again.

Listening is a quality that does not support any aggression while speaking is an aggression. During verbal spat it is seen that no one is listening and everyone is speaking. The person who speaks more is not a receptive person and the biggest quality of a wise person is to be receptive first.

The people of Shravana Nakshatra take a keen interest in creation and do not want any kind of noise that disturbs their concentration. They are a very observant person and don't like any disturbance. Planets in Shravana Nakshatra indicate that such individual prefer pin drop silence as they do not want to lose anything, that indicate a very high level of receptivity.

Receptivity means egolessness. If this person does not show arrogance, then he can become a very intelligent person. Arrogance of skills is very harmful and they can be narrow-minded, developing bigotry instead of receptivity. Such a person is not ready to listen to the voice of others, he only speaks, and others are there only to listen to him.

When the receptivity is high, such a person should always be careful what he is listening to and such people should always avoid wrong association, they should not listen to any nonsense as their mind absorbs it quickly. Receptivity also opens the door to vulnerability, so there is a need to be careful at every stage.

There are five sense organs - eyes, ears, nose, tongue and skin. Energy does not flow outward from the ears, only in an inward direction. Therefore, ears play a very important role in the development of our mind and mind controls all the senses.

Therefore, a person with a weak mind gets easily influenced to do wrong things in the company of wrong people, because the sound has an effect on the mind. The planets in this Nakshatra indicate that one should always be careful about what one is listening to, so it is good to stop at first. It is like a recording of music, where a musician stops every sound he does not want to record, only then the greatest creation is possible.

The person who holds everything in his mind has the ability to speak well and then he says from his experience. Now the words are coming from his soul not only from his throat, so his speech is totally different from others.

The biggest quality of this Nakshatra is that it leaves nothing in between; Whatever activity once started always reaches its end. That's why these people do not leave their table without completing their chapter or without completing their work. They are a very hardworking person and works till late night with full concentration after closing the room.

God's entire creation always teaches us to be receptive, so first be receptive and 'The Creator' will bless us abundantly. Such a person speaks only when necessary, what he does not know, he keeps his mouth shut and waits for the generosity of the Lord.

Negative Traits: Such people lose the power of listening and take interest only in speaking, they like to discuss on worthless matters and make everything an issue. They take interest is gossiping and backbiting. They like to collect useful information which they can use it for their benefit. They ask many questions about their friends and colleagues but never reveal anything about themselves. They know that in present days information is power, so they are ready to do anything to get that. They are flatterers and sycophants who are always on search for some information which they can use it for their own benefit.

They are much focused person and it can shift to achieve a wrong target, they can use unethical means to achieve that. When learning is important for them such a person can learn various wrong things and use his skills for manipulations.

Gender: The gender of the nakshatra is "Male", it indicates they do not hesitate to take step forward.

Animal Symbol: The animal related this is "female monkey". Its counterpart is Purva Ashadha, whose animal is a male monkey. It is the enemy of Pushya and Krittika whose animal symbol is sheep (goat).

Monkeys are known for their curiosity and intelligence. They are very social animals, quick learners, and love to swing from branch to branch. Female monkey shows that such individuals take an interest in artistry but they are moody, and when things go wrong, they immediately move to another place without saying anything.

Sun's Ingress: Sun enters this Nakshatra every year on 24th January and stays there till 6th February. January is the month of new beginnings, a time when many religious, cultural and national activities take place.

Profession: They work as; professor, teacher, trainer, freelancers, preachers, researchers, storytellers, jugglers, magicians, musicians, anchors, actors, counselors, advisors, social workers, and performers. Planets in Sharavana indicate that such a person cannot work under anyone for long, they start their career as an employee but end it as an entrepreneur.

Favourable Activities: Reading, writing, learning, counselling, drama, cinema, and music is good.

Unfavorable Activities: Any activity of aggression, risk, and ego is not good.

Gana (Type): The gana of the nakshatra is Deva. They are dignified people, take an interest in less available but fine things, they are not ready to compromise below the quality. They are open-minded, ready to give, and do not like to quarrel.

Guna (Quality): The quality of the nakshatra is "Satwik-Tamasic-Rajasic". The seeker of truth has to live in deep silence and when he knows, it is his responsibility to show the way to others.

Body Parts: Ears and Genitals are related to this nakshatra.

Tree: The tree associated with nakshatra is Arka or Madar, also known as 'Calotropis gigantea'. It is a perennial shrub up to 3–4 m high and has a bunch of flowers that are white or lavender. Its leaves are used as garlands for Lord Hanuman and flowers are used for offering to Lord Shiva. It has a milky stem that is sticky and mildly poisonous. This latex can be purified and used as a very effective antidote as well as herbal medicine.

Padas: The first pada of this asterism is 10° 00' - 13° 20' in Capricorn and ruled by Mars (Aries Navamsha). The soft quality of Moon, gets energy from Mars and that is controlled by Saturn.

Such a person is a disciplined person who does everything with structured and well-organized way. They are very energetic and passionate person who never sit before completion of the work. A weak Moon indicates that such a person may waste his energy in worthless wanderings and always be in a hurry.

The second pada of this asterism is 13° 20' - 16° 40' in Capricorn and ruled by Venus (Taurus Navamsha). They are polite, sociable and attractive people. They have sweet voice and are natural speaker. These are very creative people, never leave anything in between and are always ready to help others.

The third pada of this asterism is 16° 40' - 20° 00' in Capricorn and ruled by Mercury (Gemini Navamsha). They are very intelligent person and have strong communication skills. They are quick to learn and assimilate a lot of information in their mind. They are good writers, speakers and use witty words in their communication.

The fourth pada of this asterism is 20° 00' - 23° 20' in Capricorn and ruled by Moon (Cancer Navamsha). The level of receptivity is very high in this pada. They are very imaginative and sensitive person. They have nourishing quality and provide proper guidance to others. They are very friendly but don't like gossips. Such a person has the power to influence the public, deal with the public, sit in prominent positions where he meets the public or will do such work which will come in limelight among the public.

Chapter 23

Dhanishta

Dhanishta is the 23rd of 27 Nakshatras and is located at 23° 20' Capricorn – 06° 40' Aquarius. The Sanskrit word "Dhanishta" is made up of two words; "Dhan" means "Wealth", or "Abundance" and "Nishtha" means "Devotion", "Faith", "Deep affection", "Trust", or "Concentration". The dictionary meaning of wealth is 'a large number or amount of something'; it can be money or other valuable assets.

Dhanishta is known as "The Star of Wealth". It is the wealth of devotion and faith towards the Almighty. Its other name is "Sravishtha", which means "the most famous". Such devotion is attained when all the senses work under complete control then a harmony is born within, therefore, it is known as "The Star of Symphony".

Astronomy: In the constellation Delphinus, a small constellation in the northern celestial hemisphere and close to the celestial equator, Beta Delphini (Rotanev) is the brightest star in this constellation. With a visual magnitude of 3.64, this star appears moderately bright in the night sky. Its declination is 14° N 40' 28.19" and right ascension is 20h 38m 36.3s. Delphinus has 7 stars that make up this constellation; the others can only be seen with a telescope.

Deity: The deity of the nakshatra is "The Eight Vasus", they are the group of deities of energy and light. These eight gods are known as;

1. Apa, which means water,

2. Dhruva, meaning the fixed star,

3. Soma, meaning Moon,

4. Dhara, meaning earth or carrier,

5. Anila, meaning wind,

6. Anala, which means fire,

7. Pratyusha, meaning Sun, and

8. Prabhasa, which means ether.

These eight Vasus are the abode of all that exists in the world. The working force of eight gods to achieve a common aim indicates cooperation, hence Dhanishta people always believe in cooperation. When direction from eight forces work simultaneously for a common goal a proper synchronization is required, it indicates a rhythm with every beat that produce a perfect harmony.

A horizontal version of number 8 becomes the handcuffs symbol. It also looks like the symbol of infinity (∞) and represents the concept of eternity, endless and unlimited. Shackles are a device for restraining the wrists. The deities of the constellation indicate that this energy acts as a restraint and the energy here is excessive.

A maximum output is possible only when everything is used in an efficient manner. Therefore, the energy planet Mars becomes exalted here at 28°, because Dhanishta does not let even an ounce of energy go waste. These eight deities are responsible to create harmony and where there is disharmony they will come to correct it. They impose restrictions, tighten knots and bring harmony in the atmosphere.

Shakti (Power): Its Shakti is "Khyapayitri Shakti", i.e., the power to give fame and abundance.

The Sight of Nakshatra: It is an Urdhvamukhi Nakshatra i.e., Facing Upward.

Nature: Its nature is Chara (Movable). Chara nakshatra always looking for some engagement and prefer a physical movement.

Element: Its element is "Ether", indicates space.

Activity: Active

Planetary Ruler: Mars, the planet of energy is the ruler of this nakshatra. In a work where many forces are affecting the outcome, it is very difficult to coordinate, because the difference of even a microsecond makes a difference. It requires a deep understanding of every procedure and flow of every action. Such efficiency is possible when a person fully understands the pattern of timing, repetition, and required spacing of each element.

When to create harmony in the mundane world is difficult, so what about the creation of harmony in the inner world where multiple desires simultaneously force, it requires a lot of energy. Therefore, Mars is assigned as the lord of this nakshatra. The differences between the three Mars nakshatras are as follows;

• **Mrigashira** - A relentless seeking energy

• **Chitra** - Excellence and radiance

• **Dhanishtha** - Establishing harmony through the use of pressure and force

Symbol: Its symbol is mridangam (musical drum), tabla and flute. These musical instruments are hollow inside and produce sound with the help of air and beat. Music means rhythm and these musical instruments need to be harmonized in a proper way so that it can produce melodious sound. Dhanishta people have inclination towards music and sound, and they like to use hands to beat a drum or a table.

Sound waves travel through a medium such as air or water and the empty space of musical instruments facilitates it to produce a perfect sound. A drum or a flute are never in search of anything to fill its hollowness because any entered thing can disturb its efficiency. Hence, Dhanishta people want a distinct space in their life and they never allow anyone to enter in that space.

A musical instrument produces a pleasing sound when everything is used in a proper manner. It indicates efficiency and utilization, Dhanishta person know how to utilize every available resource and get the optimum results, and so, they never throw anything worthlessly. They can produce great wealth, because they know the utilization of every minimum resource. They have great capacity to prove the phrase 'from rags to riches', therefore, it is called the star of wealth, because their focus is always on utilization to get the maximum output.

The sound of the drum creates energy and its vibration affects our mind and compels us to act. This action can be dance or any signal. Therefore, these people produce such signals and also are excellent to identify the signals from very far. Their mind works quickly on the vibrations and they work on those places which create such vibrations. They like to listen music and use costly music system and high-quality head phones which produce high quality sound.

The empty part of the drum and a flute indicates egolessness. Hence, they are very polite person, like to mingle with people. But they also try to fill this empty space with money and as money increases their ego also increases. The melodious sound now fades away and only the beat of the drum of the ego is heard.

Caste: The caste of the nakshatra is Farmer or Servant. The farmer has good knowledge of seeds and their conservation. They wait for the right time to sow and never rush for it. They add fertilizer and water and wait for the yield. They are never in a hurry to get the fruits because they know that the fruits will come only when the plant is ready, some trees bear fruits after years and the farmer waits for that day, he takes care of the tree every day so that the tree should not die.

The farmer's work requires a proper understanding of the available resources, their timely use, and security at the initial stage, and waiting for the result. A person with such qualities earns abundant wealth, so according to the author; the ancient sages have assigned the caste of the farmer to this Nakshatra.

Characteristics: Dhanishta natives have a quick rhythmic brain, so they pick up on every beat, swing, and tone very quickly. A natural rhythm in our body is our heart, which beats continuously, so it is closely related to our heart. Dhanishtha people are quick to take the pulse of the body and they act as a physician. They take deep interest in Ayurveda whose treatment is based on the rhythm of the pulse.

Timing is in important factor for rhythm, so they are time conscious person and always like to reach on time and never do delay in their work. It indicates a proper time management and it is possible when one does not panic on seeing the circumstances. When the time for one work is over, they know they have to accomplish another task. So, they don't want to sit idle at a place.

In corporate world, they are great leaders who create a harmony among different departments, do accurate assessment of the associated risks, take timely action and prevent losses. But they are not sycophants who sit up late in the office to please their bosses, so they lack necessary tactics and lag behind in their career. If Moon is afflicted they always count time of every sitting and in lieu of that their focus is on rewards.

Their senses are strong to catch any pattern of change and they prefer to make every planning in advance. Hence, they work as a planner, risk advisor, portfolio manager, consultant, insurance agent as they have the ability to identify the changing trend and take preventive measures. They work everything as per their planning and often use these words in their discussions; procedures, strategy, organize, technique, blue print, road map, scheme, proposal, project, etc.

They can quickly identify changes in wind and season. They have a deep knowledge of the weather and prepare everything before it changes. They know that human life is full of ups and downs, so they prepare everything in advance and always prepare themselves to avoid any unforeseen event.

Dhanishta native's arrangements are very perfect because they are able to create a harmony between different groups, so they work as a large event organizer. They work in those fields where they arrange; meetings, multiple schedules, words, syllabus, electric light and colour that provides proper shades, etc. They are perfect organizer, keep everything under control and never miss anything.

Their attention is always on space and they judge time and space accurately, so they maintain a rhythm in their speech, dance and are never in a hurry. They take interest in activities where large space is required, such as dancing, yoga, driving, etc. They do not like to live in a small room and always prefer open space for their stay. They make big rooms, houses and skyscrapers.

This energy serves to understand the cyclicity of events; they have a strong understanding of the periodic occurrence of living beings. Hence, they have a deep understanding of biology and love to study the cycle of different organisms and notes their daily variations in certain activities. They work as a researcher and a scientist who study various cycles of many organisms throughout his life and reaches a conclusion which is not already known to anyone.

Such a person always follows a regular pattern of their sleep and diet, when the pattern changes they feel disturbed as their inner harmony gets disturbed. Because they like to follow a pattern, they like to eat same food and go to the same restaurant over and over again. They immediately get upset seeing the difference in the amount of oil and salt in the food, because their mind is not ready to accept any kind of disharmony.

They like to tune their music sets and spend time on arranging sequential notes. When the voice is stable, they do not like any disturbance till the end of the music, and if there is a possibility of any obstruction in between, they do not start that work. They're always armed with every necessary tool in their bag, and put everything in its place, because relocation creates disharmony which they never like. They start their journey when everything is ready and all equipment is fully functional.

They take a keen interest in automobiles and work where the rhythm of the engine or machine is important and they judge its performance by its noise. They have strong understanding of gears and use multiple gears in their work. They like to tune the vehicle to create a consistent rhythm, and use every force for a perfect tuning, they are tuners, and be it human body, engine, music or atmosphere.

In present times, the simple musical drum has been replaced by the jazz drum and the flute has been replaced by the saxophone. Dhanishta people like to play all these instruments and they like to listen to orchestras.

Pitches are very important in music, otherwise it becomes monotonous. High pitch and low pitch make music very attractive. Similarly, Dhanishta native's focus on work is sometimes high and sometimes low, but their ultimate goal is achievement. So, sometimes they work day and night and sometimes they leave it completely but they don't like anything monotonous in their life.

They are the followers of their habits and like to follow the good habits for whole life. In the same way they like to follow; web pages, subscriptions, and ideas of great leaders. Once they accept a thing, it is very difficult for change because they don't like disturbance in the rhythm, they are very loyal, strong supporters and hard-core followers.

They want to maintain peace at any cost and are ready to suppress any kind of disharmony. They work as a police officer, and always has handcuffs ready to catch culprits. They work as a military person to suppress the rebellions. They don't hesitate to beat the culprits, as they are beating the drum. They adopt every method to bring harmony in the atmosphere, so they ruthlessly suppress the rebels and establish peace. Wherever discord arises, the eight gods of Dhanishta will always come to pacify it, they are the controllers and responsible for bringing harmony in the system and they can use extreme force and go to any extent to bring it about.

The Eight Vasus also indicate group activity. These people like to attend ceremonies, parties and sit is a group to eat and discuss. This energy works to bring peace; therefore, they like to sign peace related documents, and participate in all those activities that bring peace. They shout on the roads to bring peace. Where there is a quarrel the Dhanishta person has capability to pacify the situation and convince both parties to create harmony. They are adept at getting reconciliation done, that's why people look at them with respect.

Due to their controlling nature, they control their senses and often go on fasting, when they decide not to eat or not to do a thing they never eat or do it. Once they leave a bad habit they leave it forever, because deep down they know the value of restrictions. They believe in restrictions and limitations and keep everything under firm control. On the downside, they impose too many restrictions.

Because time is always important to them, they often turn on their stopwatch to record the time. They take interest in sports which require a lot of energy. They love to run, jog, walk and all activities that require physical movement. They are good players and trainers.

The first two pada falls in Capricorn and next two pada falls in Aquarius. Capricorn in an earthy sign and indicates persevere efforts with full determination, they are runners, cyclists, bikers and like to record time on their stop watch. Aquarius is a watery sign, so they like to record time while swimming.

Capricorn part indicates a very hardworking person who has strong belief on the ideas, they are very courageous, never frustrate, discuss on logics and provide sharp arguments. Aquarius part indicates a technical expert, who always support new and innovative ideas. Capricorn is an earth sign, hence focused on material things, while Aquarius indicates a philosophical nature and such a person takes interest in meditation and occultism.

A perfect harmony is possible when the strings are not too tense or too loose. They are generous person, love to share intelligent jokes, always keep the surroundings pleasant and like to listen classical melodious songs.

On the higher aspects, this energy brings harmony to the inner world. When every sense is fully controlled and participates to produce the immortal sound, then Dhanishtha has attained his inner harmony, he is able to hear that divine music which never ceases. They always feel an abundance of joy within themselves, and their wealth never ends. It is the inner wealth which is endless and limitless and will last for eternity.

Negative Traits: On the negative side, they become misers and tight-fisted controllers of every resource. They do not like to give anything, and keep everything in their pocket. They impose too many restrictions on others, want to control everything and get angry when someone disobeys their rules.

When negative traits of Mars are high, they become argumentative, ruthless, arrogant, selfish and revengeful. Their marital life gets disturbed and legal cases are also possible. They take interest to interfere in all those activities where they can impose their will on others. They can be hard hearted, oppressive and violent individuals who are ready to use multiple forces to achieve their objective.

They are criminals who note down the daily activities of their victims before launching an attack. They become conservative individuals who do not like to change anything and follow a (wrong) routine for years. If the native is influenced by malefics, they know how to create chaos in a situation and disrupt the normal life of others.

Gender: This is a feminine constellation. Dhanishta people listen to the views of others and are always ready to adopt good points.

Animal Symbol: The animal related with this nakshatra is 'Female Lion'. Its counterpart is Purva Bhadrapada whose animal is a male lion. It is inimical to Bharani and Revati nakshatra whose animal symbol is elephant.

Lionesses are much faster and better hunter than lions and play a main role while hunting. The pride gets most of its food from her hunts and the first bite goes to the male lion. The mail lion's role is to protect the pride and goes on hunting when necessary. Lionesses are very active members of the pride, caring for and raising the lion cubs.

Sun's Ingress: Sun enters this Nakshatra every year on 6th February and stays there till 20th February. At this time people start planning for the next financial year. All these qualities are present in a Dhanishtha native.

Profession: Musician, drummer, artist, entertainer, choreographer, social worker, risk consultant, financial planners, insurance related professions, doctors, heart specialists, engineers, sports persons, coaches, administrators, managers, real estate persons, NGO workers, scientists, armed forces and police related professions.

Favourable Activities: Group activity, music, dance, manufacturing or maintaining high-tech equipment, automobiles, travel, financial transactions, business meetings, planning, restructuring, treatment of diseases, learning, research work, bringing peace and any other work that requires full concentration.

Unfavorable Activities: It is not good for leaving a partner, involve in legal cases, marriage, and imposing too much restrictions.

Gana (Type): The type of the nakshatra is Rakshasa, all nine rakshasa nakshatras are active nakshatras. These people are always in search of some activity; they sit only when they are fully tired, and rejuvenate faster than others. Rakshasa is never satisfied on small things, they always desire for abundance and they work very hard to achieve it.

Guna (Quality): The quality of the nakshatra is "Satwik-Tamasic-Tamasic". The first quality indicates that such a person initiates an action with a noble intention, and may use any tamasic activity to achieve it. On the higher aspects, such a person sits for long periods of time in meditation like an idol, in order to achieve inner harmony.

Body Parts: The back and the anus.

Tree: The tree associated with the nakshatra is "Shami", scientifically known as 'Prosopis cineraria'. It is an evergreen, medium sized plant. It has immense medicinal benefits and used for mental disorders, diarrhea, constipation, excessive heat and many other diseases. When the harmony gets disturbed it is useful to bring it, therefore, it is beneficial to plant at home, it brings peace, happiness and prosperity.

Padas: The first pada of this asterism is 23° 20' - 26° 40' Capricorn and ruled by Sun (Leo Navamsha). They are energetic, aggressive, and adventurous people. They are passionate and become ruthless to fulfill their desire. They are influential and kind but also conservative. The ego is the main problem for them and they lose a lot in their life to protect their ego.

The second pada is 26° 40' - 30° 00' in Capricorn and ruled by Mercury (Virgo Navamsha). They take an interest in diplomacy, financial planning, business activities, and innovative ideas. This is the exaltation pada of Mars because all the energy of Mars is fully utilized here. These people never waste anything. They know the usefulness of everything and are always ready with every necessary tool in their pocket. They control difficult situations and also teach others how to control them when situations are bad in life.

The third pada of this asterism is 00° 00' - 03° 20' in Aquarius and ruled by Venus (Libra Navamsha). They are very social people and keep a good network of people. They are intelligent and always adopt a practical and scientific approach. They seek materialistic pleasures, demand attention and try to bring harmony among conflicting things.

The fourth pada of this asterism is 03° 20' - 06° 40' in Aquarius and ruled by Mars (Scorpio Navamsha). They try to hide information and disclose only when it becomes necessary. They are silent workers and do not like pomp and show. They work hard and have patience for the results. They do charity and adopt a benevolent approach in their findings but; autocratic nature, dogma, anarchy, and destruction are also seen here. If the work is not done according to their wish, then they do not hesitate to throw it away.

Chapter 24

Shatabhisha

Shatabhisha is the 24th of 27 Nakshatras and is located at 06° 40' - 20° 00' Aquarius. It comes from the two Sanskrit words "Shata" and "Bhishaj". The word "Shata" means "Hundred" and the word "Bhishaj" refers to "Physician" or "Doctor". Hence, this nakshatra is deeply related with the medicines and the process of healings.

Astronomy: In the constellation of Aquarius and in the group of a hundred stars belonging to this nakshatra, its brightest star visible to the naked eye at a visual magnitude of 3.74 is known as "Lambada Aquarii", also known as Hydor or Shattaraka. Its declination is 7° S 27' 33.84" and right ascension is 22h 53m 47.2s.

Deity: The deity of the nakshatra is "Varuna, the god of Cosmic Waters". He is one of the Adityas and god of all water bodies. The constellation of Aquarius is located near other water-related constellations or sea segments of the sky. This energy rules over water reservoirs, water tanks, lakes, rivers and oceanic water.

Shakti (Power): The Shakti associated with the nakshatra is known as "Bheshaja Shakti". This energy is capable of diagnosing a disease, examining it and providing appropriate remedies for treatment.

The Sight of Nakshatra: It is an Urdhvamukhi Nakshatra i.e., Facing Upward.

Nature: Chara (movable)

Element: Ether

Activity: Active

TriMurti and Behaviour: Shiva and Dissolution

Planetary Ruler: The ownership of this nakshatra has been given to "Rahu". It is a turbulent planet, creating disorder and chaos to achieve its objective. This indicates that this energy does not rest until they solve the problem or achieve their objective. The mythological story states that Rahu did everything to get the nectar, similarly such a person does everything to achieve his objective and never remains silent. The question always revolves around in his mind and he is busy in finding the solution.

The differences between the three Rahu constellations are as follows;;

- **Ardra** - Cleaning and transformation by soaking and beating in water

- **Swati** - Purification through churning

- **Shatabhisha** - Achieving the objective at any cost

Symbol: The main symbol of this nakshatra is an "Empty circle". A circle is complete only when the end point meets the starting point. Everything in the universe is moving in a circle. The Earth revolves around the Sun in a year, and the counting of days starts again from there and this rotation continues every year.

A child becomes a young person and then he becomes old and helpless like a small child. It is said that there is no difference between an old man and a child. It signifies that the life cycle is about to reach the meeting point of its journey, only then a new journey can begin. When one day the person was born as a very weak and helpless child, now he has again become weak and helpless.

The cycle of life is about to end and the emptiness in the circle signifies that nothing will be gained by moving on, and the cycle of life and death continues. Here every cycle is completed, this is the rule and Shatabhisha completes it, this is the functioning of this energy that never leaves anything unfinished. In the same way Shatabhisha people never leaves anything unfinished. Similarly, Shatabhisha people also never leave anything incomplete. Their passion for completing the work is much more than others and these people get up only after completing the work. They leave their desk only when the work is done and many times they skip their meals to get the work done.

Caste: The caste of the asterism is 'Butcher'. The butcher's profession is quite a bloody, gory profession and the term is also used for a brutal and ruthless murderer.

This indicates that this energy shows no mercy while running after the objective. To complete the unfinished work, they never hesitate to cut down, whatever hinders them. They can immediately cut their long relations that are hindering in their way, but attainment of the goal is always important for them.

Characteristics: Shatabhisha people are independent, self-determined person and show leadership qualities. The association of number 100 with this Nakshatra signifies reaching to the point of culmination. This indicates that they will work out a hundred ways to get the answer, if one way fails their mind immediately goes to another way, again if that fails then the third and so on until they get the answer.

They are never afraid to take bold and courageous steps, for them taking steps are important, whatever it may be. They are not idle person who sit silently and wait for the decision of others. If there is a mystery or a riddle and came in contact with Shatabhisha people they will surely find the answer. The question is only of steps and they are ready to take hundred steps, but will return only when they have the answer. They never care about the chaos and anarchy they have done in their pursuit, for them getting the answer is important at any cost.

While eating, walking, sleeping, their mind keeps on working to find the solution. Even their life is full of many chaoses but it is important for them to run after the mystery and they cannot leave it without knowing the answer and one day they get it. Hence, they are the best secret agents and spies.

There are some questions in life from which their answer can't be known, if a person follows fixed rules and traditional path. That is the reason the lordship of this nakshatra is given to Rahu, who can break any barrier. To get the solution Rahu is ready to break any rules and path because answer is always important.

We have seen this type of situation in movies. If the detective will worry about rules, constraints, and order, then he will not be able to catch the person who has the answer. Hence Rahu signifies, this energy can create any disorder but will stop only when it has the answer. Shatabhisha natives are ready to break any rules to get the answer.

They have the ability to find solutions from various directions and the related word 'Bhishaj' indicates to find cure. Therefore, they are able to trace the root cause of the problem (disease), from its origin to how it should be prevented. They are excellent physicians and in the field of medicine they research the functioning of the life cycle of various germs and bacteria, plants etc. and find suitable medicines to stop this cycle. Shatabhisha natives have the ability to end any cycle. Hundred stars or hundred steps indicate that these people adopt a hundred ways to close a cycle, so they have great potential to understand and close a very complex cycle or a complex mystery.

The symbol of empty circle also represents the symbol zero. When something starts from the beginning, the pointer of the scale always moves to zero. Every start starts from zero and the journey begins, people become interested in the movement of the pointer, they become interested in watching the process and analyzing the results. A new cycle begins and Shatabhisha analyze everything. These people note down every movement of the scales and do not miss anything. In other words, these people observe every step of the happening and find a solution.

The symbol of circle indicates that the energy of this nakshatra forces to complete the cycle. Hence, this energy always supports the beginning but never stop anything in between, the circle has to be completed and whatever the process starts it must reach its conclusion, and the final conclusion of this material world is; Only emptiness remains. This circle indicates that after wandering in this world only emptiness remains in the hands.

It requires a lot of patience to complete a cycle and hence, Aquarius is the Mooltrikona sign of Saturn, and immense patience is required to search for the ultimate truth.

Therefore, Shatabhisha natives are seekers; they take deep interest in the unknown world. Where there is something hidden and unknown to the world, they will find the answer. The wavy zig-zag sign of Aquarius represents waves of water or electricity. These people are associated with water or electricity in some form or the other and this reflects the human aspect of this asterism.

Water or electricity when channelized gives fruitful results and this is the futuristic aspect of this Nakshatra. So, the planets posited here indicate such a person to take keen interest in the invention of new technology. They take keen interest in solving the puzzles and complex mathematical theorems. Their approach is very scientific and philosophical. They do as many experiments as possible to get the solution.

They do everything to get answers but no one knows their true identity. They always keep a circle around themselves and do not allow anyone to enter that circle. They can contact you whenever they want but others cannot contact them. They keep ocean of secrets in their heart but they never open in front of anyone. No one knows their whole secret, no matter how many years you've known the person. Their search for the mystery does not end until they find the truth and the ultimate truth is to find the existence of God, and their search continues.

They are hermit, seekers of God, in search of 'Him' they go everywhere and search on different paths. Energy always moves in circles, when the seeker sits in a meditative position, his spine is straight, his eyes are closed, his hands and feet are joined together, such a position forms a circle and the energy generated flows through his body. This is the upliftment of the soul and one day such a soul will know all the secrets of existence, now it has all the answers. Until that soul completes this circle, it has to come again to find such an answer.

Negative Traits: They always take interest in hiding and concealing things and want to enjoy others being unaware of it. They don't like to show their face, and do everything behind the scenes. In present days, they are computers hackers who try multiple options to crack the system and create chaos but never show their face. They have strong ability to sit at one place for long hours and rather than doing meditation they take interest in creating chaos by producing sophisticated viruses.

They take interest in making things dirty or create disturbance and laugh when they see trouble on other's face. Their thirst for alcohol is never quenched and they are always intoxicated. They never trust anyone; they are antisocial people and always like to sit in solitude. They are highly egoistic person and think that they are supreme. They are very hard and oppressive people and do not hesitate to do inhuman acts. They keep patience for years to take revenge. They prefer to do things that they can hide from the public eye and in a secluded place they live in their illusions and darkness.

Gender: The gender of the Nakshatra is "neutral", which indicates that it is a very harsh Nakshatra. The placement of neuter planets (Mercury and Saturn) in this nakshatra shows the extremely harsh nature of the person.

Animal Symbol: The animal related to the nakshatra is "Female horse". Its counterpart is Ashwini nakshatra whose animal is male horse. It is inimical to Swati and Hasta nakshatra whose animal symbol is buffalo.

Female horses tend to be less aggressive than male horses. They are more docile and less agitated in new situations. They prove to be excellent companions when properly cared for, and play an important role in running. Shatabhisha energy forces a person to run for answers.

Sun's Ingress: Sun enters this nakshatra every year on 20th February and stays there till 5th March. In India, people start running for financial closing in the month of March.

Profession: Scientific jobs, Technological experts, Aeronautical science, Medicine and drugs, Physicians, Doctors, Surgeons. They are hunters, puzzle solvers and yoga experts. They take deep interest in psychology, astrology, and other healing techniques. They work for electricity and water department.

Favourable Activities: It is a movable nakshatra, so it is good for all activities where movement is involved. It is good for; Purchasing vehicle, travelling, changing job and residence, acquiring knowledge, sitting in Meditation, search for the unknown.

Unfavorable Activities: It is not good for marriage and fertility treatment.

Gana (Type): The type of this nakshatra is Rakshasa (Demon). Demons are not social, they have vengeful tendencies and prefer to live only in their groups or in isolation.

Guna (Quality): The quality of the nakshatra is "Satwik-Tamasic-Satwik". This energy has a strong potential to elevate the soul to a higher level. Their aim starts with a noble cause, and then they go into solitude to find the solution and then generously spread it to others which they have got with the blessings of Almighty.

Body Parts: It is related to the Right Thigh.

Tree: The tree belonging to this Nakshatra is known as Kadamba, its scientific name is '*Neolamarckia cadamba*', also commonly known as Burr flower tree. It is a beautiful and large evergreen tree and its height is up to 45 meters. This tree is known for its miraculous healing properties. Its leaves are useful; in lowering the blood sugar level; relieving any kind of pain and inflammation; For the treatment of skin diseases and protection of the liver.

Padas: The first pada of this asterism is 6° 40' - 10° 00' in Aquarius and ruled by Jupiter (Sagittarius Navamsha). This is Rahu-Saturn-Jupiter energy, so they struggle hard to get what they want, along with optimism; hardness also appears in this pada. They are wanderers, explorers and have a strong desire to discover the unknown.

The second pada of this asterism is 10° 00' - 13° 20' in Aquarius and ruled by Saturn (Capricorn Navamsha). This is Rahu-Saturn-Saturn energy, so they are very secretive and want to have complete control over their surroundings. They do everything methodically and their approach is very practical, but extreme harshness also visible here. They check the working of everything, investigate every matter and always plan properly.

The third pada of this asterism is 13° 20' - 16° 40' in Aquarius and ruled by Saturn (Aquarius Navamsha). This is also Rahu-Saturn-Saturn energy; here the difference from the second pada is that there is more secrecy and less harsh behavior. They are silent workers and their approach is altruistic. They have a scientific mind, love to research and have a strong ability to sit at one place for a long time. They completely forget the outside world and get deeply involved in their project and don't leave it until they find the solution.

The fourth pada of this asterism is 16° 40' - 20° 00' in Aquarius and ruled by Jupiter (Pisces Navamsha). Again, this is Rahu-Saturn-Jupiter energy; the difference from 1st pada is that power of imagination is very high here. They are very sensitive and compassionate person. Their approach is philosophical; they are non-combative person and avoid any kind of tussle. They are moody person and unable to take right decision on time. They possess depth in their personality and keep everything in deep secret.

Chapter 25

Purva Bhadrapada

Purva Bhadrapada is the 25th nakshatra, it is the most intense of all the 27 nakshatras and is situated at 20° Aquarius – 3° 20' Pisces. Bhadra means - One who brings welfare and luck; Pada means feet and Purva means former or before. Hence, it means "One who brings luck before" or "The first lucky step".

The person who takes the first step on the path of spirituality is extremely fortunate and the name of the constellation indicates this. But before taking that "First lucky step" one must know the futility of the material world, and this requires an experience of burning. Until one burns his fingers, the worldly attraction keeps on pulling him. Only one experience of burning is enough to take that first step lucky step and such a person jump immediately into spirituality without having a second thought. Hence, this constellation has a strong connection with fire and burning.

Purva Bhadrapada is known as lightning in the sky between thunderclouds.

Astronomy: The two bright stars in the constellation of Pegasus named Alpha Pegasi (Markab) and Beta Pegasi (Scheat) represents Purva Bhadrapada at longitude 29° 37' 32" Aquarius and 05° 30' 54" Pisces. These stars are visible in the sky at magnitudes of 2.49 and 2.42 respectively; declination is 15° N 19' 36.12" and 28° N 12' 18.9"; right ascension is 23h 4m 52.1s and 0h 44m 43.1s.

Deity: The deity of the constellation is known as Aja Ekpada. In Sanskrit, Aja means "One who is never born", it is used in the sense of nature or Adi Shakti. Ek means "One" and pada means "Feet". Therefore, it means "One Footed God" or "One Legged God". It is also known as "Rudra", the destructive form of Lord Shiva. In Hindu mythology, Rudra's character is fierce and violent, and He is ready to destroy anything that comes in his way. Rudra is full of destructive energy, which spreads violent gusts of wind all around and spews fire. Rudra cannot be stopped by anyone.

Purva Bhadrapada is like a hurricane and the vortex forms the shape of "One Footed God", ready to destroy everything that comes in his way.

Shakti (Power): Yajamana & Udyamana Shakti (The power to uplift the person on spiritual level). The energy of this nakshatra is extreme and destructive. Therefore, the purpose of such destruction must be noble. Hence, the energy works for constructive destruction.

The Sight of Nakshatra: It is Adhomukhi Nakshatra – Facing Downward.

Nature: Ugra (Fierce)

Element: Ether

Activity: Passive

TriMurti and Behaviour: Brahma and Creation

Planetary Ruler: Jupiter is the ruler of this nakshatra. Such a fierce and destructive energy can be controlled only by the planet of benevolence. The energy for all three Jupiter nakshatra works for creation, so what is the difference between these energies?

- **Punarvasu** - Creation through repetition

- **Vishakha** - Creation through transformation

- **Purva Bhadrapada** - Creation after destruction

All three Jupiter-ruled nakshatras indicate getting wisdom which one learns from one's own experience.

Symbol: The first symbol of the nakshatra is "The front part of a funeral cot". In India, wooden funeral cot is used to carry the dead body to the crematorium. When everything is over and the soul leaves the body, then funeral cot is used. It is used only to remove a dead body. The front part is used to put the head and the cot moves towards the crematorium indicates exit from the material world.

The symbol of funeral cot indicates that the energy of the nakshatra works for the removal of anything dead, expired and outdated and front part indicates that they are the initiator. When any law, custom or traditions become dead or outdated, Purva Bhadrapada people are the one who takes initiative to remove it from the system. So, they act as revolutionaries and struggle to remove all those things which have become a burden to the society and it is being dragged for many years but people are not ready to throw it due to lack of courage or personal attachment.

Purva Bhadrapada people have no attachment to any dead things. Therefore, they are ruthless and immediately throw away anything that is useless or dead. They burn effigies, shout, become very furious and want to throw everything that has become dead into the system or in their surroundings. They collect garbage, dead leaves and burn it. They have a very sharp vision to find out the dead or expired things, they feel immediate repulsion. They always take care of the expiry date of each product and remove the expired items immediately.

The second symbol is "A man with two faces". The energy of the Nakshatra is so powerful that a person can have two faces at a time. The first face shows a normal and gentle person while the second face shows a fierce and violent person.

A person gets another face only after death but the symbol says that a person under the influence of this Nakshatra has two faces. This shows that such a person has to go through the process of transformation in his life.

When a person enters the path of spirituality a divine face develops which is different from the face of the material world. A fierce and cruel energy is transformed into a divine and benevolent energy. Only a well-placed Jupiter can show the path for such transformation. The energy of this Nakshatra tells that even the most dangerous criminal can get an opportunity to follow the path of God. The story of Lord Buddha and dacoit Angulimala is a symbol of spiritual transformation.

"A single ray of Sun" is another symbol of this nakshatra. This indicates that no matter how sad and disappointing a situation may arise in life, hope never ends. Where Jupiter is present there is always a hope.

Caste: The caste of Nakshatra is Brahmin. It reflects the energy of the constellation works for purification. They learn quickly and have inclination towards knowledge and wisdom. When the energy works in a proper direction, they become extremely intelligent and capable to reveal many mysterious things. This energy has strong power to create scholars.

Characteristics: The energy of Purva Bhadrapada is like a double-edged sword. It is like a storm that is ready to destroy anything but still remains wet and can prove to be a boon for areas facing summer drought. It is a very powerful transformative energy that can change the seasons. Planets in Purva Bhadrapada indicate changes are inevitable in the life of the person.

It is a highly destructive and ruthless energy which shows no mercy to anyone. Purva Bhadrapada people believe that creation can be done only after destruction. The new will come but before that old has to go and they are the initiator of removing anything which has become obsolete and dead. They break all their ties with one that has lost its relevance. They do not take any time to break those relationships which are of no use today and burn all the memories and pictures.

Many times, people get stuck in old rules and regulations, culture and traditions which have lost its value but people do not dare to take it out from their home, their society, their culture or from their country, then Purva Bhadrapada enters and revolution begins. People get furious and start shouting to throw out the old system. The process of creative destruction begins, Rudra is now activated, fire and gusty wind (heated discussions) start spreading everywhere. Purva Bhadrapada people do those courageous acts which others are afraid to do. It can happen into a family, into a society or into a country but Purva Bhadrapada is ultimately able to take the corpses (dead beliefs and rules) to the crematorium (out of the system).

When someone dies and the relatives are crying, but the dead body has to be taken to the crematorium. During this process, those who take the dead body to the cremation ground do not listen to anyone's cries and they are not kind to leave the body. The dead body has to be burnt, this is the act of purification and this has to be done.

Purva Bhadrapada people do not listen to anyone's advice or cries, they feel that what they are doing is always right. They think that it is necessary to do this and they are doing right job. Therefore, it is futile to cry in front of these people. They are merciless and ready to make sacrifices for what they think is a great cause. According to their opinion, sacrifice is necessary, they are doing something great act which will bring change to the system, and for that purpose they are ready to kill themselves and others. Hence, they often use the word "sacrifice is necessary", "sacrifice for change" and they believe that what they are doing is very pious and noble.

In general discussions they often say that they don't believe in outdated traditions and rules which has lost its relevancy. Even at home they don't like anything which is worthless or dead, they are ready to throw it immediately. They are ready to throw anything without asking others which has lost its relevancy. They look things in term of its usability and often use the word 'useful' or 'useless' in their conversation.

Purva Bhadrapada keeps no relationship with anything that is useless or expired, be it a person or an object. They are ready to give up their family traditions or even leave the family if the ideology of the family does not match with their principles. The people of PBP have no attachment to anything that has become junk, whether it is an investment made by them or an old relationship. The energy of the nakshatra works for settlement or ending;

1. This is the cut-off energy.

2. Such a person has no attachment to what has ended; he immediately abandons it, whether it is a person, an object or a relationship.

3. The thing that has lost its relevance, they don't want to pursue it.

4. What has become useless, they start avoiding it and do not bother about the past relations.

When a company is declared insolvent, the court issues an order that the insolvent company be wound up. The process of liquidation begins, which is a complicated process of selling off the company's assets and paying off its debts. This is the same process that is done to take the dead body to the crematorium on the funeral cot. Purva Bhadrapada people work in all these liquidation processes of the company. They work in various legal and financial departments and eventually bring the dead company to its destination.

They are the best in the process of dissolving something and many times they say that such matter should be dissolved quickly and why it is taking so much time. They never delay the matter voluntarily and also tell others to finish their work quickly. They are very hardworking people and hate procrastination. They follow up all their pending tasks properly. They always ask their team members about the latest follow-up. Because deep in their subconscious mind they know that time is running out and funeral cot is getting closer, hence, they prefer to take term insurance plan quickly. They can't wait for long to achieve their objective and quickly wants to see the outcome of their efforts.

Purva Bhadrapada people involved in the process of final settlement or ending of any process. In the stock market, they operate in the trade settlement cycle where shares move from the seller's account to the buyer's account and money moves from the buyer to the seller. They work for settlement of loan in financial department. They work as a perfectionist and have strong ability to catch anything wrong (mistakes).

If there is anything wrong written in the document then Purva Bhadrapada people can't forward it, and return the document with a mark of mistakes. They never compromise on anything dead in the system, hence, for that they are very rigid. This is a very powerful energy which can remove any dead object from anywhere. They check each and every item before finalizing it as they cannot allow even a single dead item to go any further in the system.

Purva Bhadrapada people tend to throw away useless things immediately. They immediately throw away what has become garbage. It is like a vacuum cleaner that sweeps away dust with its powerful air. When the wind of Purva Bhadrapada starts the process of cleaning starts. In India, March and April are the month of Vasant (Spring) and Sun enters in this nakshatra on 4th March. At this time trees shed their old leaves and the wind carries them away. Whatever has become lifeless, nature itself cleans it.

The women of Purva Bhadrapada tend to clean everything in the house. They don't like anything that is of no use and occupying space, so they utilize the space perfectly. But their cleaning behavior sometimes becomes eccentric. They always check the expiry date of a product and when they find anything old or expired, they immediately throw it away.

In the corporate world, Purva Bhadrapada bosses immediately fire their non-performing employees. They don't want to keep anything that is useless. The place of a wasted item is the dustbin and no one like to keep the garbage on the table. Similarly, they fire their non-performing employees from the company and sometimes without giving any notice. They never think about their past loyalty and dedication. They think that at present the person is of no use and keeping him in the organization is like putting garbage on the table.

When anything wrong happens or someone is doing anything wrong to make things dead, then the energy of the nakshatra immediately works to remove it. They are very honest and can't tolerate if someone is doing anything wrong, mixing something bad and outdated in the new one, etc. When something wrong is happening and comes to the notice of Purva Bhadrapada people, they immediately act to throw that wrong thing and they fight fiercely to remove it. Union leaders, revolutionaries are influenced by this Nakshatra who fight to remove anything wrong, dead or outdated.

When they see anything dead, they cannot tolerate it and the energy of the Nakshatra prompts them to remove that thing from the system. They can catch the mistakes easily, because they have strong vision to find the mistakes. If a document is getting damaged due to some mistake, then that mistake has to be rectified and they immediately catch the mistake or forgery in the document.

Counterfeit currency is a dead currency and it has to be removed from the system immediately. Therefore, they work at places that remove counterfeit currency from the system. As soon as this person touches the note, he immediately realizes that it is fake. This energy does not allow the dead to stay with the living, even if they are buried inside the wall for years. Anything dead cannot stay anywhere with the living, the dead must be burned and they will find it.

Purva Bhadrapada people have two faces and the one is totally different from the other. On the one hand; Mystery, occult, violence, cunningness, fierce anger and on the other hand; Honesty, benevolence, charity, penance, etc. If assigned a task, these people secretly complete the task and deny its completion to their co-workers, but when their boss comes over, they immediately display their completed papers from their desk. They can immediately manage their two faces which are totally opposite to each other.

Due to high energy, they are able to complete the most difficult tasks which other people are not able to do. They are very bold and don't care about the social taboos and do what they want to do.

The nakshatra energy works for both creation and destruction simultaneously. Hence, contradictory personalities witnessed in their character; Benevolence and ruthlessness, merciful and violent, sociable and secretive, helpful and rude, a very pleasant mannerism and on the other hand they don't hesitate to cut the relations immediately, etc.

They are religiously inclined person and having philosophical tendencies. They believe in occult science and put energy to learn it. They take care of each and every member of the family. They protect their family and worry about the health of their acquaintances. They work hard for their family members because it is inherent in them to protect their people. They can do strong penance and take intense pain for worship without hesitation.

They are skillful in money making. They are great warriors, fight for the truth and can create a whirlwind. They are great writers who write on revolutionary topics. Due to strong throat, they chant religious hymns loudly; they are very skillful in speaking and can speak for hours. They are great orators who speaks publicly about system change. They love listening to loud music and want to enjoy the thrill of life. They have the capacity to endure intense pain and find pleasure in torturing themselves. Once they decide to give up their food or medicine, then no one can compel them to take it.

On the higher aspect, after destruction when everything ends, there is still a hope and creation begins again. This Nakshatra signifies a new beginning. Whatever negative happens there is always 'A ray of light' and soon the life again picks up pace with full vigor. Change is always possible and can be done at any time, no matter how low one has fallen in life. The energy of this Nakshatra says that the way back is never closed.

When the villagers advised Lord Buddha not to go into the forest where Angulimala was, the Buddha replied that it never happens that all hope is lost. There is always a ray of light present. Do whatever you want but you can never go away from God, and there is always a chance to come back and change yourself. Angulimala saw the light in Lord Buddha and he was transformed.

Negative Traits: The energy of the nakshatra lacks any kind of mercy; hence, they become extremely violent and ruthless. They are fickle minded person and lack the power of foresight. They become gloomy and depressed quickly. They become very anxious, lose their temper and start shouting. They can be very harsh towards others and not ready to listen to anyone. They can adopt cynical attitude, can become eccentric then it is very difficult to control them. They are selfish people and maintain relations only till their purpose is fulfilled, after that they never recognize you.

Demons, tyrants, mass murderers, homicides, genocides, dangerous criminals, serial killers are associated with this nakshatra. They are ruthless and ready to die, but before that they can cause great destruction. The strange thing is that they consider all their actions are right and they do not feel guilty for committing heinous crimes, and think all these acts are for purification. While doing those crimes, they feel something great inside, like Angulimala felt that he was doing a great work by killing people.

They show only one face at a time to others and keep the other face in dark. Being secretive in nature they keep their activities hidden from others. Their activities do not match to the traditional society and they involve in those work which generally do not follow by others. During the day they do their normal job but at night they can work for violent and criminal activities. They can practice black magic or engage in activities of destruction.

The people of Purva Bhadrapada have the ability to make big changes but can also do big harm. The energy of a Nakshatra has a destructive effect, therefore, when the action is started it must be sure that the consequences will not be normal and the end result may be beyond the expectations, because no one can gauge the destructive power of Rudra.

One of the driving forces of a hurricane is heat energy and it dies down when it loses its energy source which is usually warm water. To prevent the destruction of Purva Bhadrapada natives it is good not to make them angry and remove all items near to them which can produce heat.

Gender: The gender of the nakshatra is 'Male'. They take initiative and don't like to wait for long.

Animal Symbol: Its animal symbol is "Male Lion", it is compatible with Dhanistha nakshatra whose symbol is a "Female Lion" and inimical to Bharani and Revati whose symbol is elephant.

The entire function of a male lion is to protect his pride and offspring at all costs. Hence, Purva Bhadrapada people feel a responsibility to protect their family. They are brave and courageous and do not easily change their beliefs. They fight to protect their money, position and business. They always protect their disciples and colleagues.

Following are some more features;

1. Lions are hunters. Hence, Purva Bhadrapada people are not afraid of hunting or how to complete the difficult task or a project.

2. Lions like to relax and do not want anyone's interference. That's why these people do not like anyone's interference while resting. Just ask them to do something while they are resting and you will hear the roar of a lion.

3. Lions take rest during the day and are more active at night when it is cooler. Purva Bhadrapada people have a capacity to sit for long hours at night without taking any rest. On negative side, most of the nefarious activities are done by them at night.

4. They are generous and donate easily, but no one can take anything from them if they are not willing to give, it is like fighting with a lion.

5. Purva Bhadrapada persons have some intense mating behaviour and feel unsatisfied with their partner unless the partner is coming from other big cat family.

Sun's Ingress: The Sun enters in Purva Bhadrapada nakshatra on 5th March to 18th March every year. The energy of the nakshatra works towards downward direction and for ending things. Dead leaves from the trees start falling. The process of cutting off starts, Sun in Purva Bhadrapada i.e. the old chapter has started closing and a new one is likely to start soon. In India, Holi is celebrated every year on the day after the full moon in the month of Phalguna. It is celebrated as a way to welcome spring, and is also seen as a new beginning where people cut all their old deadlocks and start afresh.

In the month of March students' exams start, financial year starts ending, people rush to close their accounts, but it is not right to start a new session. Therefore, the financial year in India starts from 1st April.

Profession: Reformers, revolutionists, occultists, hermit, workers at crematorium and mortuary, official liquidator, trade settlers, scrap collector, surgeons and postmortem experts, weapon scientists and researchers, astrologers, palmists and esoteric practitioners, philosophers, teachers, trainers, psychoanalysts, politicians, encounter specialists, soldiers, speakers, work related with chemical and pharmaceutical industry, work related with demolition of buildings, work related with insurance and retirement planning. They work as journalists, TV anchors, news writers etc.

Favorable Activities: In India, new financial year starts from 1st April, therefore, people start working on closing their financial statements, so they can timely finish their job at the end of March. During this time schools and colleges start working to close the session, so they can timely open for the next session. It is favorable to support all risky, dangerous and mysterious activities. It supports any activity that requires downward energy.

Like, drilling, digging for water, an act of going down, an act of demolition, etc.

Unfavorable Activities: Its energy is not supportive to start anything positive. Marriage, start a new enterprise, expansion of business, travel, taking admission in a new course, signing new collaboration, etc. should be avoided.

Gana (Type): The Gana of the Nakshatra is 'Manushya' (Human), which means they like to live and work in groups. They perform better when they work in a team. They are down to earth person and their approach is always practical. They want normal environment and adjust in any situations.

Guna (Quality): The three combined Guna of the nakshatra is 'Satwic-Satwic-Rajasic'. They do not like to sit idle and are more active when the cause is noble.

Body Parts: It is related to the Left Thigh.

Tree: The tree associated with the constellation is "Mango". Mango flowers and leaves are considered very auspicious. Mango represents the transformative power of this energy. The taste of ripe mango is completely different from that of raw mango and known as the King of fruits. In Ayurveda, mango cures all the three doshas; vata, pitta and kapha. Its wood is also used in funeral pyre.

Padas: The first three pada comes under Aquarius ruled by Saturn and last pada comes under Pisces. The first pada is situated in

Aquarius from 20° 00' - 23° 20' and is ruled by Mars (Aries Navamsha). Here, the energy level is very high and it is very aggressive. They have strong determination and possess good commanding power. Once they are determined, they never take their steps back.

The second pada comes in Aquarius from 23° 20' - 26° 40' and is ruled by Venus (Taurus Navamsha). The cut-off energy works with Venusian pursuits. They will be engrossed in longing and will start shouting if someone stops them.

The third pada comes in Aquarius from 26° 40' - 30° 00' and is ruled by Mercury (Gemini Navamsha). It indicates cleaning through communication. The native is a good speaker and motivate others. They practice esoteric science for healing purposes.

The fourth pada falls in Pisces from 0° 00' - 3° 20' and is ruled by Moon (Cancer Navamsha). The possibility of extreme two faces of the person is very high here. Pisces is ruled by Jupiter and nakshatra lord is also Jupiter. They are very generous and benign person. They are inclined towards spirituality and use their power for the benefit of others.

On the other hand, the opposite of this is also true, they can be extremely dangerous, ruthless and use their power only for destructive purposes. The position of Moon must be strong for good qualities of the person. If there is an aspect or conjunction of Jupiter then it shows the gentle nature of the person. Such a person always uses his power for the good of others.

Chapter 26

Uttara Bhadrapada

Uttara Bhadrapada is the 26th of 27 nakshatras and situated at 3° 20' - 16° 40' Pisces. Uttara means latter, left or where everything has an answer. Bhadra means auspicious and Pada means feet which represent stability and strength. Hence, it means "Latter auspicious feet", "The latter blessed one" or "Strong and auspicious answer".

The right is good for starting and the left is used for closing. When the answer is found, all questions cease to exist. The energy of this constellation works to find solutions and the search continues till the answer is found.

Astronomy: In the constellation of Pegasus, a star named Gamma Pegasus (Algenib), and in the in the constellation of Andromeda a star named Alpha Andromeda (Alpheratz), these two stars create this nakshatra and are visible to the naked eye with a visual magnitude of 2.84 and 2.06 respectively.

Deity: The deity of the nakshatra is known as "Ahir Budhanya", a form of Rudra who brings rain. Ahir Budhanya is also known as the serpent of deep water.

Ahir Budhanya has the vital power of cleaning. An unclean person is not allowed to enter the temple of God. Before entering one should be completely free from the desires of the material world. This energy compels the person to go to this world and clear the ashes of desires time and again until he is completely clean to enter the temple of the God.

Shakti (Power): This energy works to "Bring rain". It converts barren land into fertile land, it is a gentle energy for healing purposes. When a dead body is cremated near a river, water is used to clean it and all the ashes are thrown into the river. When it rains, all the dust in the atmosphere gets washed away. It is a calming and soothing energy that is used to cleanse and rejuvenate.

The Sight of Nakshatra: It is an Urdhvamukhi Nakshatra i.e., Facing Upward.

Nature: Dhruva (Stable)

Element: Ether (Akash)

Activity: Balanced

TriMurti and Behaviour: Vishnu and Maintenance

Planetary Ruler: Legs represent stability and stability requires balance. Hence, the lord of balance, 'Saturn' is the ruler of this nakshatra. The energies of the three Saturn nakshatras prove the old adage "slow and steady wins the race."

The differences between them are as follows:

• **Pushya** – A very hard working and diligent person who has to do everything to win the odd circumstances.

• **Anuradha** – Fighting all difficulties and overcoming every obstacle in life and still maintaining a smile on the face with a sweet voice.

• **Uttara Bhadrapada** – This compassionate, deep, and productive energy can bring about change from the roots.

Symbol: The main symbol of the constellation is "The back legs of a funeral cot". The back legs always support the front legs. Front legs provide the direction and the back legs follow them. As its predecessor star, the funeral cot signifies the passing out of dead things.

Caste: The caste of the nakshatra is Kshatriya (Warrior). They are duty bound person and never wave to fulfill their duty.

Characteristics: The deity in the deep water indicate how deep and intense the personality of these people are. They take much time to open their mouth and to say a single word. Their vision is sharp, they see everything minutely, but instead of reacting, they first try to tolerate it. Rulership of Saturn indicates they prefer to control their anger and emotions. They are very deep, and the personality that others see on the surface is like the tip of the iceberg. They can bear immense pain without any complaint and weep alone.

This warrior star indicates they are fully aware of their duty. They work with full dedication and never run away from the situation. In Mahabharata, Lord Krishna says to Arjuna, "As a Kshatriya, you are bound for your duty to engage in a battle to protect Dharma. You can't run after seeing the situation". They are very hard-working people and determined to find the solution, no matter how much it will take time. Once they decide they will always come back with the answer and never run from the situation. They have sharp eyes and are very efficient in finding the root of the problem; hence, their advice is always valuable. This compassionate, deep, and productive energy can bring about change from the roots.

They are ready to do sacrifices like their predecessor star but the difference between Brahmin and Kshatriya comes here. Brahmin is ready do to sacrifice for a noble cause and purification purposes, while Kshatriya is ready to do sacrifice for the fulfillment of his duty. Therefore, the people of Uttara Bhadrapada sacrifice food for the sake of duty and the people of Purva Bhadrapada sacrifice food for the sake of religion. Both Bhadra people can fast easily. They are very religious and whenever the day of fasting comes according to the lunar calendar, they give up their food.

Once they have decided to give up their food for medical purposes, then no temptation can tempt them. Uttara Bhadrapada is a very powerful energy for sacrifice, once they have made up their mind, they never retrace their steps. They can even stop taking medicines once they decide to leave the body.

The back legs of the funeral cot cannot decide to move, it has to follow the front part. That's why the energy of this nakshatra is supportive; they act as supporters and followers. Once they support, they are like pillars and never waver under any circumstances. They never distract by any temptation, that's the working of the energy of this nakshatra.

Once decided Uttara Bhadrapada people are firm with their decisions. Feet represent stability, a guard has firm legs, and he can stand for hours and prevent intruders. This energy removes any form of dust (intruders) and they work as protectionists. They prevent everything from getting dusty and are very careful about their clothes.

The back of the cot indicates patience; so, they never take prompt action. They always ask how to do, what to do and prefer a consensus opinion. They are never in a hurry and always take decisions with full consideration. No matter if it will take time they are ready to wait for that. Such a quality supports its meaning "The latter blessed one". The decision is taken without any haste and after careful consideration is the right decision.

They have a strong ability to find solutions. They never sit calmly and rush to find answers when the situation demands. They provide strong and bold answers. Their one answer is sufficient to keep the mouth shut of many people and produce an atmosphere of deep silence in a meeting.

They have an excellent quality of writing answers. They work for the research department to find solutions. They work for those jobs where answer writing is required. They prepare answer notes for publishing companies. They write article for newspapers and magazines; they work as a news editor and can quickly find fault because this energy can't bear the wrong answer (dust). They like to write a conclusion in their articles and often use the word "conclusion" in discussions. They are those who speak at the last in a meeting and provide a conclusion.

Like its predecessor star, this energy works to throw away useless things and cannot tolerate dust anywhere, but they are not initiators. They prefer to take a second opinion because they don't like to take a risk on any matter. They always take a back foot when they see the possibility of any danger. They are always cautious about danger and buy insurance and term loan policies quickly.

They are always cautious about the time, deep in their mind they know that the funeral cot is coming, it indicates that the time to leave everything is coming, but is has not come yet, so be ready for that. Therefore, they often use the words 'Time is running out' or 'Time is short' in their discussions.

In the corporate world, Uttara Bhadrapada bosses are liked by their subordinates. They always inspire their team members to learn and grow. Before taking a final call, they listen to everyone's advice, hence, they often conduct team meeting and provide everyone a chance to speak not like Purva Bhadrapada where only one speaker and others are listeners.

Uttar Bhadrapada's bosses do not fire non-performers immediately and value their dedication and loyalty. They have a generous attitude and they are ready to provide a second chance.

Utara Bhadrapada people are very cautious about their legs and like to have multiple pair of shoes. They like to change their shoes because the focus of this energy is more on the feet and females like to apply henna on her feet. These natives walk slowly and never hurry in doing things. They want a peaceful environment to work where they can think deeply and are not distracted by noise or sound. They work as perfectionists and catch mistakes easily.

They are very talented but they like to sit on the back benches in the colleges and in the meetings. They are not initiators and prefer not to show their face. They do the work with full dedication but never beat the drum of doing so. They are full of sympathy and always like to help others. Sometimes, others fool them for their generosity but they don't care.

A team surrounded by Uttara Bhadrapada people is an excellent team. They never leave their master or boss under any circumstances. They are ready to provide their full cooperation as long as the Master maintains their dignity.

This constellation has a deep connection with water. Pisces is the water of the celestial ocean; Jupiter is the lord of Pisces and the deity is also of water quality. People of Uttar Bhadrapada like to live in watery surroundings, they like to visit watery places and go for swimming.

They are always busy with water related activities at home and are misfit to live in places where there is scarcity of water. In cities they keep a big water storage tank at home. They immediately throw the buckets full of water if a signal particle of dust comes; because the symbol of funeral cot says that they will throw it immediately if they find anything worthless, then the dust should be thrown away immediately. They prefer to take a water pipe and clean everything.

This energy serves to throw debris out of the system, be it a dead body or a particle of dust and clean with water. They always keep their dustbin clean as it is used to remove the household wastes, whatever becomes junk they immediately throw it away. Like his predecessor star, they also like to throw away anything from the house that is old, dead, dusty or out of date, but the difference is that they listen to the opinion of others and prefer to donate it.

They are busy in cleaning the house whole day and sometimes it becomes a problem for other people. They keep checking which product has expired. They can forget anything but never forget the expiry date of a product.

Remember, this energy only throws off dead things, if something is alive, they never throw it away. Therefore, they are able to detect whether there is any sign of life left. Where others fail, they are quick to catch the sign of life and then keep it under complete protection. They are very protective of useful things, adept at handling valuables, and always have some money saved for emergencies.

This energy does not allow carrying anything dead. Therefore, before entering into the temple people remove their leather belt, shoes and anything made from carcass. People clean their feet with water, without cleaning a person is not allowed to enter in the temple.

On the higher aspects, it indicates a person who is not satisfied with the answers given by others. A man in search of truth will not be satisfied by reading books and scriptures. They want their own answers and are not ready to copy from others. Such a person wants to learn from his own experience and his search continues till he finds the truth.

One must be completely clean and rid of all mortal things, only then he is entitled to enter the temple of God. Hence, this nakshatra has strong power to create great mystics, hermits and saints who know that everything is going to die one day.

The last Nakshatra is Revati where Venus is exalted at 27°. It is the location of the crown chakra and exaltation of Venus means salvation (moksha). A funeral cot indicates, only they will be entitled to ultimate knowledge when they are completely out of materialistic desire. One should leave all the attachment in this world where everything is dying and burning. Only then he is allowed to enter in the temple of God. A person who is carrying the carcass (of desires) and is not clean will come again and then process will continue till he is purely cleaned. As long as one does not transcend the desire for things that can be dead, one is not entitled to the ultimate knowledge. They have to return from outside the temple with their leather belt and shoes.

Negative Traits: They take a long time to take decisions and are often indecisive. Hence, they are unable to control the crisis situation. They immediately feel panic and look for solutions because it takes time for them to find solutions and there is no time in an emergency. They are always dependent on others and like to follow the path shown by them.

Procrastination is their biggest problem, and they get upset when it comes to getting things done quickly. Although they are very hardworking in the office but become lazy at home. They perform their duties half-heartedly, when there is lack of zeal and enthusiasm. They are fearful and timid person and always look for someone's company.

Individuals of this Nakshatra are not mature enough in their young age and need support and counseling; otherwise, they will work hard but will not be able to achieve results. This energy needs proper nurturing and guidance until the individual is mature enough to be independent.

Gender: Male

Animal Symbol: The animal symbol of the nakshatra is "Cow". Its counterpart is Uttara Phalguni whose animal symbol is the bull. It is the enemy of Vishakha and Chitra Nakshatra, whose animal symbol is tiger.

These people have many talents and are very productive individuals. They are very social and like to spend time together. They are very generous and take care of everyone in the family. They give their best results when they are properly nourished.

They cannot take the risk and want proper care. They have a group of friends and like to chat with them. They like to go for gatherings, marriage ceremony and parties.

A cow becomes dangerous when someone tries to harm her calf. Then she uses all the energy to throw off the offender using her horns. In the same way, the people of Uttara Bhadrapada are very protective of their children and ready to fight with anyone when they know that their child is in trouble. As they grow older, they have gas problems because cows tend to produce methane gas.

They are very skilled in turning bad things into good as the cow eats grass and gives us milk. When a situation in an organization is getting out of hand and no one is able to control it, a back-bencher person who rarely comes in the limelight shows the courage to control the situation. He is the Uttara Bhadrapada person who is capable of providing the ultimate solution and his dazzling presentation finally silences many critics. But they are not interested in coming in limelight so they are not aggressive person, they sit silently and watch others doing monkey dance.

Sun's Ingress: Sun in Uttara Bhadrapada nakshatra on 18th March to 31st March every year. Where Purva Bhadrapada ends, Uttara Bhadrapada begins. After burning, the ash starts getting cleaned by the shower of rain.

Profession: They are excellent in those jobs where a person has to write reports after research and findings. In financial market, they work as an analyst, who do research and write reports. They work as a news writer in media industry. They are eloquent speakers and they work as radio jockeys or TV anchors. This energy works for facial cleansing, Uttara Bhadrapada people often wash their face and like to apply make-up, women like to apply eyeliner (the same process of removing dust from water and in this case, surface is face).

They work for; Editing and Writing, Activity related to support someone, Research, Librarian, Work for humanitarian activities and for non-profit organizations, Charity organizations, Professor, Psychologist, Healers, Counselors, Waste Management, Cleaning something with water like Car cleaners, Floor cleaners, Make-up professionals, Watering related activities, Irrigation, Drainage, Fertilization activities. Profession related to catharsis, yoga and meditation. This energy says that the time is coming to leave everything; hence, they work as insurance and retirement solution providers.

Favourable Activities: Doing research and start writing findings, activity start for recycling. This energy supports to throw all wastage of mind, so it is good for Yoga and meditation. This energy support for slow detachment, so it is good for retirement plans.

Unfavorable Activities: This benign energy is not good for taking first step in life where the outcome is unknown. It is not good for taking quick decisions and emergency like situations.

Gana: The Gana of the nakshatra is Manushya (Humans). Humans are common people, this nakshatra energy is utilized for common welfare activities of human being.

Guna: Under three level of categorization, the Guna of the nakshatra is "Satwic-Satwic-Tamasic". Among the many virtues of religiousness, piousness, devotion and liberal attitude, the quality of laziness also exist in this nakshatra.

Body Parts: The body parts related with the nakshatra is "Ankles", which provide support to the whole body.

Tree: The tree associated with the constellation is Neem, which is used for purification. Neem leaves purify the blood, people burn neem leaves to drive away mosquitoes. Every part of Neem is useful, showing how useful the energy of this Nakshatra is.

Padas: All the four pada of the nakshatra comes under Pisces. The first pada situated at 3° 20' - 6° 40' in Pisces and ruled by Sun (Leo Navamsha). The liberal part of the Sun comes here and they are very polite and benevolent. They are warm, passionate and dignified person. They have great desire for creation. They are learned in arts and culture. They are magnanimous person and always ready to help others.

The second pada situated at 6° 40' - 10° 00' and ruled by Mercury (Virgo Navamsha). Under this pada the energy moves to create a highly intelligent and analytical mind person with strong business acumen. They like to cooperate with others. They are perfectionists and very good at planning and organizing.

The third pada situated at 10° 00' - 13° 20' and ruled by Venus (Libra Navamsha). They are social, religious, knowledgeable and pious persons. This pada reflects many positive qualities of Venus and they are proficient in many arts. They are bright, straight forward and experts in their field. They are very active person and good advisor.

The fourth pada situated at 13° 20' - 16° 40' and ruled by Mars (Scorpio Navamsha). The Martian energy move towards investigation and search for the mystery. They can easily spot hidden things that others fail to notice. They are strong in arguments and skilled in writing reply letters. They have strong control over their emotions and use the energy for transformation. They are interested in occult and practice meditation and tantric techniques. They have a deep understanding of medicine, surgery and toxicology. If Jupiter and Moon are strong in a horoscope, then the person will use his knowledge for the benefit of others.

Chapter 27

Revati

Revati is the last of 27 Nakshatras and is located at 16° 40' - 30° 00' Pisces. Revati comes from the Sanskrit word Revat, which means wealthy and prosperous. It is related to brilliance and abundance. The planet of beauty and luxury Venus gets exalted here at 27°.

Astronomy: In the constellation of Pisces and a visual magnitude of 5.24, the star of this nakshatra is known as "Zeta Piscium". Its declination is 7° N 41' 37.35" and right ascension is 1h 14m 54.6s. Higher magnitude indicates that the star is not easily visible in the sky with the naked eye

Deity: The deity of the nakshatra is Pushan (Protector of flocks and herds). He is one of the twelve Adityas and carries a golden scepter which is a symbol of his constant movement. He is the god of travel and roads and the protector of travelers. He is also the god of the journey of departed souls to the afterlife. He always protects the travelers from accidents, removes obstacles and shows the right direction to travel. He is the patron of travel and makes every journey successful, with his blessings a person overcomes every obstacle in his path and reaches his destination safely.

He is the lord of all things that move from one place to another. He is the god of marriages and meetings. A new journey of life begins after marriage and Pushan bestows good luck to the couple. The god of marriage and union indicates that people of this nakshatra are very much interested in the matters and activities related to marriage and couple matching and they go on to attend wedding parties. They are very busy people when it comes to matters related to marriage.

One has to travel in order to make a successful meeting with someone. Therefore, Revati people take interest in meetings and make various trips to make them successful. Nowadays, these people keep talking on their mobile phones continuously to fix various meetings and run from one meeting to another.

Pushan is known as the god of nourishment and protector of flocks, herds, cattle and crops. He is a helpful deity who provides the person with crops and cattle, which means wealth. In ancient times, a person who had more crops and cattle was considered a wealthy person. Hence, the people of Revati take interest in agricultural activities; they love animals and fight for their protection.

According to ancient texts, it is believed that the deity Pushan does not have teeth and consumes only liquid food.

Shakti (Power): The Shakti of the nakshatra is Kshiradhyapani Shakti (The power to protect and nourish with condensed milk).

The Sight of Nakshatra: Tiryanga-mukha (Sideways)

Nature: Mridu (Soft)

Element: The element of the Nakshatra is Ether, which provides expansion of ideas and inclination towards adaptability to new ideas and innovations.

Activity: Balanced

TriMurti and Behaviour: Shiva and dissolution

Planetary Ruler: This is the third nakshatra ruled by Mercury. Revati comes under the sign of Pisces that is ruled by Jupiter. It is a place where Venus is exalted; indicating that supreme knowledge is present at this place and after knowing it one attains salvation. Mercury signifies children; children are innocent, pure in heart and away from the tricks of the material world.

Mercury being the lord indicates that naive state of mind where the person has seen through the fallacies of all tricks and is no longer interested in any tricks. He has again attained the innocence of children and become lord for the supreme wisdom.

The energy of all three Mercury nakshatras is related to intelligence.

- **Ashlesha** - Tenacious energy with bending quality

- **Jyeshtha** - Planning, preparation and progress

- **Revati** - A dynamic energy that protects and nourishes

Symbol: The symbol of the nakshatra is a swimming fish which signifies constant movement. The fishes keep moving here and there in the water and there is no purpose for their movement. The constant movement of the fish indicates a restless person who is very busy in his life. People of Revati walk in a gentle manner and they are not in a hurry to move from place to place, they enjoy pleasant movement.

It's another symbol is a drum; it is also the symbol of Dhanishta nakshatra. It indicates synchronicity, rhythm and timing. People of Revati know the value of time, hence they are very punctual. There exists a synchronicity between the natural clock in the body and the time they keep for their work. So, they follow the order given by the natural clock and always work accordingly. They practice music early in the morning and when the sun sets below the horizon, they stop worldly activities and prefer to follow the natural rhythm.

Caste: The caste of the nakshatra is 'Shudra'. Such people are very helpful in nature and takes interest in serving others. They run for others requirements and take pressure upon themselves on the matter of others. They show genuine concern for the problems of others, and take upon themselves the burden of overcoming them.

Characteristics: The natives of Revati Nakshatra looks very sober and attractive, they are very social person and always behave politely. They have a refined nature and show proper etiquette and manners. They look for joy, prefer light jokes in their discussion, and remain optimistic in difficult situations in life. It is always their instinct to nurture others, so they are always ready to provide necessary help to others.

Revati is the last Nakshatra, the journey that started with Ashwini ends here. This is the exaltation star of Venus; the energy starting from the Mooladhara Chakra reaches the Sahasrara Chakra, which is located at the top of the head. To complete this journey a soul has to go through many lives. Hence, Revati is related to travel and comes in the 12th house. If the journey is not completed then the next cycle again starts from Aries which is the first house, therefore, a Gandanta exists between these two signs. Either the cycle of birth and death has to be stopped forever or the next cycle has to be started from the next zodiac.

To cross this Gandanta requires a lot of energy, but Planets in Revati indicates that such a person doesn't want to cross that Gandanta, he is more interested in closing than opening his karmic balance. So, he is a very humble person and works for the settlement of accounts and other things. Such a person knows that if he keeps his ego alive he will create a karmic imbalance and he will be thrown again in the next cycle with the baggage of unclosed accounts, so he prefers to close it.

Revati people never take an interest in any type of argument, fighting, and involvement in cutthroat competition. They are generous, gentle, and kind-hearted people who are always ready to help others. Revati indicates a liberal person who has less attachment to material things and easily donates costly items to others.

Revati is soft nakshatra, so they do everything very softly, take an interest in physical beauty, and like to do sober makeup before appearance. They work as musicians, make-up artists, and jewellers. They don't like haste of any kind and like to work peacefully.

Revati means the end of the journey, so most of the Revati people do those jobs where they often say goodbye to the people. As TV hosts, travel helpers, flight attendants, customer care executives, etc. They meet every day new people and politely say welcome and goodbye.

Revati is a balanced Nakshatra. Equilibrium is possible when more opposite forces work together on the same plane and all are ready to cooperate. Revati works to pacify all the forces and bring them to the meeting table so that a balance can be established and people can live in peace.

The symbol of the asterism is a swimming fish, it represents life and balance. Millions of years ago, life first appeared in the water in the form of fish. Revati people make every possible effort to protect and save lives and they bring a balance among different activities. As a mother tells her children that when it is time to sleep, it is good to go to bed and Revati does all such things.

Revati people take an interest in the medical field saving the life of a person. They provide equipment to the needy person so that they can bring balance to their daily life. They work as a medical practitioner, open hospitals and blood banks, and write articles to save lives and bring balance to society. The water of Pisces is seawater, so they take an interest in swimming, fishing, and boating.

Being social people, they do activities for the welfare of the society. They donate to good causes and actively participate in facilitating the same. They monitor all the developments and strictly remove all hindrances.

Once started any project their task is to successfully complete it and as the deity, Pushan protects travelers from thieves and dacoits, they protect their every work from falling into the hands of mischievous persons.

The deity of the Nakshatra always provides guidance for the right path, Revati people are well aware of choosing the right path, it may not always be the physical path but the path of any business. They know in which direction they should lead the successful operation of the business, so they act as an entrepreneur. They are well aware of the ups and downs of the business and manage time properly to reduce losses.

This Nakshatra is related to roads and transport and the various vehicles moving on the roads are like fishes swimming in the sea where they go on their way, do not disturb others, and move towards their destination. If someone creates an obstacle, then the smooth movement is disrupted, which Pushan never allows to happen. It has to be corrected soon and make the road clear for smooth movement. Hence, Revati people work in the maintenance department where they are always ready to clean every block that restricts the movement.

The deity of the Nakshatra always watches the flow of every movement and extends their every support for the successful completion of the journey. They bestow the person to bring balance and come up with peaceful and joyful outcome after every meeting that brings happiness among all participants. Revati people work as a comedian where many people laugh at a gathering.

This energy works to remove all obstacles that create any hindrance to the free flow of movement, be it road or life, or blood. So, Revati person works in the medical field and removes blood obstructions, they provide medicines and equipment that support the body and bring normal life to the person.

Revati is related to motherhood, this energy is related to the development of children. She teaches lessons in a very polite manner and also punishes like a mother. Revati takes care of the baby and gives him the necessary food so that the baby is nourished and his body develops properly. Revati deals with the flow of nourishment and provides every support for life, so they take care of their dependents and always suggest to take medicines on time. A Revati person never gives any harsh punishment to anyone; they always take a protective approach and believe in parenting.

It is the star that supports flow in every area of life. Therefore, these people listen patiently to the sorrows of others, wipe their tears and help them to re-establish themselves in life.

On the higher aspect, it is the path of life and one should not create any obstacle in the path of another, as the deity of the Nakshatra is there to remove it and punish that person who created such an obstacle because that person has disobeyed the deity. When a person leads his life in peace then the gods show the necessary path to the other world. Revati people take a keen interest in religion and like to take a dip in the deep ocean of spirituality.

Negative Traits: These natives' eyes are blurred to see the reality and they often take wrong decisions as they do not see both sides of the coin. They are emotionally attached to their imaginary world and are unable to accept the truth. They live in their own world and do not want to come out of it.

They get disheartened quickly and are unable to fight the situation. When things do not go according to their wish, they get frustrated and go into a state of depression. They feel insecure and suspect everybody. They are daydreamers and change their decisions quickly. They suffer from an inferiority complex and lack courage.

The deity of the nakshatra consumes only liquid food, indicating that Revati can become that evil one who consumes only blood.

Gender: It is a female nakshatra. It lacks the aggressiveness of the male, and favors all kinds of gentle activities.

Animal Symbol: Its animal symbol is 'Female Elephant'; its counterpart is Bharani whose symbol is a male elephant and it is inimical to Purva Bhadrapada and Dhanishta whose animal is lion.

Elephants are incredibly intelligent animals and female elephants tend to be more sociable than males. Female elephants constantly protect each other from predators and help with each other's calves (baby care). They form close and long-lasting relationships with their friends and family members.

Sun's Ingress: Sun enters this Nakshatra every year on the 1st April and stays there till the 14th April. This is the time for the April holidays for kids and celebrates activities. This time is pleasant and people take an interest in fun activities. This season is the beginning of summer, people like to travel, take an interest in social activities and spend more time outside.

Profession: Travel related, Publisher, Editor, Journalist, Flight Attendant, Actor, Film Director, Artist, Musician, PR Personal, Comedian, Fiction Writer, Maintenance Personal, Magician, Hypnotist, Doctor, Surgeon, Teacher, Nurse, Baby Care, Customer Care.

Favourable Activities: It is good for travel, starting a new venture, and auspicious for marriage. It is good for humanitarian work and charitable activities. It is good for business meetings, financial matters, exchanges, and construction-related activities. It is good for healing, music, art, and customer care activities. It is good for occult and spiritual practices.

Unfavorable Activities: Aggression, fighting, and taking any bold and drastic action are not good.

Gana (Type): This is Dev Gana Nakshatra. Such persons do not take aggression, they prefer to wait till they reach their destination and always adopt a sober approach.

Guna (Quality): The guna of the nakshatra is "Satwik Satwik Satwik". This is the place in the celestial ocean where supreme knowledge exists and the lord of that place is Brihaspati. He will allow a person to reach that destination only when only "Sattva" is left in him.

Body Parts: Feet and Ankles are related to this nakshatra.

Tree: The tree associated with this Nakshatra is Mahua or Butter Tree or *Madhuca Longifolia.* It is a tall tree and reaches a height of 20 m. The tree blooms between March and April, with light green or pink flowers. The tree bears its fruit between June and August. It is used to make skin care, vegetable butter and soap. It is used to make vinegar and alcoholic beverages.

Padas: The first pada of this asterism is 16° 40' - 20° 00' in Pisces and ruled by Jupiter (Sagittarius Navamsha). They are positive, enthusiastic, and confident people. They are philosophical people and take an interest in religious literature. They are patient and take decisions after careful observation. They are true to their word and stick to their beliefs.

The second pada of this asterism is 20° 00' - 23° 20' in Pisces and ruled by Saturn (Capricorn Navamsha). They are realistic people, good at planning but conservative, and believe in setting limits. They are hardworking and dutiful people. Such people follow religious rules strictly and impose their rules on others.

The third pada of this asterism is 23° 20' - 26° 40' in Pisces and ruled by Saturn (Aquarius Navamsha). They have an amazing ability to understand and connect with different types of people. They love friendship and teamwork but also like to enjoy their independence and don't allow anyone to enter that. They are deep thinkers and always interested in innovation and technology that can change lives. They are lazy people, busy with themselves, and do not listen even when someone shouts.

The fourth pada of this asterism is 26° 40' - 30° 00' in Pisces and ruled by Jupiter (Pisces Navamsha). They are humble and loyal individuals and can adapt to any kind of situation. They are receptive people, give good advice to others, and have a sense of security for each member. They are a very moody person, always in dilemma and unable to take the right decision.

Nakshatra Tables

Table 1: Animal Symbol and Inimical Yoni

Sr. No.	Male	Female	Animal Symbol	Inimical Yoni
1	Ashiwini	Satabhisha	Horse	Buffalo
2	Bharni	Revati	Elephant	Lion
3	Pushya	Krittika	Sheep (Goat)	Monkey
4	Rohini	Mrigashira	Snake	Mongoose
5	Mula	Ardra	Dog	Deer
6	Aslesha	Punarvasu	Cat	Rat
7	Magha	Purva phalguni	Rat	Cat
8	Uttara phalguni	Uttara bhadrapada	Cow	Tiger
9	Swati	Hasta	Bufallo	Horse
10	Vishakha	Chitra	Tiger	Cow
11	Jyeshtha	Anuradha	Deer (Hare)	Dog
12	Purva ashadha	Shravana	Monkey	Sheep (Goat)
13	Purva bhadrapada	Dhanishta	Lion	Elephant
14	Uttara ashadha	-	Mongoose	Snake

Table 2: Nakshatra, Deity & Symbol

Sr. No.	Nakshatra	Deity	Symbol
1	Ashwini	Ashvini Kumaras	Horse head
2	Bharani	Yama	Vagina
3	Krittika	Agni	Axe, sharp edge
4	Rohini	Prajapati - Lord of creation	Chariot
5	Mrigashira	Soma - God of immortality	Head of a deer
6	Ardra	Rudra - The Lord of Storms	Teardrop, Diamond
7	Punarvasu	Aditi - the universal mother	Quiver of arrows
8	Pushya	Brihaspati	Milk yielding by the teat of a cow
9	Aslesha	Naga	Coiled snake
10	Magha	The Pitris - The Ancestral Fathers	Throne
11	P. Phalguni	Bhaga - God of love and marriage	Hammock, front legs of bed
12	U. Phalguni	Aryama - God of vows and	Bed, legs of a cot
13	Hasta	Savitar - God of sunrise	Hand or fist
14	Chitra	Tvastar - Vishwakarma	Multifaceted jewel
15	Swati	Vayu-Wind	Sword, coral
16	Vishakha	Indragni- Gods of lightning and	Potter's wheel
17	Anuradha	Mitra - the God of friendship	Lotus flower
18	Jyeshtha	Indra	Umbrella, Earring
19	Mula	Nirritti – Alaksmi	Bunch of roots tied together
20	P. Ashadha	Apas - goddess of Waters	Tusk of an elephant - left, Fan
21	U. Ashadha	Vishvadevas-Universal Gods	Tusk of an elephant - right
22	Shravana	Vishnu	Three footprints, trident, ear
23	Dhanishta	The eight Vasus	Musical drum
24	Satabhisha	Varuna	Empty circle or a charm
25	P. Bhadrapada	Aja Ekapada - Unicorn	Front of a funeral cot, Two faced man
26	U. Bhadrapada	Ahir Budhya	Back legs of a funeral cot
27	Revati	Pushan – The Nurturer	Fish swimming in the water, Drum

Table 3: Nature

Light	Mridu (Soft)	Mixed (Sharp+Soft)	Dhruva (Fixed)	Ugra (Dreadful)	Tikshna (Sharp)	Chara (Movable)
Ashvini	Mrigashirsha	Krittika	Rohini	Bharani	Ardra	Punarvasu
Pushya	Chitra	Vishakha	Uttara phalguni	Magha	Aslesha	Swati
Hasta	Anuradha		Uttara ashadha	Purva phalguni	Jyeshtha	Dhanishta
	Revati		Shravana	Purva ashadha	Mula	Satabhisha
			Uttara bhadrapada	Purva bhadrapada		

Table 4: Caste

Brahmin	Kshatriya	Vaishya	Shudra	Outcaste / Mleccha	Servant	Butcher
Krittika	Pushya	Ashwini	Rohini	Bharani	Mrigashira	Ardra
Purva phalguni	Uttara phalguni	Punarvasu	Magha	Aslesha	Chitra	Swati
Purva ashadha	Uttara ashadha	Hasta	Anuradha	Vishakha	Jyeshtha	Mula
Purva bhadrapada	Uttara bhadrapada		Revati	Shravana	Dhanishta	Satabhisha

Table 5: Marriage

Auspicious	Not auspicious
Rohini	Ashwini
Magha	Bharani
Purva phalguni	Krittika
Uttara phalguni	Mrigashira
Hasta	Ardra
Swati	Punarvasu
Uttara ashadha	Pushya
Uttara bhadrapada	Aslesha
Revati	Chitra
	Vishakha
	Anuradha
	Jyeshtha
	Mula
	Purva ashadha
	Shravana
	Dhanishta
	Satabhisha
	Purva bhadrapada

Table 6: Direction

Upward	Downward	Sideways
Rohini	Bharani	Ashwini
Ardra	Krttika	Mrigashirsha
Pushya	Aslesha	Punarvasu
Purva phalguni	Magha	Hasta
Uttara ashadha	Uttara phalguni	Chitra
Shravana	Vishakha	Swati
Dhanishta	Mula	Anuradha
Satabhisha	Purva ashadha	Jyeshtha
Uttara	Purva bhadrapada	Revati

Table 7: Activity

Active	Passive	Balanced
Krittika	Ashwini	Bharani
Aslesha	Mrigashirsha	Rohini
Magha	Punarvasu	Ardra
Chitra	Pushya	Purva phalguni
Vishakha	Hasta	Uttara phalguni
Jyeshtha	Swati	Purva ashadha
Mula	Anuradha	Uttara ashadha
Dhanishta	Shravana	Purva bhadrapada
Satabhisha		Uttara bhadrapada
		Revati

Table 8: Trimurti

Brahma	Vishnu	Shiva
Ashwini	Bharani	Krittika
Rohini	Mrigashirsha	Ardra
Punarvasu	Pushya	Aslesha
Magha	Purva phalguni	Uttara
Hasta	Chitra	Swati
Vishakha	Anuradha	Jyeshtha
Mula	Purva ashadha	Uttara
Shravana	Dhanishta	Satabhisha
Purva bhadrapada	Uttara bhadrapada	Revati

(Note: Brahma – Creation, Vishnu – Maintenance, Shiva – Dissolution)

Table 9: Gana

Dev	Manusha	Rakshasa
Ashwini	Bharani	Krittika
Mrigashira	Rohini	Aslesha
Punarvasu	Ardra	Magha
Pushya	Purva phalguni	Chitra
Hasta	Uttara phalguni	Vishakha
Swati	Purva ashadha	Jyeshtha
Anuradha	Uttara ashadha	Mula
Shravana	Purva bhadrapada	Dhanishta
Revati	Uttara bhadrapada	Satabhisha

Table 10: Guna

Sr. No.	Nakshatra	Guna (1)	Guna (2)	Guna (3)	Guna (Combined)
1	Ashwini	Rajasic	Rajasic	Rajasic	Rajasic-Rajasic-Rajasic
2	Bharani	Rajasic	Rajasic	Tamasic	Rajasic-Rajasic-Tamasic
3	Krttika	Rajasic	Rajasic	Satwic	Rajasic-Rajasic-Satwic
4	Rohini	Rajasic	Tamasic	Rajasic	Rajasic-Tamasic-Rajasic
5	Mrigashirsha	Rajasic	Tamasic	Tamasic	Rajasic-Tamasic-Tamasic
6	Ardra	Rajasic	Tamasic	Satwic	Rajasic-Tamasic-Satwic
7	Punarvasu	Rajasic	Satwic	Rajasic	Rajasic-Satwic-Rajasic
8	Pushya	Rajasic	Satwic	Tamasic	Rajasic-Satwic-Tamasic
9	Aslesha	Rajasic	Satwic	Satwic	Rajasic-Satwic-Satwic
10	Magha	Tamasic	Rajasic	Rajasic	Tamasic-Rajasic-Rajasic
11	Purva phalguni	Tamasic	Rajasic	Tamasic	Tamasic-Rajasic-Tamasic
12	Uttara phalguni	Tamasic	Rajasic	Satwic	Tamasic-Rajasic-Satwic
13	Hasta	Tamasic	Tamasic	Rajasic	Tamasic-Tamasic-Rajasic
14	Chitra	Tamasic	Tamasic	Tamasic	Tamasic-Tamasic-Tamasic
15	Swati	Tamasic	Tamasic	Satwic	Tamasic-Tamasic-Satwic
16	Vishakha	Tamasic	Satwic	Rajasic	Tamasic-Satwic-Rajasic
17	Anuradha	Tamasic	Satwic	Tamasic	Tamasic-Satwic-Tamasic
18	Jyeshtha	Tamasic	Satwic	Satwic	Tamasic-Satwic-Satwic
19	Mula	Satwic	Rajasic	Rajasic	Satwic-Rajasic-Rajasic
20	Purva ashadha	Satwic	Rajasic	Tamasic	Satwic-Rajasic-Tamasic
21	Uttara ashadha	Satwic	Rajasic	Satwic	Satwic-Rajasic-Satwic
22	Shravana	Satwic	Tamasic	Rajasic	Satwic-Tamasic-Rajasic
23	Dhanishta	Satwic	Tamasic	Tamasic	Satwic-Tamasic-Tamasic
24	Satabhisha	Satwic	Tamasic	Satwic	Satwic-Tamasic-Satwic
25	Purva bhadrapada	Satwic	Satwic	Rajasic	Satwic-Satwic-Rajasic
26	Uttara bhadrapada	Satwic	Satwic	Tamasic	Satwic-Satwic-Tamasic
27	Revati	Satwic	Satwic	Satwic	Satwic-Satwic-Satwic

Table 11: Gender

Male	Female	Neuter
Ashwini	Bharani	Mrigashirsha
Pushya	Krttika	Mula
Punarvasu	Rohini	Satabhisha
Hasta	Ardra	
Anuradha	Aslesha	
Shravana	Magha	
Purva bhadrapada	Purva phalguni	
Uttara bhadrapada	Uttara phalguni	
	Chitra	
	Swati	
	Vishakha	
	Jyeshtha	
	Purva ashadha	
	Uttara ashadha	
	Dhanishta	
	Revati	

<u>Table 12: Planetary Lordship and Quality</u>

Planetary Lordship	Quality		
	Rajasic	Tamasic	Satwic
Ketu	Ashwini	Magha	Mula
Venus	Bharani	Purva phalguni	Purva ashadha
Sun	Krittika	Uttara phalguni	Uttara ashadha
Moon	Rohini	Hasta	Shravana
Mars	Mrigashira	Chitra	Dhanishta
Rahu	Ardra	Swati	Satabhisha
Jupiter	Punarvasu	Vishakha	Purva bhadrapada
Saturn	Pushya	Anuradha	Uttara bhadrapada
Mercury	Aslesha	Jyeshtha	Revati

Table 13: Nakshatra and its Various Properties

Sr. No.	Nakshatra	Caste	Nature	Activity	TriMurti	Gender	Gana	Guna	Naksh. Goal
1	Ashwini	Vaishya	Swift	Passive	Brahma	Male	Deva	Rajasic	Dharma
2	Bharani	Mleccha	Ugra	Balanced	Vishnu	Female	Manusha	Tamasic	Artha
3	Krittika	Brahmin	Mixed	Active	Shiva	Female	Rakshasa	Satwic	Kama
4	Rohini	Shudra	Dhruva	Balanced	Brahma	Female	Manusha	Rajasic	Moksha
5	Mrigashira	Servant	Mridu	Passive	Vishnu	Neuter	Deva	Tamasic	Moksha
6	Ardra	Butcher	Tikshna	Balanced	Shiva	Female	Manusha	Satwic	Kama
7	Punarvasu	Vaishya	Chara	Passive	Brahma	Male	Deva	Rajasic	Artha
8	Pushya	Kshatriya	Swift	Passive	Vishnu	Male	Deva	Tamasic	Dharma
9	Aslesha	Mleccha	Tikshna	Active	Shiva	Female	Rakshasa	Satwic	Dharma
10	Magha	Shudra	Ugra	Active	Brahma	Female	Rakshasa	Rajasic	Artha
11	P. Phalguni	Brahmin	Ugra	Balanced	Vishnu	Female	Manusha	Tamasic	Kama
12	U. Phalguni	Kshatriya	Dhruva	Balanced	Shiva	Female	Manushya	Satwic	Moksha
13	Hasta	Vaishya	Swift	Passive	Brahma	Male	Deva	Rajasic	Moksha
14	Chitra	Servant	Mridu	Active	Vishnu	Female	Rakshasa	Tamasic	Kama
15	Swati	Butcher	Chara	Passive	Shiva	Female	Deva	Satwic	Artha
16	Vishakha	Mleccha	Mixed	Active	Brahma	Female	Rakshasa	Rajasic	Dharma
17	Anuradha	Shudra	Mridu	Passive	Vishnu	Male	Deva	Tamasic	Dharma
18	Jyeshtha	Servant	Tikshna	Active	Shiva	Female	Rakshasa	Satwic	Artha
19	Mula	Butcher	Tikshna	Active	Brahma	Neuter	Rakshasa	Rajasic	Kama
20	P. Ashadha	Brahmin	Ugra	Balanced	Vishnu	Female	Manushya	Tamasic	Moksha
21	U. Ashadha	Kshatriya	Dhruva	Balanced	Shiva	Female	Manushya	Satwic	Moksha
22	Shravana	Mleccha	Dhruva	Passive	Brahma	Male	Deva	Rajasic	Artha
23	Dhanishta	Servant	Chara	Active	Vishnu	Female	Rakshasa	Tamasic	Dharma
24	Satabhisha	Butcher	Chara	Active	Shiva	Neuter	Rakshasa	Satwic	Dharma
25	P. Bhadrapada	Brahmin	Ugra	Passive	Brahma	Male	Manushya	Rajasic	Artha
26	U. Bhadrapada	Kshatriya	Dhruva	Balanced	Vishnu	Male	Manushya	Tamasic	Kama
27	Revati	Shudra	Mridu	Balanced	Shiva	Female	Deva	Satwic	Moksha

Bibliography

Brihat Parashara Hora Sastra by Maharshi Parasara

Uttara Kalamrita by Kalidas

Mansagari, Translation by Shree Sitaram Jha, Shree Thakur Prasad Pustak Bhandar, Varanasi, India

Brihat Jatak, Translation by Prof. P.S. Sastri, Rajan Publications, New Delhi

Jatak Parijat, Translation by V. Subramanya Sastri, Rajan Publications, New Delhi

Hora Sara, by Prithuyasas (Translation by R. Santhanam)

Hindu Science of the Future by Harihar Majumder

The Book of Nakshatras, by Prash Trivedi

Scientific Hindu Astrology Vol 1 &2 by P.S. Sastri

Yoga and Vedic Astrology by Sam Geppi

Importance of Sky Gazing, Bhartiya Vidya Bhavan, Mumbai

About The Author

Ajay Srivastava is the founder of www.lotuswisdom.in and holds 'Bachelor of Science' from Deen Dayal Upadhyay Gorakhpur University, Gorakhpur (UP) and 'Masters Programme in International Business' from PSG Institute of Management, Coimbatore (Tamil Nadu).

He has extensive experience in the capital market as a Lead Analyst, Investment Banker, Consultant, and Advisor in identifying investment opportunities and formulating strategies. In his career, he has written various research notes and has done in-depth research from a commercial and financing point of view in multiple deals. With diverse industry experience and wide understanding, he started imparting his knowledge in the industry since 2013.

He has deep knowledge of graphology and since childhood he is very much interested in analyzing a person by handwriting and has analyzed the handwriting of hundreds of persons in his life.

He is very much passionate to learn about astrology and palmistry in deep and has completed 'JyotirVid' and 'JyotirVisharad' in Astrology from Bharatiya Vidya Bhavan, Mumbai. His various research articles have been published in the renowned Indian magazines "The Astrological eMagazine" and "Planets & Forecast".

Email ID: ajay.vastav@gmail.com

Web Site: www.lotuswisdom.in

Books Written by the Author

1. Psychology and Investment

2. Vedic Astrology: The Light of Wisdom

3. Midlife Crisis: An Astrological Appraoch

4. Jupiter: The Planet of Fortune

5. The Joy of Creation and Success

6. The Light of Nakshatras

7. Sun: The Supreme Creator

8. Astrology & Predictions

9. Animal Symbols of Nakshatras

10. Astrology & Profession

11. Rahu & Ketu: The Invisible & Mysterious Planets

12. Planets & Human Life

<u>Astrology Courses</u>

1. <u>Vedic Astrology for Beginners {Level – 1 (Basics)}</u>

Module – 1: Basics of Astrology

Introduction; The Zodiac; Elements

Module – 2: Signs

Meaning of the Signs, Elements of the Signs, Qualities of the Signs, Odd and Even Signs, Sheershodaya & Prishtodaya Signs, Direction, Colors, Caste, Fruitful and Barren Signs, Masculine & Feminine Signs, Places, Other Major Qualities

Module – 3: Houses

Meaning of the 12 Houses, Types and Classifications of Houses

Module – 4: Planets

Planets and their Characteristics, Planetary Relationship, Exaltation, Debilitation & Mooltrikona, Natural Karakas, Karakas in Jaimini Astrology

Module – 5: Planets in Groups

Natural Benefic and Malefic Planets, Gender; Color; Caste; Guna and Places; Planet and Tastes; Nature of Planet; Elements; Metals; Age; Cloth and Height; Vegetable and Fruits; Physical Constituents and Tendency; Maturity Age of Planets; Planetary Aspects; Seasons

Module – 6: Planetary Strengths and Weaknesses

Strength of Planets based on its degrees, Direction; Direction Strength; Maran Karaka Sthana; Yog Karaka; Vargottam Planet; Shadabala

Module – 7: Retrograde and Combust Planet, Gandanta

2. <u>Vedic Astrology for Beginners {Level – 2 (Advanced)}</u>

Module 1: Vimshottari Dasha System

Nakshatra and Planetary Lordship, Change of Dasa and Results

Module 2: Basics of Nakshatra

Deity, Animal Symbol, Caste, Activity, Gana, Guna, Gender

Module 3: Important Yogas

Know the 30 most important astrological combinations

Module 4: Ashtakvarga

Interpretation of Ashtakvarga Table

Module 5: Transit of Planets and their impact

Understand the effect of transit of Jupiter, Saturn, Rahu-Ketu

Module 6: Planets and Profession

Identify the influence of the planet and the direction of profession

Module 7: Weak Planets and Remedies

Identify the signal of weak planets and useful remedies

Module 8: Key Steps to Chart Interpretation

Course Offerings:

- 30 hours of live sessions (Level 1 & Level 2)

- Learn various astrological concepts with practical examples

- Mode - Online Classes

- Recordings available

3. <u>Nakshatra Course</u>

Knowledge of Nakshatra is very important in astrology, without it one cannot understand how energy works and what will be the result of the transit of planets. Do not limit yourself to the movement of planets, explore the world of Nakshatra and understand the hidden secrets.

What You'll Learn

• How the knowledge of Nakshatra helps to understand the characteristics and negative traits of the person

• Effect of transit of planets and time of activation

• Meaning of each symbol and its influence

• Influence of the associated animal on the personality of the person

• When to start a new venture and when not to go ahead

• Related Profession

• Understand each concept with logic

Course Offerings:

• 60 hours of live sessions

• Learn various astrological concepts with practical examples

• Mode - Online Classes, Recordings available

• Medium - English

Contact Us:

Mobile No.: +91 9867581379

Email ID: ajay.vastav@gmail.com

Blog: https://lotuswisdomonline.blogspot.com/

Web Site: http://www.lotuswisdom.in/

4. <u>A Course on Animal Symbols of Nakshatras</u>

In the ancient scriptures, a total of 14 animals are related to the 27 nakshatras, and the behavior of every person is limited to these 14 animals. To understand the various merits and demerits of a person, it is necessary to understand the different characteristics of these animals.

How to Utilize Such Knowledge

• You will be surprised to know that these animals decide whom we form a relationship in our life.

• These animals determine our relationships with our friends, our spouse, our partners, our juniors and superiors.

• This knowledge helps to channelize your energy in pursuit of higher goals in life.

• The human mind is a very complex creation and it is difficult to say why a person behaves in a certain way and why his behavior changes. Knowledge of animal traits can provide proper guidance in this regard.

Course Offerings:

· 14 hours of live sessions

· Learn various astrological concepts with practical examples

· Mode – Online Classes

· Recordings available

Sun:
The
Supreme
Creator
A Research Work on
Astrological Aspects of the Sun
Ajay Srivastava

The Light
of
Nakshatras
A Comprehensive Work to Explain the
Functioning of 27 Mystical Energies
Ajay Srivastava

Jupiter:
The
Planet of
Fortune
Ajay Srivastava

Vedic Astrology
The Light of Wisdom
Astrology for Beginners,
Learn the Language of Stars
Ajay Srivastava

PSYCHOLOGY
AND
INVESTMENT
The Art of Investing in Stocks with an
Explanation of Human Psychology
AJAY SRIVASTAVA

The Joy
of
Creation and Success
Ajay Srivastava

Midlife
Crisis: An
Astrological
Approach
Understand The Timing Of Crisis,
Learn How To Turn A Crisis Into An Opportunity
Ajay Srivastava

Astrology
&
Predictions
The Predictive Techniques of
Ancient Scriptures: Redefined
Ajay Srivastava

Animal Symbols
of
Nakshatras
Ajay Srivastava

Astrology
&
Profession
Astrological Principles Behind Career
Selection, Downfall and Resurrection
Ajay Srivastava

Rahu & Ketu
The Invisible and Mysterious Planets
An Extensive Research Work to Demystify
the Mystery of Lunar Nodes
Ajay Srivastava

Planets
&
Human Life
A Research Work on The Impact of
The Nine Planets on Human Life
Ajay Srivastava

<u>Notes</u>

* 9 7 8 9 3 5 9 6 7 8 7 9 5 *